Tracy M. Soska, MSW
Alice K. Johnson Butterfield, PhD
Editors

University-Community Partnerships: Universities in Civic Engagement

University-Community Partnerships: Universities in Civic Engagement has been co-published simultaneously as *Journal of Community Practice*, Volume 12, Numbers 3/4 2004.

Pre-publication
REVIEWS,
COMMENTARIES,
EVALUATIONS . . .

"**E**XCELLENT. . . . IMPORTANT. . . . RECOMMENDED READING for university administrators, scholars and students in professional schools and in the applied social sciences, and leaders of community organizations. This book raises the discussion on university-community partnerships to a higher level of academic inquiry and interpretation. It succeeds in illuminating university-community partnerships and charting the existing experience and knowledge. The chapters are thoughtfully selected, wellorganized, and worthwhile."

Michael Sherraden, PhD
Benjamin E. Youngdahl
Professor of Social Development
and Director, Center
for Social Development,
George Warren Brown School of Social
Work, Washington University in St. Louis

More Pre-publication
REVIEWS, COMMENTARIES, EVALUATIONS . . .

"A MUST for those interested in action-oriented projects through a highly engaged university community. The scope and diversity of this book is surprising! It OPENS UP NEW AVENUES FOR MACRO-PRACTICE FOR FACULTY AND STUDENTS who wish to increase their impact on local, state, or national entities, as well as neighborhoods in need. It will be of great importance to students, educators, and researchers committed to social change, especially those who wish to turn their academic environment into a rich and interactive learning experience."

Yossi Korazim-Korosy, DSW
*Community Social Work
Specialist; Chair,
The Interdisciplinary Forum
for Community Development,
Jerusalem, Israel*

"AN EXTREMELY VALUABLE RESOURCE. . . . Universities must be engaged with the communities in which they exist if they are to remain at all relevant. And the kind of engagement that is necessary must be based on true university-community partnerships that move away from the more traditional types of gown/town interactions. This book PROVIDES MANY USEFUL EXAMPLES AND MODELS that will be of benefit to any university personnel considering ways to bring about a higher and more effective level of engagement between their institutions and communities."

Richard L. Edwards, PhD
*Alumni Distinguished Professor
The University of North Carolina
at Chapel Hill*

The Haworth Social Work Practice Press
An Imprint of The Haworth Press, Inc.

New York • London • Victoria (AU)
www.HaworthPress.com

University-Community Partnerships: Universities in Civic Engagement

University-Community Partnerships: Universities in Civic Engagement has been co-published simultaneously as *Journal of Community Practice*, Volume 12, Numbers 3/4 2004.

University-Community Partnerships: Universities in Civic Engagement, edited by Tracy M. Soska, MSW, and Alice K. Johnson Butterfield, PhD (Vol. 12, No. 3/4). *Community Outreach Partnership Centers (COPC) sponsored by the United States Department of Housing and Urban Development (HUD) have identified civic engagement and community partnership as critical themes for higher education. This unique book addresses past, present, and future models of university-community partnerships, COPC programs, wide-ranging social work partnerships that involve teaching, research, and social change, and innovative methods in the processes of civic engagement.*

Innovative Approaches for Teaching Community Organization Skills in the Classroom, edited by Donna Hardina, PhD (Vol. 7, No. 1, 2000). *This accessible and comprehensive book will help social work educators efficiently teach students methods of practice that they need to know in order to offer the best services to clients with a variety of different needs, in a variety of different settings.*

Research Strategies for Community Practice, edited by Ray H. MacNair, PhD, MSW (Supp. #1, 1998). *"An excellent compilation of materials. A key sourcebook for ideas on community organization research." (John Tropman, PhD, Professor, School of Social Work, University of Michigan, Ann Arbor)*

Community Economic Development and Social Work, edited by Margaret S. Sherraden, PhD, and William A. Ninacs, MS, CED (Vol. 5, No. 1/2, 1998). *"The major value of this book is its potential to bring together the two opposing streams of thinking about social welfare. Both liberals and conservatives can rally around the approach explicated in this book." (Roland Meiner, PhD, President, Missouri Association for Social Welfare)*

Community Practice: Models in Action, edited by Marie Weil, DSW (Vol. 4, No. 1, 1997). *"The text stands alone among macro tests in its timeliness, comprehensiveness, and contribution to strategy development–it could well become a classic." (Moses Newsome, Jr., PhD, Dean, School of Social Work, Norfolk State University; President, Council on Social Work Education)*

Community Practice: Conceptual Models, edited by Marie Weil, DSW (Vol. 3, No. 3/4, 1996). *"Presents diverse views on approaches to community practice and provides a compilation, critique, and analysis of current models while illustrating how these approaches have developed over time." (Public Welfare)*

African American Community Practice Models: Historical and Contemporary Responses, edited by Iris Carlton-LaNey, PhD, and N. Yolanda Burwell, PhD (Vol. 2, No. 4, 1996). *"If you're a social worker who cares about today's and tomorrow's African American communities, read this book. . . . It's likely to become a classic in its own right." (Paul H. Ephross, PhD, Professor, School of Social Work, University of Maryland at Baltimore)*

Diversity and Development in Community Practice, edited by Audrey Faulkner, PhD, Maria Roberts-DeGennaro, PhD, and Marie Weil, DSW (Vol. 1, No. 1, 1993). *The contributing authors provide current knowledge and practice models for community work in diverse settings.*

University-Community Partnerships: Universities in Civic Engagement

Tracy M. Soska, MSW
Alice K. Johnson Butterfield, PhD
Editors

University-Community Partnerships: Universities in Civic Engagement has been co-published simultaneously as *Journal of Community Practice*, Volume 12, Numbers 3/4 2004.

The Haworth Social Work Practice Press
An Imprint of The Haworth Press, Inc.

New York • London • Victoria (AU)
www.HaworthPress.com

Published by

The Haworth Social Work Practice Press, 10 Alice Street, Binghamton, NY 13904-1580 USA

The Haworth Social Work Practice Press is an imprint of The Haworth Press, Inc., 10 Alice Street, Binghamton, NY 13904-1580 USA.

University-Community Partnerships: Universities in Civic Engagement has been co-published simultaneously as *Journal of Community Practice*, Volume 12, Numbers 3/4 2004.

The development, preparation, and publication of this work has been undertaken with great care. However, the publisher, employees, editors, and agents of The Haworth Press and all imprints of The Haworth Press, Inc., including The Haworth Medical Press® and The Pharmaceutical Products Press®, are not responsible for any errors contained herein or for consequences that may ensue from use of materials or information contained in this work. Opinions expressed by the author(s) are not necessarily those of The Haworth Press, Inc.

Cover design by Kerry E. Mack

Cover photos were provided by: Alice K. Johnson Butterfield, Nathan L. Linsk, Ken Thompson, MD, Angela DeVan, George Berkeley, and George Pivet.

Library of Congress Cataloging-in-Publication Data

University-community partnerships: universities in civic engagement / Tracy M. Soska, MSW and Alice K. Johnson Butterfield, PhD, editors.
       p. cm.
       "Co-published simultaneously as Journal of community practice, volume 12, numbers 3/4, 2004."
       Includes bibliographical references and index.
       ISBN 0-7890-2835-2 (hard cover : alk. paper)–ISBN 0-7890-2836-0 (soft cover: alk. paper)
       1. Universities and colleges–United States–Public service. 2. Community and college–United States. I. Soska, Tracy II. Butterfield, Alice K. Johnson. III. Journal of community practice.
LB2331.44.U65 2005
378.1'03–dc22   2004025962

Indexing, Abstracting & Website/Internet Coverage

This section provides you with a list of major indexing & abstracting services and other tools for bibliographic access. That is to say, each service began covering this periodical during the year noted in the right column. Most Websites which are listed below have indicated that they will either post, disseminate, compile, archive, cite or alert their own Website users with research-based content from this work. (This list is as current as the copyright date of this publication.)

Abstracting, Website/Indexing Coverage . . . . Year When Coverage Began

- *Alternative Press Index (print, online & CD-ROM from NISC)*
  The most complete guide to alternative & radical media
  <http://www.altpress.org> **1995**

- *Applied Social Sciences Index & Abstracts (ASSIA)*
  (Online: ASSI via Data-Star) (CDRom: ASSIA Plus)
  <http://www.csa.com> **1994**

- *Business Source Corporate: coverage of nearly 3,350 quality*
  magazines and journals; designed to meet the diverse
  information needs of corporations; EBSCO Publishing
  <http://www.epnet.com/corporate/bsourcecorp.asp> **2002**

- *CareData: the database supporting social care management*
  and practice <http://www.elsc.org.uk/caredata/caredata.htm> . . . **1994**

- *CINAHL (Cumulative Index to Nursing & Allied Health*
  Literature), in print, EBSCO, and SilverPlatter, DataStar,
  and PaperChase (Support materials include Subject Heading
  List, Database Search Guide, and instructional video)
  <http://www.cinahl.com> **1996**

- *EBSCOhost Electronic Journals Service (EJS)*
  <http://ejournals.ebsco.com> **2001**

(continued)

(continued)

(continued)

*Special bibliographic notes related to special journal issues
(separates) and indexing/abstracting:*

- indexing/abstracting services in this list will also cover material in any "separate" that is co-published simultaneously with Haworth's special thematic journal issue or DocuSerial. Indexing/abstracting usually covers material at the article/chapter level.
- monographic co-editions are intended for either non-subscribers or libraries which intend to purchase a second copy for their circulating collections.
- monographic co-editions are reported to all jobbers/wholesalers/approval plans. The source journal is listed as the "series" to assist the prevention of duplicate purchasing in the same manner utilized for books-in-series.
- to facilitate user/access services all indexing/abstracting services are encouraged to utilize the co-indexing entry note indicated at the bottom of the first page of each article/chapter/contribution.
- this is intended to assist a library user of any reference tool (whether print, electronic, online, or CD-ROM) to locate the monographic version if the library has purchased this version but not a subscription to the source journal.
- individual articles/chapters in any Haworth publication are also available through the Haworth Document Delivery Service (HDDS).

University-Community Partnerships: Universities in Civic Engagement

University-Community Partnerships: Universities in Civic Engagement has been co-published simultaneously as *Journal of Community Practice*, Volume 12, Numbers 3/4 2004.

University-Community Partnerships: Universities in Civic Engagement

CONTENTS

ABOUT THE EDITORS

Tracy M. Soska, MSW, is Continuing Education Director and a Community Organization and Social Administration Program faculty member at the University of Pittsburgh's School of Social Work. Co-Director/PI of the University's Community Outreach Partnership Center, he is also PI for the University-Community Career Development Partnership and the Catalyst for Community Building projects. A recipient of the Chancellor's Distinguished Public Service award, he is Chair of the University Senate's Community Relations Committee. He is on the Editorial Boards of the *Journal of Community Practice* and *Professional Development: The International Journal of Continuing Social Work Education* and the Editor of ACOSA's national newsletter. *ACOSA Update!* He was formerly a community human service executive for over 15 years.

Alice K. Johnson Butterfield, PhD, is Professor at the Jane Addams College of Social Work, University of Illinois at Chicago. Her research in the United States focuses on policy and service delivery for homeless families, as well as innovative teaching methods and curriculum development in community practice. Her international work includes technical assistance, training, and research on the nonprofit sector and child welfare organizations in Romania. She has written about the development of international curriculum and the use of E-mail partnerships as an innovative teaching method for linking social work students with students and practitioners in other countries. Currently she is Principal Investigator of a university-to-university partnership grant to establish a School of Social Work at Addis Ababa University in Ethiopia. Dr. Johnson is the author of more then 35 journal articles and book chapters. She is Editor of the *Journal of Community Practice*.

Preface

Armand Carriere

In the early 1990s, under the leadership of then-Secretary Henry Cisneros, the Department of Housing and Urban Development (HUD) sought to create an office that would assist colleges and universities in bringing their considerable resources to bear on the problems of urban America. An Urban Planner and former Mayor of San Antonio, Texas, Secretary Cisneros understood the roles being played by the institutions of higher education in their communities and, more importantly, knew and understood the potential these institutions possessed for being significant agents for positive change in what could be described as distressed communities. A team consisting of Dr. Michael Stegman, HUD's Assistant Secretary for Policy Development and Research (PD&R), Dr. Marcia Marker Feld, an academic on loan from the University of Rhode Island, and Jane Karadbil from the PD&R staff established the Office of University Partnerships in 1994.

The signature program within the Office of University Partnerships was then and continues to be the Community Outreach Partnership Center (COPC) program. Utilizing 3-year grants of up to $400,000, COPC

Armand Carriere is Associate Deputy Assistant Secretary for University Partnerships, Office of University Partnerships, U.S. Department of Housing and Urban Development, 7th Street, SW Room 8106, Washington, DC 20410 (E-mail: Armand_W._Carriere@hud.gov).

For more information, contact: University Partnerships Clearinghouse, 8737 Colesville Road, Suite 1200, Silver Spring, MD 20910 (E-mail: oup@oup.org).

[Haworth co-indexing entry note]: "Preface." Carriere, Armand. Co-published simultaneously in Journal of Community Practice (The Haworth Social Work Practice Press, an imprint of The Haworth Press, Inc.) Vol. 12, No. 3/4, 2004, pp. xxv-xxviii; and: University-Community Partnerships: Universities in Civic Engagement (ed: Tracy M. Soska, and Alice K. Johnson Butterfield) The Haworth Social Work Practice Press, an imprint of The Haworth Press, Inc., 2004, pp. xv-xviii. Single or multiple copies of this article are available for a fee from The Haworth Document Delivery Service [1-800-HAWORTH, 9:00 a.m. - 5:00 p.m. (EST). E-mail address: docdelivery@haworthpress.com].

was designed to enable the college or university to respond to community issues *as identified by the community*. The architects of the program went to great lengths to ensure that this program would not be perceived as yet another research or field work foray into the community, regardless of how well intentioned, by the local college or university.

The word "Partnership" in the program title is the operative term. Examples contained in the articles that follow all emphasize partnering with the community. And as the examples further describe, the partnerships are with a variety of organizations, some mainstream, some grassroots, but all representing the interests of the communities to be served.

While attempting to focus the resources of colleges and universities on the problems of urban America was new to HUD and comparatively new to the government, the concept of college or university outreach is as old as American higher education itself. Readers are encouraged to pursue the writings and speeches of Dr. Ira Harkavy, a historian and nationally renowned leader in the field of campus-community engagement at the University of Pennsylvania. Dr. Harkavy traces the history and development of campus-community engagement from colonial days, through the establishment of land grant colleges and their attendant extension services (Harkavy, 1992; Harkavy & Puckett, 1994), right up to current times and the work of trail blazing institutions like the University of Pennsylvania, Portland State University, and Trinity College.

Latter day trends, with modest support from HUD over the past 10 years, have seen a greater emphasis on linking a broad range of disciplines to outreach activities. HUD's contribution also coincides with the rapid growth and influence of organizations like Campus Compact and the Learn and Serve Office of the Corporation for National and Community Service, two organizations promoting service learning. During its 10-year history HUD/OUP has been privileged to provide seed money to approximately 150 colleges and universities, many of whom have understood that a key factor in sustaining these outreach efforts involves adapting curriculum to community engagement efforts.

Present at the creation with COPC back in 1994 was the Community Development Work Study Program (CDWSP). Transferred into the Office of University Partnerships from HUD's Office of Community Planning and Development, the Work Study Program has sought to enroll low-income, minority students in graduate-level community building curricula through direct grants to universities ranging from $90,000 to $150,000. In their Introduction, Tracy Soska and Alice Johnson Butterfield take HUD to task for historically ignoring the field of Social

Work in HUD's definition of what constitutes a community-building curriculum. They accurately point out that concentrations and majors within social work have long fostered the development of professionals serving with distinction in a variety of public service roles. Through their efforts and the efforts of their colleagues in the field of social work, HUD's 2004 Notice of Funding Availability for the CDWS Program was expanded to include appropriate majors and concentrations within social work. I believe this decision will ultimately strengthen the program and provide additional opportunities for deserving graduate students.

Over the past 10 years other programs have been added to OUP's portfolio. These programs, many of which target minority-based institutions, have greatly enriched the Office and have enabled us to assist more institutions addressing the needs of distressed communities. We are building on the legacy of institutions of higher education serving the African American, Latino, and other minority communities.

We have also developed doctoral research grant programs that inform HUD's research agenda and help develop a cadre of scholars dedicated to studying important housing and community development issues. These research grants, ranging from $15,000 to $55,000, have helped tie the mission of OUP more closely to the overall mission of the Department. Specific grants programs targeting second year PhD students, students preparing to write a dissertation, and junior faculty members establishing their career pre-tenure have provided HUD with scholarly studies of contemporary and relevant topics. Successful proposals have been received from a variety of disciplines, including the social sciences.

But the flagship of the Office remains the COPC program. Starting back in 1994 with what could be euphemistically referred to as the "usual suspects," i.e., Cal-Berkeley, UCLA, Trinity, Yale, etc., the program has evolved to now include a variety of institutions more representative of the total academic landscape, including liberal arts colleges, minority-based institutions, and community colleges.

Along with this deeper, richer applicant base has come a broadened curricular involvement, especially among professional schools. The Graduate School of Social Work at the University of Maryland-Baltimore took the lead in the University's COPC application and has developed an outstanding program serving a number of neighborhoods through a network of Village Centers in the West Baltimore Empowerment Zone. Students and faculty from the School of Social Work help organize residents in on-going problem-solving activities.

The University of Pittsburgh's School of Social Work has done a similar thing, serving as the catalyst at the University in an outstanding outreach effort in 5 neighborhoods that are a part of the city's Enterprise Community. The COPC grant grew out of multi-year assessments that the University conducted, in partnership with its community, to identify urgent needs of the neighborhoods. In both of these examples, the School of Social Work is successfully linking classroom activities with outreach work, responding to needs identified by their community partners.

I am delighted to introduce this publication and take great pride in the accomplishments of the institutions highlighted within. The articles provide testimony to the benefits to be derived by both the institution of higher education and the community. The kinds of activities inherent in a social work curriculum, including applied research, field assignments, internships, and the clients you serve, including public and non-profit agencies, all fit extremely well with the goals and aims of COPC. For those of you who are doing this work, I hope you share my feeling of pride in what is being accomplished. And for institutions that have not sought COPC or other OUP resources to assist you in your work, I hope you will be inspired by these wonderful success stories.

As important as partnerships are for individual campuses, so too are partnerships important for the greater Office of University Partnerships. I appreciate the opportunity to join the Association of Community Organization and Social Administration and Haworth Press, Inc. in this publication and look forward to additional opportunities to collaborate in the future.

REFERENCES

Harkavy, I. (1992). The University and social sciences in the social order: An historical overview and "Where do we go from here?" *Virginia Social Science Journal*, 27: 1-25.

Harkavy, I., & Puckett, J.L. (1994). Lessons from Hull House for the contemporary urban university. *Social Service Review*, 68(3), 299-321.

University-Community Partnerships:
An Introduction

Alice K. Johnson Butterfield, PhD
Tracy M. Soska, MSW

The title of this work is "University-Community Partnerships: Universities in Civic Engagement." This publication responds to the growing trend of university-community partnerships and campus civic engagement. Community Outreach Partnership Center (COPC) programs, sponsored by the U.S. Department of Housing and Urban Development (HUD), have provided new financial incentives for universities and communities to partner in community building. Reports on higher education from the Kellogg Commission on the Future of State and Land Grant Universities (1999) and the Carnegie Foundation for the Advancement of Teaching (Ehrlich, 2000) have identified civic engagement and community partnership as critical themes for institutions of higher education (IHEs). University-community partnerships have emerged as vital for teaching, research, and practice. Reports of these interdisciplinary efforts are found in urban planning, higher education, and community development literature.

Our intention in soliciting manuscripts for this publication was also prompted by the particular lack of attention to university-community partnerships in social work. While we acknowledge the new interdisciplinary nature of these partnerships in this publication, we take special

[Haworth co-indexing entry note]: "University-Community Partnerships: An Introduction." Butterfield, Alice K. Johnson, and Tracy M. Soska. Co-published simultaneously in *Journal of Community Practice* (The Haworth Social Work Practice Press, an imprint of The Haworth Press, Inc.) Vol. 12, No. 3/4, 2004, pp. 1-11; and: *University-Community Partnerships: Universities in Civic Engagement* (ed: Tracy M. Soska, and Alice K. Johnson Butterfield) The Haworth Social Work Practice Press, an imprint of The Haworth Press, Inc., 2004, pp. 1-11. Single or multiple copies of this article are available for a fee from The Haworth Document Delivery Service [1-800-HAWORTH, 9:00 a.m. - 5:00 p.m. (EST). E-mail address: docdelivery@haworthpress.com].

notice of the role of social workers in university-community partnerships.

THE CALL FOR PAPERS AND ITS OUTCOME

The response to the "Call for Papers" was excellent. Fifty-two manuscripts were submitted for peer review, and twelve articles were selected for publication. The first two articles focus on the history, contemporary context, and models of university-community partnerships. The remaining articles are grouped into three sections: (1) HUD-funded Community University Partnership Center (COPC) programs; (2) wide-ranging social work partnerships involving teaching, research, and social change; and (3) innovative methods in the processes of civic engagement.

Before introducing the reader to each article, we take a moment to discuss what is meant by the terms *university-community partnership*. While the term is rather straight-forward, it is perhaps so general that it is difficult to outline just what is meant by a university-community partnership. This was certainly evident in the papers submitted for consideration in this publication. There were papers on service learning, applied research, reports of community meetings and conferences, participatory research, and so on. From this broad range of topics, we learned a lot about what one might call the "individual" perspective of university-community partnerships–individual faculty members or programs working with communities in some type of participatory research or collaboration. Other papers gave us much better idea of university-community partnerships as an "institutional" response. These types of partnerships are those in which the university institutionalizes a structure within itself such as a Center or nonprofit organization to engage with the community. It was also somewhat disconcerting to learn how few schools of social work are connected to these institutional partnerships. However, schools of social work did document creative individual faculty and program partnerships with communities and demonstrated they were on a "learning curve" in regards to institutional partnerships.

AN OVERVIEW OF LEAD ARTICLES

In the lead article, *Robert Fisher*, *Michael Fabricant*, and *Louise Simmons* provide an overview of the increasing civic engagement of institutions of higher education. The contemporary movement arose out of Bok's (1982) argument for a more engaged university and Boyer's (1990) challenge to institutions of higher education (IHEs) to engage with local communities in solving social problems. "Understanding contemporary university-community connections: Context, practice, and challenges" traces major historical developments and raises critical questions about the context of contemporary university-community relationships. What contemporary forces drive the movement? The authors point out the far-reaching trend of privatization which "load sheds" the social welfare elements of the state on to non-profits and community institutions.

> Consider, for example, the dramatic decline in percentage of income directed to public institutions from the state, and the increasing pressures of universities to raise more external funds, to be more entrepreneurial, and to load shed costs or to transfer costs to students whose tuition keeps rising. . . . Of course, the vacuum created in communities, especially urban areas, does provide new opportunities for those who have been trying–sometimes for more than 30 years–to engage IHEs to reassume their broader civic mission and role.

Rather than substitute for declining public responsibility, IHEs are urged to engage as part of a larger force for civic responsibility and social change.

"University Civic Engagement with Community-Based Organizations: Dispersed or Coordinated Models?" by *Elizabeth A. Mulroy* compares and contrasts two case studies of large research universities involved in civic engagement projects with urban nonprofit community-based organizations and neighborhood associations. Each uses a different approach to achieve a university-community partnership. The University of Hawaii's *dispersed* model encourages an entrepreneurial approach for individual faculty and student involvement, while the University of Maryland's *coordinated* model invites faculty and students from different departments to work together. Whether the university delivered what community organizations wanted was based on five factors, including geographic proximity, institutional leadership, community-based research, funding, and curriculum flexibility. Mulroy outlines the need for further research on models of civic engagement. Theses two contributions underscore several topics also addressed by other authors in the works that follow.

COMMUNITY OUTREACH PARTNERSHIP CENTER (COPC) PROGRAMS

One image of university-community partnerships is the urban university engaged with a local community in close geographic proximity to its campus. Typically, university faculty and/or the university have a history of relationships (good, bad, or otherwise) with neighboring communities. The majority of contemporary civic engagement work by institutions of higher education falls in this category. But, is close geographic proximity necessary? In "Connecting a University to a Distant Neighborhood: Three Stages of Learning and Adaptation" *Margaret Bourdeaux Arbuckle* and *Ruth Hoogland DeHoog* offer a candid analysis of three developmental stages of a COPC partnership between the University of North Carolina at Greensboro and the Macedonia neighborhood that is 30 minutes driving time from the university. In addition to its "distant community" aspect, the article emphasizes the need for the university (and its COPC program) to shift roles, methodology, and project focus as the community changes and develops its own strategies and funding sources. What one gleans from this article is the importance of university leadership that is responsive to the dynamics of community change. University-community partnerships can evolve, and thereby, bring the university to a deeper understanding of the partners and the community. In this case, the authors acknowledge how an "unplanned process" moved the partnership from technical assistance to self-help.

Next, "The Role of Evaluation in Developing Community-Based Interventions: A COPC Project," also deals with issues of community change, but from the perspective of evaluation research. *Sondra SeungJa Doe* and *Daniel Lowery* point out that evaluating COPC programs presents problems because the partnerships are supposed to evolve over time through the participation of community members. Reporting on the initial stages of the evaluation of a COPC initiative at Indiana University Northwest in Gary, Indiana, the article describes four distinct COPC components: education, neighborhood revitalization, community organizing and economic development. Their paper highlights the use of logic modeling–an evaluation method that is increasingly required by many federal funding agencies.

In the contemporary period, research is a major component of contemporary civic engagement. However, not all efforts by IHEs involve research. In "Seven Ways of Teaching and Learning: University-Community Partnerships at Baccalaureate Institutions," *Steven R. Timmermans* and *Jeffrey P.*

Bouman discuss the Service Learning Center at Calvin College, a small liberal arts college in Grand Rapids, Michigan. At this COPC program, civic engagement is not based on research, but on various forms of teaching and learning. The article details a range of *curriculum-linked* and *partnership-driven* activities suitable for helping baccalaureate educational institutions fulfill their teaching missions in partnership with the local community. Those readers from baccalaureate institutions may be inspired by these creative approaches in civic engagement through internships, independent studies, resident hall partnerships, work study, and various models of service learning.

SOCIAL WORK
AND UNIVERSITY-COMMUNITY PARTNERSHIPS

In a reflective essay on books in higher education and their implications for community practice, David Moxley (2003) wrote:

> I am puzzled by the relative dearth of knowledge about social work practice in higher education, and by the absence of literature that explicates the role of community practitioners in higher education as force for institutional change and development. There is a real need for literature that illuminates the distinctive contributions social workers with community practice focus can bring to higher education. (p. 106)

Perhaps we as social work educators don't write an adequate amount about our work in higher education for several reasons. Too often, data are descriptive; methods are perceived as lacking rigor for tenure venues. Or, perhaps, we have not taken the time to write about civic engagement efforts that more likely "fit" into categories of teaching or service. Whatever the reason, the profession suffers when funding agencies, government officials, and the like don't realize that social workers are involved.

For example, HUD's Office of University Partnerships (OUP) has funded grants through the Community Development Work Study Program (CDWSP) since 1996. CDWSP provides a two-year $150,000 grant to support up to five economically disadvantaged and minority students who are enrolled full-time in a graduate community building program. CDWSP pays tuition, fees, books, and a work stipend of up to $1000 per month, or an average of $15,000 per year, per student.

Sounds good, doesn't it? Disadvantaged and minority students. . . . Working in community building. . . . Are these community practice students in social work? Not likely. Since CDWSP's inception, social work has been listed as an *ineligible*! Only now, as we write this introduction to the special issue in June 2004, are *social work programs eligible to apply for funding!* And this happened only after intense ACOSA and NASW advocacy and education with HUD's Office of University Partnerships–an effort to raise awareness of schools of social work with strong and active programs and curriculum in community building, community organizing and community development. It was surprising that HUD did not realize or recognize the role of social work schools in developing community building practitioners; they saw social work from a narrow, clinical perspective not at all connected to their community initiatives.

This is not a critique of HUD or of its officials. Rather it is a critique of social work, of our lack of participation and particularly of our *lack of visibility* in community building as a part of higher education. The Office of University Partnerships has been consistent in its effort to develop and disseminate curricula and teaching methods related to community building skills and strategies in colleges and universities. For example, in July 2000, OUP sponsored a conference billed as "the first-ever assembly of community building curricula programs" (OUP, 2000a, p. 1). Only two or three social workers were among the 100 or so representatives of HUD-funded projects involving faith-based organizations, urban planning, public policy, and COPC programs. Three major conference reports discuss the amount of curriculum work going on at undergraduate and graduate levels (McNeely et al., 2000; Thomas, 2000; OUP, 2000b). "An influential paper by Victor Rubin (Rubin, 1999) who spearheaded the HUD effort, reported that community building education is happening in all kinds of majors. No mention is made of social work!" (Johnson, 2004, p. 320).

The next four papers recognize and document the efforts of social work faculty engaged in university-community partnerships through education, research, and social change. We hope that these few articles begin a dialogue about what social workers are doing in civic engagement through higher education. Our impression is that social workers are involved in many forms of civic engagement. Certainly, more is being done than has been recorded in the literature. We hope these articles encourage others to write about the social work role in higher education and civic engagement.

This section begins with "University-Community Partnership Centers: An Important Link for Social Work Education" by *Mary E. Rogge* and *Cynthia J. Rocha*. Although the School of Social Work at the University of Tennessee did not play a major leadership role within the University's COPC program and its Community Partnership Center, the authors consciously planned and measured their involvement as individual social work faculty. What we like about this article is its "nuts and bolts" illustration of how pretenure faculty can meet requirements for research, teaching, and service through involvement in university-community partnerships. Their dynamic participation maximized student learning, shaped community service, and resulted in scholarly publications. Students engaged in legislative lobbying, advocacy, and social change; Community Fellows contributed to classroom teaching. The article outlines the challenges and mutual benefits derived from faculty involvement with an established center for university-community partnerships.

Mindy R. Wertheimer and her social work colleagues at Georgia State University present the development of a unique MSW program structured around a single concentration of community partnerships. Recognizing how devolution and cutbacks in social service funding have affected agencies, a case is made that today's service delivery environment requires agencies to collaborate and form partnerships. "Community Partnerships: An Innovative Model for Social Work Education and Practice" describes specific courses and outlines how the curriculum model works in view of accreditation standards, course offerings, and field placements. The MSW program is anchored to the centrality of partnership for service delivery and community building. In addition, a unique aspect of this new curriculum is its concept of organizing around skill sets rather than objectives, which allows for flexibility in meeting community needs.

"The collaborative research education partnership: Community, Faculty, and Student Partnerships in Practice Evaluation" describes another creative mechanism for developing university-community partnerships. *Marla Berg-Weger* and colleagues at Saint Louis University discuss the founding and operation of the Emmett J. and Mary Martha Doerr Center for Social Justice Education and Research, an endowed non-profit organization located within the School of Social Service. Each year, the Center requests proposals and community agencies respond with a letter of intent. The proposals are reviewed, matched with faculty interests, and faculty-agency teams write proposals. Funded projects involve students as research assistants through field practicum, independent study, or part-time employment. These research education partnerships emphasize issues of social justice and evaluations of evidence-based practice.

The last article in this section adds an international perspective for our consideration. How often do schools of social work sponsor a major change in public policy? What challenges face the university in the role of catalyst and organizer? *Roni Kaufman* addresses these questions in "A University-Community Partnership to Change Public Policy: Pre-Conditions and Processes." In collaboration with community service and social advocacy organizations, faculty and students at the Department of Social Work at Ben-Gurion University in Israel join forces to identify hunger as a social problem, and promote the right to food security in Israel. The outcome of their multi-faceted advocacy effort is the establishment of a governmental task force to prepare guidelines for a National School Lunch Program Bill. The article considers the necessary preconditions for university-community collaboration in policy change, including competent and committed faculty, university and organizational environments that back social actions, and organizational structures that enable collaboration.

THE PROCESSES OF CIVIC ENGAGEMENT

One theme that runs consistently through the articles in this special issue is the process of engagement with the community. Several authors refer to the "town-gown" phenomenon to depict the inequalities inherent in relationships between universities and local communities. Many central city areas have been battered by segregation, riots, disinvestment, toxic waste disposal, deindustrialization, natural disasters, and so on. Such urban areas exist in the shadow of many local universities with its academic way of life, bureaucratic power, complicated committee structures, administrative policies, research grants, expansion plans, and multi-million dollar budgets. Compounding these problems is the "memory" of the community. Community members often cite examples of when university faculty parachuted into the community to "study it" through needs assessments and various research projects–only to abandon them when studies were completed, research reports written and not shared with community, and the university's funding lapsed. Many local communities haven't forgotten their "ivory tower" encounters.

Through innovative methods that bridge these aforementioned inequalities, the articles in this section add new voices to our dialogue about the concept of university-community partnerships. We have chosen these articles because they highlight varied roles and innovative engagement methods, including processes involving consultants, a post-disaster response coalition, and community organizing by community-based agencies.

The first article in this section addresses the general lack of literature about the role of consultants in community practice. In some ways, even the word "consultant" conjures up the idea that those in positions of power and authority have hired experts to help them get what they want. "Partnerships and Processes of Engagement: Working as Consultants in the US and UK" by *Jeremy Kearney* and *Denys M. Candy* reveals a different aspect of consultancy. Since current social policy in the US and UK has made partnership a key element of most community-based activities, requiring partnership can lead to "the very social hierarchies that such collaboration is intended to defuse." Drawing from organizational consulting, group work, and methods originally developed by family therapists, the authors demonstrate the use of *high engagement techniques* to facilitate successful partnerships.

The next article provides another take on the engagement process. "Community and University Participation in Disaster-Relief Recovery: An Example from Eastern North Carolina" by *Stephanie Farquhar* and *Noelle Dobson* challenges conventional wisdom that IHE civic engagement should always involve long-term commitment. In this example, the School of Public Health at the University of North Carolina is approached by a coalition of agencies for emergency assistance in the aftermath of Hurricane Floyd. Because engagement is fueled by the community, the authors, a post-doctoral fellow and research assistant at the time, emphasize the time-limited nature of their work by naming it a "community-university" partnership. This case is also a good example of how community-based participatory research can benefit marginalized groups that are disproportionately affected by the hardships of natural disasters, and usually excluded from recovery policy and decision-making.

We have chosen the final article because it recaps the major sections and themes of this publication. "Addressing Barriers to University-Community Collaboration: Organizing by Experts or Organizing the Experts?" discusses the history of COPC as social policy and summarizes a major evaluation of university-community partnerships (Vidal, Nye, Walker, Manjaerrez, & Romanik, 2002). Authors *Donna J. Cherry* and *Jon Shefner* outline how class, race, and organizational differences are barriers to equity and equality in civic engagement processes. Drawing from the literature in social work and sociology, they suggest several methods that can be used by community organizers to disrupt these structural inequalities and bring about authentic partnership. In organizing the experts, community-based organizers also need to resist taking the expert or buffer role in bringing traditionally segregated groups together in collaborative relationships.

In a complementing segment, "Engaged Research in Higher Education and Civic Responsibility Reconsidered: A Reflective Essay," *David P. Moxley* examines higher education research and explores how civic engagement is helping to redefine the university's role in relation to community partnerships and applied participatory research. Moxley examines two books that present new insights, case studies, and models for enhancing our "engaged research." This essay analyzes how these engaged efforts are challenging and reshaping our higher education research enterprise and its long-standing paradigm.

As the editors of this publication, our closing commentary provides a summary introduction to the growing literature and rich dialogue that is emerging on university-community partnerships and civic engagement. From the historical connection of cities and universities (Bender, 1988) to the outstanding websites of Campus Compact and the National Service Learning Clearinghouse on service learning in civic engagement, to the wealth of information from and connections to the many colleges and universities that are part of HUD's Office of University Partnerships, there is a plentiful array of information available to those interested. We outline a number of the more notable journals and books that have begun to reflect the "scholarship of our engagement" as well as its pedagogy in higher education, and invite our readers to explore this literature further and make their own contributions.

REFERENCES

Bender, T. (Ed.). (1988). *The university and the city: From medieval origins to the present.* New York: Oxford University Press.

Bok, D. 1982. *Beyond the ivory tower: Social responsibilities of the modern university.* Cambridge, MA: Harvard University Press.

Boyer, E. (1990). *Scholarship reconsidered: Priorities of the professoriate.* Princeton, NJ: Carnegie Foundation for the Advancement of Teaching.

Ehrlich, T. (Ed.). (2000). *Civic responsibility and higher education.* Phoenix, AZ: Oryx Press.

Johnson, A.K. (2004). Social work is standing on the legacy of Jane Addams: But are we sitting on the sidelines? *Social Work, 49*(2), 319-322.

McNeely, J., Hull, P., Motley, S., Johnson, V., Johnson, S., & Sharer, M. (2000, July). *Competency study of leaders who facilitate successful community building initia-*

tives (pp. 1-23). (Draft report prepared for the National Community Building, United Way, and the Annie E. Casey Foundation by Development Training Institute and IORD, Inc.). Retrieved January 3, 2004 from *http://www.oup.org/curriculum/files/competencystudy.doc*

Moxley, D.P. (2003). Books on higher education and their implications for community practice: A reflective essay. *Journal of Community Practice, 11*(3), 103-111.

Office of University Partnerships. (2000a). HUD awards $7.5 million to 24 colleges and universities to revitalize neighborhoods near their campuses (p. 1). Retrieved June 22, 2004 from *http://www.oup.org/about/collegeawards.html*

Office of University Partnerships. (2000b). *Teaching and learning for community building: New roles, new skills, and stronger partnerships.* Washington, DC: U.S. Department of Housing and Urban Development. Retrieved January 2, 2004 from *http://www.oup.org/about/teachandlearn.html*

Office of University Partnerships. (2004). Community development work study program (CDWSP9). Retrieved June 22, 2004 from *http://www.oup.org/about/aboutcdwsp.html*

Rubin, V. (1999, December 7). *How community building is finding its way into the graduate curriculum* (pp. 43-55). (Remarks by Victor Rubin to Conference on "Community Building: How Can Higher Education Make a Difference?") Washington, DC: U.S. Department of Housing and Urban Development. Retrieved January 2, 2004 from *http://www.oup.org/about/confpapconfpap.pdf*

The Kellogg Commission on the Future of State and Land-Grant Universities. (February, 1999). *Returning to our roots: The engaged institution.* Washington, DC: National Association of State Universities and Land-Grant Colleges. Retrieved June 30, 2004 from: *http://www.nasulgc.org/Kellogg/kellogg.htm*

Thomas, N.L. (2000). Community perceptions: What higher education can learn by listening to communities. In Development and Training Institute & IORD, Inc., *Competency study of leaders who facilitate successful community building initiatives* (pp. 26-42). Retrieved June 22, 2004 from *http://www.oup.org/about/confpapconfpap.pdf*

Vidal, A., Nye, N., Walker, C., Manjaerrez, C., & Romanik, C. (2002). *Lessons from the community outreach partnership center program.* Retrieved June 22, 2004 from *http://www.huduser.org/publications/commdevl/lessons_complete.html*

LEAD ARTICLES

Understanding Contemporary University-Community Connections: Context, Practice, and Challenges

Robert Fisher, PhD
Michael Fabricant, PhD
Louise Simmons, PhD

SUMMARY. This article contextualizes the contemporary phenomenon of university-community partnership initiatives. Because changes in the university must always be understood in context, recent efforts to build and strengthen relationships between institutions of higher educa-

Robert Fisher is Professor of Social Work and Director of Urban and Community Studies at the University of Connecticut. Michael Fabricant is Professor and Director of the PhD program at Hunter College/CUNY School of Social Work. Louise Simmons is Associate Professor of Social Work and Director of the Urban Semester Program at the University of Connecticut.

Address correspondence to: Robert Fisher, PhD, School of Social Work, University of Connecticut, 1798 Asylum Avenue, West Hartford, CT 06117 (E-mail: robert. fisher@uconn.edu).

[Haworth co-indexing entry note]: "Understanding Contemporary University-Community Connections: Context, Practice, and Challenges." Fisher, Robert, Michael Fabricant, and Louise Simmons. Co-published simultaneously in *Journal of Community Practice* (The Haworth Social Work Practice Press, an imprint of The Haworth Press, Inc.) Vol. 12, No. 3/4, 2004, pp. 13-34; and: *University-Community Partnerships: Universities in Civic Engagement* (ed: Tracy M. Soska, and Alice K. Johnson Butterfield) The Haworth Social Work Practice Press, an imprint of The Haworth Press, Inc., 2004, pp. 13-34. Single or multiple copies of this article are available for a fee from The Haworth Document Delivery Service [1-800-HAWORTH, 9:00 a.m. - 5:00 p.m. (EST). E-mail address: docdelivery@haworthpress.com].

tion and communities must be situated in the broader social sites that produce them. To that end the article surveys the university-community intersect through an historical lens which emphasizes the relationship between the larger political-economy and civic engagement efforts. Subsequently, types of contemporary initiatives are broadly and selectively discussed. Lastly, challenges to both universities and communities embodied in the current initiatives are posed. *[Article copies available for a fee from The Haworth Document Delivery Service: 1-800-HAWORTH. E-mail address: <docdelivery@haworthpress.com> Website: <http://www.Haworth Press.com> © 2004 by The Haworth Press, Inc. All rights reserved.]*

KEYWORDS. University-community partnerships, civic engagement, service learning, political economy, social work education, history of university-community partnerships, institutions of higher education

INTRODUCTION

In 1996 Ernest Boyer, then President of the Carnegie Foundation for the Advancement of Teaching, proposed that the missions of higher education achieved their greatest fulfillment when they served larger purposes such as building a more just society. He denounced the ivory tower and profession-oriented dimensions of the university which caused it to withdraw from the larger society, to turn inward and away from the most pressing civic, social, economic, and moral problems (Boyer, 1996). Derek Bok (1982), then President of Harvard, argued similarly more than a decade earlier for a more engaged university, one that would help address basic social problems, better prepare more teachers, and play a role in societal moral development. Boyer and Bok are two of the best known proponents of a new wave of educational theory and practice that developed in the 1980s and has gained significant momentum in the past two decades throughout the nation. Of course, few things happen quickly in institutions of higher education. Universities and colleges are highly complex organizations, with multiple missions, many of them currently in tension with a vision of civic engagement. Further challenging any generalization across higher education is the fact that institutions of higher education (IHEs) extend across a broad spectrum, from community colleges to small private and public liberal arts colleges to large private and public research universities. Nevertheless, these and other caveats aside, higher education is increasingly engaged in a discourse regarding university-community relations, a discussion about "preparing America's undergraduates for lives of moral and civic responsibility," not to mention developing applied initiatives in nearby communities, towns, cities, and throughout their states (Colby, Ehrlich, Beaumont, & Stephens, 2003, p. iii).

The proliferation of university-community projects is dramatic. Cortes (2003) writes that universities, especially ones in cities, are significantly affected by and therefore usually most likely to be engaged with adjacent communities. To address this problem the academy increasingly applies specialized expertise to local communities. This contributes to the development of programs and community service which seek to correct long-standing community problems. In 1999, the U.S. Department of Housing and Urban Development reported 342 colleges offering almost 600 university-community partnership initiatives, more than double the totals that HUD reported four years earlier. Critically, HUD was not simply recording the change. It helped to fuel this development through its Community Outreach Partnership Center (COPC) program, which since 1994 has awarded upwards of $50 million to more than 100 institutions of higher education. Increasingly, financial revenue sources such as HUD provide additional incentive to participate and thereby make university-community initiatives even more compelling.

In an age of declining public resources for IHEs, the impact of targeted, expansive funding from both public and foundation sources linked to societal improvement can not be easily overestimated. Certainly funding for civic engagement helps drive IHE interest in working with potential community partners. But university motives to pursue civic engagement are much more complex than needing additional financial support (Cortes, 2003). For example, often universities find themselves unable to remain aloof from their surrounding communities. In some cases the area around them begins to decay, forcing the local environment and its problems on the college or university. And unlike more mobile corporations, which might choose to leave the area, most universities are place bound. In response to declining adjacent communities, the initial IHE reaction was separation. Put up walls. Expand police forces. These responses exacerbated town and gown tensions. But as this tension increased, many universities and colleges have come to prefer more durable, community friendly approaches that contribute to strengthened relationships with their neighbors (Maurrasse, 2001). Also, universities have been forced to acknowledge their obligation to the world around them as they have come under increasing scrutiny as affluent institutions with resources to help affect larger societal issues. IHEs increasingly realize that knowledge production, a central mission of higher education institutions, can be enhanced by university-community connections. Civic engagement adds new voices and ideas to the intellectual process, ideally adding new perspectives and insights, just as it helps ground and give broader meaning to the world of ideas and the work of academics (Young, 1995; Cortes, 2003). Moreover, there is a close correlation between civic engagement initiatives and recent efforts of universities to more effectively prepare students for democratic moral and civic responsibility.

This article seeks to contextualize this phenomenon longitudinally and cross-sectionally. It argues that changes in the university must always be understood in context, that recent efforts to build and strengthen relationships between IHEs and communities must be situated in the broader social sites that produce them. These efforts are rooted in deep historic and recent trends. We will first discuss the phenomenon of university-community intersect through an historical lens that emphasizes the relationship between the larger political-economy and civic engagement efforts. Subsequently, types of contemporary initiatives in the contemporary context will be broadly and selectively discussed. Lastly some challenges to both universities and communities embodied in the current initiatives will be posed.

IHEs AS DYNAMIC AND STABLE INSTITUTIONS

This discussion will first consider the tension between the socially dynamic and staid or insular qualities of the university and the impact of this tension on current trends in local civic engagement. The university has always been a dynamic developing institution, and much of this dynamism results from IHEs responding to historical forces both within and without the university. At various historic moments the university has been heavily influenced by new challenges which changed its mission, role in society, understanding of students, and relations with adjacent and broader communities. At any given time they are vanguard institutions filled with innovation and an atmosphere that encourages change within and without the university. Over its 350 year history the American university, according to Clark Kerr (2002), noted higher education theorist and administrator, has confronted and adapted to six major changes, developments heavily influenced by changes in the larger context outside the university. Over time IHEs accommodated the British model of college to a frontier society, accepted a land-grant mission of serving the larger society with the passage of the Morrill Act in 1862, moved from being elite to mass institutions and simultaneously took on a more scientific-research role after World War II, and were transformed as sites of democratic deliberation and struggle in the 1960s and early 1970s. The Morrill Act, for example, changed the landscape of higher education by expanding the number of schools, increasing access to college, creating publicly funded land grant colleges whose central mission included not only providing liberal and practical education but also improving the broader society. Among the dramatic contemporary changes in IHEs is the recent reexamination of the relationship between the university and the communities in which it is situated.

But while the history of IHEs is characterized by their innovation and change, many of which serve as the basis for current civic engagement efforts, IHEs, especially large public universities, are also easily characterized as bureaucratic institutions grounded in deep traditions and continuities. Consider the challenges of the long standing tradition of the university not thinking of itself as a local institution (Ferruolo, 1988). Out of this tradition three related tensions develop within IHEs which affect the civic engagement model. Should research be pure or applied? Should the audience for the university be a local or global one? And finally, should the ideal university environment offer students an ivory tower removed from local parochialism or a learning experience engaged directly with the world? For example, universities still debate whether there is a proper role for applied research in the liberal arts and sciences and whether the world of ideas, the search for truth, and pure research should be driven by current needs or external constituencies. Similarly, universities and faculties have oft argued that their primary audience was global rather than local, and indicated that a more parochial understanding of role delimited the schools' focus, reach, and appeal. Bender (1988b) declares the university has always claimed the world as its domain. Regardless of its local communal and knowledge building roots, the university has historically striven for learning that at least reaches toward universal significance. The University of Paris from its inception in the Medieval Age drew faculty and students from outside Paris with few ties to the local environment. It was in the language of the time a *studium generale* not a *studium particulare* (Ferruolo, 1988, p. 23). It always saw its audience and its work as more global than local. Paradoxically, there is also the tendency of the university to isolate itself and for the faculty to retreat into the university as an ivory tower. Proponents argue that the ivory tower conceptualization offers faculty and students the opportunity to consider larger questions unencumbered by parochial local or contemporary pressures. Walter Lippmann articulated this best in his renown Phi Beta Kappa Address in 1932, in the midst of the Great Depression, arguing that within the university some pushed for a "civic conscience" that would engage with the world's problems and there were others who promoted a "conscience of the scholar" which sought to "preserve a quiet indifference to the immediate" (cited in Peters et al., 2003, pp. 75-76). Lippmann urged scholarly detachment.

At the time, however, in the midst of the Great Depression, there were, of course, many, especially those influenced by John Dewey and the social movements of the day, who saw the university as a base for and means of civic engagement. In the sociology and social welfare departments at the University of Chicago, for example, Ernest Burgess, building on the earlier work of Robert Park, and Edith Abbott, building on the earlier work of Jane Addams and the social settlement house pioneers, pushed students to study, engage with, and help improve the world around them. Around the same time that Lippmann called for scholars and college students to withdraw from the world, Burgess helped initiate the Chicago Area Project which persuaded graduate students to live in working-class neighborhoods with high rates of crime and juvenile delinquency. And then, in partnership with community leaders and neighborhood youth, the graduate students were expected to help address criminal behavior and neighborhood issues (Shils, 1988). Noted community organizer Saul Alinsky got his start with the Chicago Area Project. Of course most civic engagement projects, then and now, are more paternalistic, that is treating the neighborhood as an object of study or development rather than as real partners who both participate in and benefit from the projects with IHEs (Maurrasse, 2001). But the University of Chicago model in the 1930s, while flawed, is more the exception than the norm. While Boyer and others suggest that contemporary changes make anachronistic such traditional tensions about pure and applied research and local vs. global audience, they are still very much part of a lively discourse within colleges and universities. Equally important this discourse continues to affect IHE willingness to venture into civic engagement projects.

CONTEXTUALIZING CONTEMPORARY COMMUNITY RELATIONS

There are multitudinous reasons for the transformation of IHEs overtime and for the interest in and opposition to IHE involvement in civic engagement. These include not only changes in the broader politi-cal-economy of an era, but also such critical factors as changes in fund-ing, demography, the academy, communities, educational theory and practice, not to mention the initiatives of faculty, students, organiza-tions, and community residents. Given the limited space for this article, the historical dimension of the analysis will emphasize the impact of broad contextual factors such as shifts in the larger political economy.

Because human actions and writings about university-community in-teraction are always specific to a particular time and place, a brief his-tory leading up to the current period must situate civic engagement practice in the context of the broader political economy as well as the varied social sites which generated civic engagement. These contextual factors, as well as daily practice, need to be understood in order to com-prehend better the potential as well as challenges inherent in the civic engagement phenomenon in IHEs. For example, the very question of whether university-community partnerships are encouraged or discour-aged is to no small extent a product of the larger historical context. It is not by accident that the renowned British historian E.P. Thompson (1971) referred to history as the discipline of context. What follows is not designed as a definitive history obviously, but rather to make clear that civic engagement has a rich past, that it's not simply a recent phe-nomenon. Also this section argues for the critical effect of the larger po-litical economy at any given time on the civic engagement practice of IHEs.

As Ross writes, since IHEs first began participating in their commu-nities during the Colonial era, the nature of their engagement has con-tinued to evolve in response to world and national events (Ross, 2002). In the colonial era and into the 19th century, institutions tended to view their mission as the education of citizens and civic leaders. With the passage of the Morrill Act in 1862, however, establishing land-grant universities, and then later with the Hatch Act of 1887, extending land-grant missions beyond agricultural communities, the Federal gov-ernment initiated support for university-community linkages and estab-lished a new role more directly linked to the improvement of society. Unfortunately, this new emphasis on applied research and community service ended up largely relegated to and limited by its role as an agri-cultural extension service function. Such extension services have changed over time–providing needed services and education–but while they continue to provide valuable services, they do so as a community service which resides outside the mainstream of land grant colleges (Ross, 2002). But at least the acts established by the late 19th century that education had a democratic function and the university should play a role in shaping communities. In her study of New York University, Stevenson (1988) concurs but broadens the historical lens. Whereas in 1800 the goal of IHEs was to create citizens of the republic and whereas by the mid-late nineteenth century the objective was to prepare students for public life, by 1900 the focus was on educating students to enter a profession.

Professionalism aside, university-community partnerships were stimulated by the broader civic engagement and reform movements of the so-called Progressive Era, beginning in the late 19th century and culminating more or less with the end of World War I. The best of the settlement house movement was connected in New York and Chicago with local universities. It underscored the potential for community building and social change that could accrue from university-educated community workers involved in partnership with neighborhood residents (Fabricant & Fisher, 2002; Fisher & Fabricant, 2002). Jane Addams and the other settlers at Hull-House in Chicago worked closely with the University of Chicago, helping to provide a model of civic engagement and social research for its Sociology Department and the School of Social Administration. In New York City, Seth Low, President of Columbia University, sought to build on the social reform ferment in the city and nation. He responded to the widespread class tensions of the time by articulating a new progressive vision of the university which called upon students and faculty to address contemporary social issues and needs (Bender cited in Ross, 2002, p. 4). Settlement leader Vida Scudder saw the era as a "cleavage of classes, cleavage of races, cleavage of faiths: an inextricable confusion" (Scudder cited in Shapiro, 1978, p. 215). In response to these broad challenges, reformers built organizations and redefined institutions to help address the needs of local communities and the broader public.

A shift in political economy ended this movement. The progressive impulse receded in the "return to normalcy" of the 1920s, characterized by a retreat from social reform in general and a turning-inward to individualism and business perspectives rather than collective need and a broader concern for the public good. World War I was a horrific experience and conservatives took advantage of it to attack radicals during the "Red Scare" and to push discourse away from progressive reform conceptualizations. Higher education followed suit, though of course not everywhere and not uniformly. But in general universities turned inward as well, once again emphasizing research as separate from social reform, emphasizing that the mission of the university was not to engage directly with the world around it (Harkavy, 1996; Fabricant & Fisher, 2002; Ross, 2002).

In the 1930s, plagued by the Great Depression, the political economy shifted again, sparking social activism and civic conscience intended to ease some of the horrific human need and desperation of the era. Curiously, for IHEs the decade was characterized by the ongoing tension between the "ivory tower" views of Lippmann and the engaged university ideas of Dewey and others. More dramatic change in terms of Federal support would not come until the GI Bill, which expanded university access to veterans after World War II, and the Great Society programs of the 1960s. But the sheer magnitude of the problems of the Depression and the consequent broad social movements and social policies that surfaced during this era transcended campus life. Critically, however, this context of ferment and change pushed discourse on campuses towards a focus on the public realm and the public good.

The 1960s and early 1970s had even more profound results on campuses. The Federal government had already begun in the 1950s to invest in public sector programs and by the time of President Johnson's Great Society there was widespread acceptance for the role of the Federal government in funding and encouraging social reform initiatives. IHEs, since World War II a major recipient of federal student scholarships and scientific research funds, now became a critical site for civic engagement initiatives. Stimulated by the pressures of the Cold War and the civil rights and black power movements, the Federal government passed a broad number of community-based initiatives out of the Office of Economic Opportunity (OEO) many of which targeted college students and faculty. For example, Peace Corp and ACTION programs provided the platform for student volunteerism directed at improving poor communities to reenter the public imagination. Spurred on by the civil rights, new left, antiwar, and emerging women's movements and coupled with massive Federal funding for faculty projects, college campuses were increasingly dominated by an interest in public issues and social change. Contrary to earlier calls for a withdrawn ivory tower, there was a swelling clamor for "relevance" and engagement, both intellectual and applied, with the issues and problems of the day. One example of such engagement was the Students for a Democratic Society (SDS) Education Research and Action Projects (ERAP) efforts to help mobilize and improve conditions in poor neighborhoods (Frost, 2001).

It was an exciting time on campus for those interested in public issues and civic engagement. As Clarke Chambers (1996), a history professor and founder of the Social Welfare History Archive at the University of

Minnesota, described the atmosphere and the role of Federal support for public initiatives:

> You talk about luck. You come back [from the war] and Congress in its wisdom had passed the GI Bill. . . . Certainly in the liberal arts, which I know best, any number of my generation who were working class families, poor hard scrabble farming families, second generation immigrant families would never have gone to school without the GI Bill. When they come into the profession in the 1950s, it takes a while to get established. But by the 1960s they're all in place and they change the nature [of things], at least in social science and the humanities. It's a remarkably lucky and exciting kind of breakthrough that takes place. . . . The things that excited me [about the 60s and early 70s] were the Women's Movement, and the environment, and the anti-war movement. [Others] it turns out were excited by lots of money. [One colleague, for example] got into the Center for Urban and Regional Affairs. There was money there and he was its first director. He could reach out into depressed ghetto neighborhoods and establish effective programs, and housing, and transportation. I'll tell you, it was exciting.

LOAD SHEDDING THE PUBLIC SECTOR, GLOBALIZATION, AND IHEs

One can debate the extent and impact of civic engagement on the part of contemporary IHEs, but not the increased interest in the idea in the past few decades. Embedded in the renewed interest in civic engagement is a dynamic dialectic between the broader contemporary context and the reaction of educators and community activists to it. One cause of interest in IHE civic engagement is the broader privatization (or corporatization) of the political economy which "load sheds" the social welfare elements of the state on to non-profits and community institutions, including universities, many of which are situated in or near communities that are collapsing under current neo-conservative policies and politics. These policies began, more or less, with the Reagan administration in the 1980s and continue to expand since then, especially with the current Bush regime. This essay has argued that in order to understand the change in practices at IHEs one must understand the larger context which helps produce them. In terms of the contemporary context, we find ourselves increasingly in a private as opposed to a public world, with profound implications for IHEs and communities. As the societal context becomes more a social and focused on private needs and institutions and divorced from social concerns, public life increasingly declines and the concept of a public good becomes more conservative and exclusionary (Fisher & Karger, 1997; Fabricant & Fisher, 2002; Simmons, 1998). We propose that the privatization of our contemporary context has several central features: It reflects a society dominated by a culture of private individuals, a physical world of private spaces, and a political economy of private institutions. We use the term privatization broadly to reflect these three trends, not simply as a shift from public to private ownership and control, though that is part of the broader definition.

These developments are not new (Bellah, Madsen, Sullivan, Swidler, & Tipton, 1985; Warner, 1968). But the current privatization of life is occurring with a massive speed and grander reach than ever before. In the past generation, an extraordinary social, political, and economic transformation and the neo-conservative response to it, has dramatically accelerated and expanded the privatization process, profoundly reshaping the context for IHEs and communities. The context of privatization forces almost all social and political agendas away from social welfare conceptualizations toward laissez-faire ones. Social problems and the public good are ignored as much as possible as new corporate agendas of unfettered capitalism come to dominate global, national, and local decision making. Critics argue that in the new global economy, nations or cities can not afford costly public programs except those for war and some protection functions. Critically, privatization diminishes revenue sources of the state and curbs the transfer of social costs onto the corporate sector and the affluent, those segments of the population assumed to be the engines of economic growth. As noted above, privatization is used here as a broad orientation toward this objective, which includes but is much more than a specific set of policy alternatives. Neoconservatives take pride in curbing big government, ending welfare as we know it, hammering at the costs of government, lowering taxes on the rich, undermining regulatory agencies, and delegitimizing public and social welfare programs. By undermining the citizenries sense of the proper role of government in American life, problems and solutions are pushed out of public spaces onto individuals, families, and communities that lack the resources to address deep-rooted social problems. It is this load shedding of public responsibility which has contributed to IHEs and non profits being asked to assume greater responsibility for specific aspects of community life that in an earlier era would have been shouldered by the public sector.

Curiously, as capital and power centralize in the new global economy, the function of both implementing its tasks and cleaning up its mess are increasingly decentralized. "Decentralization of production" accompanies "concentration of control" (Montgomery, 1995, p. 461). This leads, paradoxically, to significant new forms of public life. Nonprofits and voluntary-sector for-profits proliferate worldwide to address problems as diverse as ecological disasters, crime prevention and AIDS. Of course, this proliferation of voluntary and nonprofit organizations and groups is a mixed blessing, as it represents both a response and adjustment to the current context. What such a trend ultimately yields is a push away from the public and an overemphasis on the individual as the source of problems and the source of solutions. Such tendency has also contributed to a similar restructuring of urban space throughout the world, and the diminishing of public costs as much as possible. The load shedding of public responsibility away from the state increasingly falls on the still relatively substantial and surviving community institutions. Consequently, there is increasing pressure for IHEs to help address problems in communities which are, like most of society, being asked to do more with less. It is not happenstance that Boyer and other advocates of increased civic engagement raise the question of the public purposes of higher education at the same time as the public realm (outside of the military and protection services) faces increased attack, disinvestment, and dismantling (Colby, Ehrlich, Beaumont, & Stephens, 2003). Consider, for example, the dramatic decline in percentage of income directed to public institutions from the state, and the increasing pressures of universities to raise more external funds, to be more entrepreneurial, and to load shed costs or to transfer costs to students whose tuition keeps rising. This represents yet another form of privatization. Of course, the vacuum created in communities, especially urban areas, does provide new opportunities for those who have been trying–sometimes for more than 30 years–to engage IHEs to reassume their broader civic mission and role. But it needs to be contextualized within the larger restructuring of the public realm and the public good, so that IHE engagement serves as part of a larger force for civic responsibility and social change, not as a small substitute for declining public responsibility.

The preceding discussion of broad trends associated with IHE community collaboration must be tethered to descriptions of specific kinds of local initiative if a more dynamic understanding of this phenomenon is to be developed. It is on this basis we now turn our attention to describing dominant forms of contemporary university-community engagement.

PRIMARY FORMS
OF CONTEMPORARY CIVIC ENGAGEMENT

This section will briefly categorize and summarize some of the primary types of IHE civic engagement projects. It does not attempt to provide a complete catalogue of civic engagement, but rather seeks to illustrate the features of several key modes. One thread of the discussion explores the marginal relationship of social work to these civic engagement projects and the forces responsible for its exclusion. Finally, a number of the challenges and tensions associated with building collaborative projects between the university and communities will be described. The concluding discussion will more fully explore the power imbalance between IHEs and their communities which can impede building such partnership.

Service Learning

Some of the best known and most common endeavors include service learning and student engagement projects. Students may be involved in service oriented internships, class projects in which students help tackle community issues or assist local organizations, and other opportunities for students to learn from and contribute to the community around them. One of the critical ingredients of service learning, as opposed to engaging in community volunteer service projects, is a reflective component that helps students analyze their experience and its multiple contexts. Service learning projects afford students and faculty the opportunity to develop and nurture institutional and individual relationships with community organizations, activists and local residents (see for example, O'Grady, 2000; Ferrari & Chapman, 1999; Zlotkowski, 1998). While urban based IHEs generally have ready environments in which to develop service learning programs, there are also abundant types of service learning initiatives in rural and suburban communities that institutions can establish. Moreover, efforts are underway in many disciplines not typically associated with service to develop new opportunities to engage in service learning, including the natural sciences, engineering and business programs, along with the more typically service-oriented educational programs in social work, health fields, and others.

Local Economic Development

In some instances institutions have been involved in redevelopment projects to upgrade their immediate environs. They may partner with local community based organizations or larger institutions which are engaged in community development. Or they may sponsor activities or create entities in communities in order to have an economic impact, such as bookstores, restaurants, schools, childcare centers and more. Some are involved in housing development and, of course, they can and most often do employ local residents. As discussed by Cortes (2004), IHEs impact local housing markets and can undertake proactive strategies in the housing arena, using their market leverage to upgrade or stabilize neighborhoods. As employers, local hiring practices likewise impact living standards in host communities. For the largest IHEs, this role may have singular importance in the local labor market. IHEs have also offered computer resources and training to local residents.

Community Based Research

Sometimes called participatory action research or community-based research, IHE faculty and students have helped community residents, organizations, and agencies solve problems through research. Certainly they have offered the necessary technical expertise so that local organizations can more successfully frame issues and press their case in the policy arena. Health, environmental, and educational problems represent part of the nexus of faculty research focus and local entity problem solving. Local groups often lack their own internal research capacity but need data and analysis to pursue specific agendas (Minkler, 1997). Problems like the epidemic of asthma among urban children, diabetes among urban elderly, effective strategies to reduce HIV/AIDS transmission, or the disproportionate siting of toxic waste facilities adjacent to poor and urban neighborhoods are but a few examples of community problems that have brought together academics and local community activists in collaborative research.

Social Work Initiatives

In varying degrees social work embodies all of the three aforementioned types of IHE engagement, but because of the unique perspective and mission of social work, we offer it as a fourth type of category, perhaps even as a megacategory. For those involved in social work education and practice, particularly macro and community practice, the idea of civic engagement and IHE involvement in the larger community are fundamental and essential to social service education. Indeed social work education has a great deal to offer the proponents of IHEs outside of social work who seek to become more engaged with their surrounding communities. For macro social work, again particularly community practice, the social world is its arena and the issues and problems of the community are precisely its terrain of practice. This is what we do and continually struggle to do better. Moreover, it is interesting that while the structure of social work education includes a highly developed field education component in which many of the challenges of civic engagement arise and must be addressed, the conversation about civic engagement and even service learning within higher education has not yet fully included social work. In fact, leading proponents of service learning and civic education such as McKnight (1995) are highly critical of what they see as the "clientelism" and "professionalism" inherent in social work and social work education which undermines democratic and reflective civic engagement. Instead of considering how they might build on and learn from the long and deep history of social work education's engagement with the community, they flatly reject such possibility while creating the space and legitimacy for their own work. Of course social work with its penchant to focus on the individual and professional issues such as licensure oft appears divorced from initiatives for civic engagement, democratic process, and community ownership (Johnson, 2004). But we see the process between social work and civic engagement as more complex. Imbedded in professionalism is the development of skills of various kinds which to be effective must be tethered to the practice of community building (Fabricant & Fisher, 2002). We find the civic engagement critique that marginalizes social work to be comparable to Saul Alinsky's relationship to and rejection of the work of social settlement houses. Alinsky dismissed them as paternalistic (most were) but the work of settlements provided a substantial part of the knowledge base and experience for his own model (Fabricant & Fisher, 2002). This special issue, while not exclusively focused on social work's role, still adds an important perspective on the contributions of social work education to university-community efforts.

CHALLENGES AND OPPORTUNITIES

Engaging with local communities poses challenges and opportunities for IHEs and raises many questions regarding the structure, content, process and possible outcomes of collaborative research and education projects. The analysis below offers selective questions and analysis regarding some critical concerns about IHE civic engagement and does so from a social work perspective informed by social justice values, ethics, reciprocity, and participation. Critically, however, many of these very specific concerns are driven by the power imbalance that exists between the university and community. The final part of the discussion will therefore explore aspects of the relationship that are weighted in favor of the university and factors that might provide corrective.

Questioning the Educational and Research Agenda

First, and most familiar to social work educators and practitioners, are the challenges and opportunities flowing from the educational function and role of the college and university. Within this arena, one finds varied types of programs: service learning, community service options for students, participatory action research, as well as the discussion of how faculty can contribute expertise to the surrounding community and receive recognition within the reward structure of higher education for their efforts. There are local, regional and national conferences, professional organizations, student organizations, formal partnerships, grants from various levels of governments and foundations, all devoted to fostering student learning and faculty engagement in the community. From internships or field practicum to research projects to two-way or three- (or more) way partnerships, an entire range of activities is taking students and faculty out of the ivory tower and into social problem-solving.

Within these activities are various value and ethical questions. For example, one significant discussion that social workers can readily intuit is that of justice or charity (see Morton, 1995). Are we teaching and providing service from the standpoint of doing charity work or are we facilitating the means to achieve social justice in these endeavors? What do students learn, for example, by serving food at a soup kitchen? Do they understand the relationship between the service offered at the soup kitchen and our national and state social welfare policies, welfare reform, economic trends and the like? What happens when legions of students from IHEs trek into inner cities to tutor children in under-achieving schools? Do they have the opportunity to examine the structural inequities inherent in urban-suburban educational systems or the mandates under federal legislation around under-performing schools? How do students see themselves vis-à-vis the community residents with whom they interact? Do they view their role as "helping the underprivileged" or "fixing" deficient human beings, rather than understanding the "big picture" as well as learning from the people in the community and appreciating the cultural resiliencies and survival skills inherent in the communities where they work? Does the experience politicize their understanding of social problems or contribute to a depoliticized analysis? (Farnen, 2003). These and similar issues are at the essence of the question of contextualization.

Or consider the research area. When faculty alone or faculty and students undertake research projects focusing on issues of importance to the community, do community representatives have a say in the nature and content of the research? What protections are there for "subjects" of research? How will the findings be used and disseminated? These issues lead to the question of reciprocity within the relationships between the community and the IHE. What types of partnerships are constructed? What do community residents and institutions get out of these arrangements? All of these serious questions (and many more) emerge as the academy meets the community.

Understanding and Redressing the Power Imbalance Between the IHE and the Community

Any effort to develop collaboration between IHEs and communities must be mindful of the complex power imbalance between these actors. To begin with, universities aspire toward an expertise, as was noted in the first section, which is often theoretical, global, technical and formalized. Residents of local communities, however, construct their expertise from the experiential or local, often non-technical and informal information that coheres about their lived experience. Critically, the knowledge that is more often ascribed value is that which accrues to the university and its faculty. This imbalance can mute or silence community voice in such collaboration. When university administrators or faculty for example cite statistics or refer to sources to document points or use a language that is foreign to almost anyone outside their field of study, its impact may be to reduce rather than open dialogue. Critically, the IHE must respect the particular expertise community members bring to the project and open the conversation in ways that enables residents to feel like full participants rather than exotic guests. This is not a simple task. The kinds of distrust that exist between IHEs and many surrounding communities are daunting. Some part of that distrust can be traced to the university historically asserting prerogative on matters such as land use or service need on the basis of superior expertise. However, too often that expertise was perceived by community residents as weapons of language and ideas advancing self interest. The community's alternate forms of expertise which depended on anecdote and personal relationship were often no match in public forum for the data marshaled by the university. And so, in small as well as large meetings called to convene partnership, the IHE must struggle to rethink how it uses and presents its own expertise and how it hears and values the expertise of community members.

Moreover, the power relationship between the university and adjacent communities is often highly imbalanced. On the one hand, the university is a relatively powerful institutional player with relatively steady revenue streams, constituent groups of alumni, and access to power brokers. Especially in a world of shrinking alternatives, it is often perceived as a motor for economic development. On the other hand, the community, whether residents or organizations, often has few organized groups that identify themselves as constituents, at best unstable revenue sources, little access to power brokers and too often perceived as the source of problems and an impediment to economic development. How then can members of the community participate in collaborative efforts when the power differential is so great? The question might be restated to ask, how can the university begin to level the playing field? Critically, some part of the success of IHE collaboration has been contingent upon the university more freely sharing some part of its power with community groups. As this journal issue underscores, only in this way has the first step of repairing past damage and of building the trust necessary to presently create authentic partnership or relationship been taken.

Why would the university redistribute its power to communities? This question is answered as IHEs assess the potential benefits of strong, expansive university-community relationship and projects. To what extent do IHEs imagine that community partnership will promote various kinds of knowledge development, strengthen proposals to raise public or private money, stimulate dynamic teaching and learning experiences, and lend legitimacy with communities and politicians, especially from inner-city communities of people of color? Only when the IHE recognize and value such mutual benefit can a more reciprocal relationship of fuller partnership be built. The benefit is clear to many commentators; universities must develop greater linkage with communities and serve more useful purpose in helping address major issues or they risk social irrelevance and institutional decline (Ostrander, 2004).

Additionally, the IHE is under increasing pressure to identify new forms of revenue. The public dollars it has historically counted on are rapidly being cut back or eliminated. Consequently, new income has to be generated. The choices are generally quite stark: raise tuition or further privatize costs, locate corporate or private sector sponsorship for specific programs or pursue new forms of public financing. It is within this context that IHE community partnerships are being pursued. Clearly some part of the incentive for forging such relationship and developing collaborative programming is that it opens up new revenue streams for the IHE, both public and private. As public and private sources of funding realize that problems and solutions rest more in communities than they do within single individuals and families (preferred foci of funding in the 1980s and early 1990s), there are increasing revenue sources for community-based initiatives. The pursuit of such resources in the name of collaboration but without attention to power imbalance and without a clear understanding of university role and community contribution can temper the development of a dynamic, authentic relationship of partnership. Financial incentives for collaboration are of course both necessary and expected, but they cannot be the singular or even primary reason for pursuing such relationship. The scent of short term opportunism will be identified very quickly by community groups and will paradoxically likely lead to further distancing of IHEs from the community members and organizations with whom they seek to work. Of course more than community rejection is at stake. The absence of clear intellectual and theoretical moorings for civic engagement will instantly weaken faculty interest in and support for university civic engagement (Ostrander, 2004).

Certainly such tensions are endemic to forming IHE community partnerships. That said, it is equally apparent that never has it been more critical for universities to collaborate with communities to upgrade their quality of life. Poor and working class communities are struggling with a range of social problems while simultaneously experiencing substantial cutbacks in health care, social services and basic infrastructural supports of fire, police and transportation. As if this dynamic of cutback and intensifying social problem weren't enough, many communities are also experiencing the further break-down of their economic base as more and more jobs are outsourced to other parts of the world. Such globalization brings this analysis full circle. It begins with the global university, moves to the increasingly tenuous circumstance of the communities in which IHEs are situated, and finally shifts to a global economy that due to the hyper-mobility of capital can rapidly and dramatically affect the fortunes of local communities including residents and institutions, among them IHEs. The IHE and community can function in reciprocal relationships fostering resource development that mutually benefit both parties. In order for this to occur, however, the IHE must be willing to reimagine its relationship to knowledge production, learning and the community. Critically, such a reimagining cannot happen in the absence of a visionary leadership which develops a deepened commitment to collaboratively reinvigorating the space in which it is situated and the world in which it is located. And they reimagine the university not simply because it is the right thing to do but also because the future of the university and the community are understood to be part of a fragile ecology of mutual dependence and possibility (Ramaley, 2003).

REFERENCES

Bellah, R., Madsen, R., Sullivan, W., Swidler, A., & Tipton, S. (1985). *Habits of the heart: Individualism and commitment in American life.* NY: Harper & Row.

Bender, T. (Ed.). (1988a). The University and the city: From medieval origins to the present. NY: Oxford University Press.

Bender, T. (1988b). Afterword. In T. Bender (Ed.), *The University and the city: From medieval origins to the present* (pp. 290-297). NY: Oxford University Press.

Bok, D. 1982. *Beyond the ivory tower: Social responsibilities of the modern university.* Cambridge, MA: Harvard University Press.

Boyer, E. (1996). The scholarship of engagement. *Journal of Public Service and Outreach, 1*(1), 11-20.

Chambers, C. (1996). Personal communication with R. Fisher. Interview by Karen Strauss, 3/15/96, and 3/18/96. Unpublished. University of Minnesota Library Archives.

Cohen, A. (1998). *The shaping of American higher education.* San Francisco: Jossey-Bass.

Colby, A., Ehrlich, T., Beaumont, E., & Stephens, J. (2003). *Educating citizens: Preparing America's students for lives of civic and moral responsibility.* San Francisco: Jossey-Bass.

Cortes, A. 2004. Estimating the impacts of urban universities on neighborhood housing markets: An empirical analysis. *Urban Affairs Review, 3*(3), 342-375.

Fabricant, M., & Fisher, R. (2002). *Settlement houses under siege: The struggle to sustain community organizations in New York City.* NY: Columbia University Press.

Farnen, R. (2003, September). Service Learning, volunteerism, and democratic civic education in North America: Is it worth the effort? Paper presented at ECPR conference, Marburg Germany.

Ferrari, J., & Chapman, J. (Eds.). (1999). *Educating students to make-a-difference: Community-based service learning.* NY: The Haworth Press, Inc. [Co-published as *Journal of Prevention and Intervention in the Community, 18.]*

Ferruolo, S. (1988). Parisius-Paradisus: The city, its schools, and the origins of the University of Paris. In T. Bender (Ed.), *The University and the city: From medieval origins to the present* (pp. 22-43). NY: Oxford University Press.

Fisher, R. (1999). The importance of history and context in community organization. In J. Rothman (Ed.), *Reflections on community organization: Enduring themes and critical issues* (pp. 335-353). Itasca, IL: F.E. Peacock Publishers, Inc.

Fisher, R., & Fabricant, M. (2002). From Henry Street to contracted services: Financing the settlement house. *Journal of Sociology and Social Welfare, 29*(3), 3-28

Fisher, R., & Karger, H. (1997). *Social work and community in a private world: Getting out in public.* NY: Longman.

Harris, R. (2003, August 27). Critical elements of a sustainable service-learning program. Audio Conference, National Conference on Student Services.

Johnson, A.K. (2004). Social work is standing on the legacy of Jane Addams: But are we sitting on the sidelines? *Social Work 49*(2), 319-322.

Kerr, C. (2002). Shock wave II: An introduction to the twenty-first century. In S. Brint (Ed.), *The future of the city of intellect* (pp. 1-15). Palo Alto: Stanford University Press.

Maurrasse, D. (2001). *Beyond the campus: How colleges and universities form partnerships with their communities.* NY: Routledge.

Mayfield, L. (2000, April 29). Building partnerships: Stronger communities and stronger universities. Discussion paper at Community-Campus Partnerships for Health, Fourth Annual Conference, Washington, DC.

McKnight, J. (1995).*The careless society: Community and its counterfeits.* NY: Basic.

Minkler, M. (Ed.). (1997). *Community organizing and community building for health.* New Brunswick, NJ: Rutgers University Press.

Montgomery, D. (1995). What the world needs now. *The Nation,* April 3, 461-63.

Morton, K. (1995). The irony of service: Charity, project and social change in service learning. *Michigan Journal of Community Service Learning, 2,* 19-32.

O'Grady, C. (Ed.). (2000). *Integrating service learning and multicultural education in colleges and universities.* Mahwah, NJ: Lawrence Erlbaum Associates Publishers.

Ostrander, S. (2004). Democracy, civic participation, and the university: A comparative study of civic engagement on five campuses. *Nonprofit and Voluntary Sector Quarterly, 33*(1), 74-93.

Peters, S. (2003). The craft of public scholarship in land-grant education. *Journal of Higher Education, Outreach, and Engagement, 8*(1), 75-86.

Ramaley, J. (2003). Seizing the moment: Creating a changed society and university through outreach. *Journal of Higher Education Outreach and Engagement, 6*(1), 13-27.

Ross, L. (2002). American higher education and community engagement: A historical perspective. In *Springfield College, lasting engagement: Building and sustaining a commitment to community outreach, development, and collaboration: Volume 1* (pp. 1-17). Washington DC: US Department of Housing and Urban Development.

Shapiro, E. (1978). Robert Woods and the settlement house impulse. *Social Service Review, 52*(2), 215-226.

Shils, E. (1988). The University, the city, and the world: Chicago and the University of Chicago. In T. Bender (Ed.), *The University and the city: From medieval origins to the present* (pp. 210-230). NY: Oxford University Press.

Simmons, L. (1998). A new urban conservatism: The case of Hartford, Connecticut. *Journal of Urban Affairs, 20*(2), 175-198.

Stevenson, L. (1988). Preparing for public life: The collegiate students at New York University, 1832-1881. In T. Bender (Ed.), *The University and the city: From medieval origins to the present* (pp. 150-177). NY: Oxford University Press.

Warner, S. (1968). *The private city: Philadelphia in three periods of growth*. Philadelphia: University of Pennsylvania Press.

Young, W.B. (1995). University-community partnerships–Why bother? *Metropolitan Universities, 6*(3), 71-77.

Zlotkowski, E. (Ed.). (1998). *Successful service learning programs*. Bolton, MA: Anker Publishing.

University Civic Engagement
with Community-Based Organizations:
Dispersed or Coordinated Models?

Elizabeth A. Mulroy, PhD

SUMMARY. This article compares and contrasts two case studies of large research universities involved in civic engagement projects with urban nonprofit community-based organizations and neighborhood associations. The article uses a community building framework in which organizational, interorganizational, and community-level features are examined. The study found that each university used a different approach through which to achieve a university-community partnership. A *dispersed* model favored an entrepreneurial approach for individual faculty and student involvement, while the *coordinated* model requested faculty and students from different departments to work together toward a community-driven goal. The extent to which these different models of civic engagement delivered what community organizations wanted was based on five factors: (1) the university's geographic proximity to a tar-

Elizabeth A. Mulroy is Associate Professor, School of Social Work, University of Maryland at Baltimore, 525 West Redwood Street, Baltimore, MD 21201 (E-mail: emulroy@ssw.umaryland.edu).

An earlier version of this article was presented at the Association for Research on Nonprofit Organizations and Voluntary Action (ARNOVA), Montreal, Canada, November 15, 2002.

[Haworth co-indexing entry note]: "University Civic Engagement with Community-Based Organizations: Dispersed or Coordinated Models?" Mulroy, Elizabeth A. Co-published simultaneously in *Journal of Community Practice* (The Haworth Social Work Practice Press, an imprint of The Haworth Press, Inc.) Vol. 12, No. 3/4, 2004, pp. 35-52; and: *University-Community Partnerships: Universities in Civic Engagement* (ed: Tracy M. Soska, and Alice K. Johnson Butterfield) The Haworth Social Work Practice Press, an imprint of The Haworth Press, Inc., 2004, pp. 35-52. Single or multiple copies of this article are available for a fee from The Haworth Document Delivery Service [1-800-HAWORTH, 9:00 a.m. - 5:00 p.m. (EST). E-mail address: docdelivery@haworthpress.com].

Digital Object Identifier: 10.1300/J125v12n03_03

get low-income neighborhood, (2) leadership for institutional social commitment, (3) use of community-based research, (4) funding as a social strategy, and (5) a flexible curriculum. Challenges faced by faculty, students, and practitioners are addressed, and directions for future research are suggested. *[Article copies available for a fee from The Haworth Document Delivery Service: 1-800-HAWORTH. E-mail address: <docdelivery@ haworthpress.com> Website: <http://www.HaworthPress.com> © 2004 by The Haworth Press, Inc. All rights reserved.]*

KEYWORDS. Civic engagement, university-community partnerships, community-based organizations, community-based research, community building

INTRODUCTION

Universities have the opportunity and resources to advance community building in low-opportunity neighborhoods through outreach to community based nonprofit organizations, particularly when they are their neighbors. University civic engagement has been recognized as a positive force for civil society with the resources to help mitigate environmental factors beyond a nonprofit organization's control. The rationale for university civic engagement can be compelling, given the deteriorating social and economic conditions that exist in urban neighborhoods surrounding many resource-rich institutions of higher education (Benson, Harkavy, & Puckett, 2000; Boyer, 1990). Even universities not located in poor neighborhoods are increasingly called upon to share their expertise and resources with organizations committed to community building.

In Community Outreach Partnership Center (COPC) programs sponsored by the U.S. Department of Housing and Urban Development (HUD), learning is expected to be bi-directional, as in systems of exchange. Thus, just as nonprofits and their consumers are expected to derive benefits from university civic engagement, universities have important lessons to learn from local leaders and community residents. Community improvement and long-term commitment to community strengthening through collaboration are common goals shared by all partners (HUD, 2000). But to what extent, and under what conditions, can university civic engagement actually attain these goals? This is the central question this article will examine. This article begins with a review of literature to offer theoretical guidance for the analysis of two case studies of university civic engagement that follows. Then implications and conclusions for community-based organizations and for universities will be considered.

UNIVERSITY-COMMUNITY PARTNERSHIPS AND COMMUNITY BUILDING

The Civic Engagement Movement

The university-community partnership movement is well along in establishing indicators for success (Maurrasse, 2002), particularly at the micro level. However, examining the effects of a university-community partnership in a macro framework puts the spotlight on community building where organizational, interorganizational, and community-level features can be examined. Weil (1996) suggests that community building involves the development of structures that include activities and policies that foster positive relationships among individuals, groups, organizations, and neighborhoods. Community building concerns the empowerment of local residents and community organizations through the acquisition of financial, physical, and social capital. It is typically created through the collaborative labor of diverse multi-sector partnerships that include residents as leaders and equal partners (Naparstek & Dooley, 1997). Scholars from different disciplines have recently suggested that social capital is a concept that requires more scrutiny (Salamon, 2001; Skocpol, 1996). These scholars are calling for critical investigations and empirical research using community-based methods that are capable of examining social processes. Some scholar/practitioners prefer to use the term *social capacity* instead of social capital because they believe it more accurately reflects terminology and intent used by participants in the practitioner-oriented community building movement (Mattessich & Monsey, 1997).

A key role for the academy, as a member of the formal community, is its potential to link resources that could increase capacity in informal communities experiencing disinvestment and decline. The extent to which university actors are motivated to participate typically depends on institutional rewards systems offered to administrators, faculty, and students. Boyer (1990) suggests that a new scholarship of civic involvement is needed, one that is conscious of building bridges between theory and practice, of seeing connections, communicating research knowledge to students, and valuing the implications of scholarly work for the larger world.

Community-Based Nonprofit Organizations and Social Change

While diversity exists among types of nonprofit community based organizations in America's cities, those with a mission of community building are increasingly at-risk. Formal community-based organizations such as settlement houses and family support centers have been identified with group formation and solidarity, community building, and collaborative practice. However, in the era of decentralization and privatization of social services (associated with large, hierarchical for-profit or nonprofit organizations), community-based, social change organizations have lost their progressive edge and fallen on difficult times (Fabricant & Fisher, 2002).

One continuing and deepening challenge to community-based, social change nonprofits is the economic uncertainty posed by public and philanthropic funding sources, each with specific expectations, requirements, and changing investment strategies in the post-welfare era. The depth and scope of contracting with the state provides much-needed revenues, as long as structures and cultures allow nonprofits to meet specific requirements. These typically include the capacity to: (1) implement mandated social programs targeted to varying individual-level needs, such as welfare-to-work job training, case management, or treatment programs for victims of child abuse and neglect, or persons with physical and mental impairments; (2) meet public sector standards for accountability; and (3) demonstrate corporate standards of efficiency and effectiveness (Gibelman, 2000). These requirements pose constraints for managers of small, cash-strapped community based organizations who need more revenue but want to hold firm to nontraditional neighborhood-level programming, informal organizational structures, and participatory management styles (Perlmutter, 1995).

Two case studies of university civic engagement will be discussed next. The first is the case of Homeless Prevention in Hawaii, and the second is the case of Community Building in East Baltimore. The focus of the next section is on the context of the civic engagement process from university and community perspectives. Specific requests for assistance made by nonprofits to the universities will be identified, and the methods and approaches used by faculty, administrators, and students to meet these community needs will be presented. An evaluation of the approaches used in the cases is then set forth.

HOMELESS PREVENTION IN HAWAII

There was an informal mandate in the mid-1990s from executive leadership at the University of Hawaii-Manoa for faculty involvement in community problem solving. State legislators were eager for the flagship campus to help resolve some of the deepening problems in a depressed Hawaiian economy. The message was conveyed downward through the Council of Deans to faculty. Implementation was left to individual faculty on an informal department-by-department basis. Inter-departmental collaboration for civic engagement was encouraged and attempted, with mixed results (Matsuoka, Mulroy, & Umemoto, 2002).

This case concerns university civic engagement with a nonprofit child and family agency located in a large Honolulu public housing project. The agency operated sixteen programs in a range of areas such as community development, child welfare, and Head Start. Some University and Community College faculty from diverse departments were interested in the agency's work, and in an entrepreneurial spirit, sponsored their own student projects on site. Thus, the agency was linked to individual faculty members who provided resources and student experiential learning, but was not linked to the university as an institutional community actor. During a three year period, faculty-led projects ranged from computer training for residents and staff training in the use of the ACCESS computer program, to a Ph.D. dissertation on organizational development and change. Because faculty did not know each other, these activities were not coordinated for either implementation or evaluation purposes. In addition, several university undergraduate and graduate departments independently placed student interns in a variety of agency programs for either academic course credit or service learning.

In one example of faculty entrepreneurship, personal contact was made with the agency out of interest in their community-based work, and an agency-faculty member relationship began to develop. The faculty member offered pro bono assistance with grant applications for the Family Support Center, one of the agency's programs. Over a one-year period, management and staff got to know the faculty member and her areas of expertise, and the faculty member got to know agency programming, operations, and the community in which the agency was located. About a year later, the faculty member received a request for proposal from the Family Support Center announcing the Center's need for program evaluation. A proposal was submitted it in a formal bid process and it was ultimately selected.

Community-Based Methods

It was clear at the outset that this was to be a local-level evaluation (Marquant & Konrad, 1996) of the Center's homeless prevention program, one of six demonstration sites funded by a three-year federal grant from the U.S. Department of Health and Human Services, Office of Community Services. Unlike typical evaluations of demonstration projects that focus on the federal- or state-level, the funder in this case wanted the focus to be on community-level systems, and therefore each demonstration site in the country selected its own external evaluator.

Identified clients were the families who lived in the project and had either been homeless prior to living in public housing or were identified as most at-risk of becoming homeless, primarily for nonpayment of rent. However, the Family Center considered all of the approximately 2,500 residents to be near-homeless because of their very low incomes and thus potential clients. This was problematic for setting boundaries for the study. Management and staff wanted to establish usable outcomes that would help them do their jobs better, and to involve the direct participation of graduate social work students as skilled labor. Program personnel had limited access to computers with appropriate software programs. While client contacts were informal in keeping with family support principles and practices, confidential case files were kept for 93 clients who received supportive counseling, and detailed handwritten case notes were recorded chronologically. Given this context, an embedded single-case study (Yin, 1994) was conducted with the program as the level of analysis. A developmental approach was used that incorporated staff's request for organizational learning and professional development (Quinn-Patton, 1998; Yin, Kaftarian, & Jacobs, 1996). A management information system was developed as a graduate student project, tested out with staff, and left with staff for their future use when the study ended (Stevenson, Mitchell, & Florian, 1996).

The first step in the evaluation was to understand the intervention as a conceptual framework (Weiss, 2000) and to detail its processes and functions (Mulroy & Lauber, 2002). This early phase of engagement leading to the development of the conceptual model opened a process for face-to-face, structured dialogue on-site that continued at the Center office in the public housing project over the life of the study. Logic modeling (Alter & Murty, 1997) was used as the framework for analysis. Logic modeling is often required by funders to assist nonprofit organizations in their efforts to systematically engage in program planning, management and evaluation. The method first asks participants to identify "theories of change," or some principles that will serve as overarching guideposts for program development. Second, participants are asked to select desired outcomes for program beneficiaries. Third, appropriate activities are selected to help reach the intended outcomes (Connell, Kubisch, Schorr, & Weiss, 1995; Weiss, 1995). Fourth, the framework allows practitioners to set benchmarks that need to be attained as stepping stones on the pathway to achieving long term outcome objectives.

The logic model format used in this case was further modified for practitioner use. With new data collection procedures and a management information system, program-level interventions and client-level patterns of service utilization were traced out. These were identified as important milestones, or interim outcomes. This approach allowed staff to understand, plan for, and measure interim outcomes as important elements in the overall evaluation process. (For further discussion of the research methods, see Mulroy & Lauber, in press.) While these participatory methods met both the staff's and faculty member goals, the process was labor-intensive and very time consuming. The one-year study stretched to two years time, and in the end, an evaluation of both the program's second and third years was completed with in-depth involvement of a total of eight graduate social work students.

COMMUNITY BUILDING IN EAST BALTIMORE

Community building in East Baltimore was framed by requirements of a three-year grant from the Fannie Mae Foundation awarded to the University of Maryland to facilitate university civic engagement through collaboration of graduate faculty from several university departments on two different campuses–College Park and downtown Baltimore. Faculty members were expected to work in a coordinated way with local organizations to better serve the affordable housing and community development needs of low-income residents in Baltimore's urban neighborhoods.

Executive directors of four nonprofit community based organizations located in East Baltimore met with the faculty team from the School of Social Work, Department of Urban Planning, and School of Public Policy to articulate what they wanted from the grant's activity.

The organizations were all located in East Baltimore, an area with a recent history of commercial disinvestment, housing abandonment, sale and use of illegal drugs, and a perception of "white flight." The organizations varied in terms of size, purpose, and target populations. The directors clearly stated that their greatest need was for help with strategic planning. They asked for a two-step approach. First, they requested assistance from the university with a strategic planning process for each organization. Second, they requested assistance in the development of a neighborhood-wide strategic plan to address some critical local social and economic problems. The executive directors of these cash-strapped organizations wanted more control over the destiny of their own organizations, and more power and influence to change the neighborhood in which they worked and about which they cared.

Community-Based Methods

Action research was the method of choice for this engagement process because it offered a theoretical framework based on the confluence of research, action, and participation to address the concrete, real-life issues presented by the community based organizations (Greenwood & Levin, 1998). It was also consistent with the goals of the executive directors, which were to generate knowledge for the purpose of taking action to promote organizational improvement and social change in their community, and faculty goal for social analysis.

The agencies' request for assistance with strategic planning, however, proved problematic. Strategic planning is best implemented when nonprofits are stable, relatively secure, and capable of self-assessment and organizational change (Bryson, 1995). In reality, initial assessment revealed that of the nonprofits at the table, only one organization, a housing and community development corporation, fit that profile. The others were experiencing a range of management dilemmas that included rapid turnover of executive leadership, financial cutbacks, and downsizing-all indicators of instability that suggested internal strategic planning was untimely.

Given these realities, the faculty member from the School of Social Work concentrated on conducting an in-depth organizational analysis at the most planning-ready of the agencies, the Community Development Corporation (CDC). Rather than dabbling in patchwork strategic planning at four agencies, the goal was to complete one plan successfully before the grant terminated. Other faculty began to work with the remaining organizations to help them meet goals for neighborhood planning. The CDC was formed in 1995 with a mission to revitalize and stabilize the neighborhood through the rehabilitation and development of affordable housing for home ownership and rental. It started small with four principal specialists and grew to a current staff of 20. Funding sources primarily included housing and community development grants from federal, state, and city governments.

The organizational analysis utilized formal protocol of the strategic planning process (Berry, 2000; Bryson, 1995). Data were collected and analyzed qualitatively (Miles & Huberman, 1994). The most critical issues were found to be dilemmas in moving from a small, informal organization with a horizontal structure, participatory, self-management style fueled by a shared passion for neighborhood improvement to an organization of medium size. Growth resulted in a need to develop personnel policies and procedures and to put them in place. The study identified the impacts of these changes on organizational culture. Draft findings were discussed with management in a face-to-face meeting to solicit their feedback and analysis.

Graduate social work students fully participated in the study, helped draft the final report, and co-presented it with faculty at a staff meeting attended by all CDC employees. Faculty and students facilitated the discussion and helped to mediate a dialogue that dealt with controversial issues. As follow up, the CDC's executive leadership requested development of a plan that would help the agency respond to the report's findings by recommending new personnel policies, procedures and administrative practices for their consideration. A draft plan was prepared, presented, modified, and finalized. The faculty/agency relationship continued long after the grant terminated, and the executive director became a regular "community expert" guest in management and planning classes.

Other faculty completed two other projects. In the Highlandtown neighborhood faculty coordinated student interns and local residents in conducting a building condition and land use survey of more than 1,000 parcels over a two-day period. Palm pilot hand-held computers known as personal data assistants (PDAs) were used as a data collection tool. Data were then analyzed quantitatively, maps were constructed, and findings given to the community organizations for their own use as more active participants with City Hall in an on-going neighborhood revitalization effort. This was facilitated by the integration of another partnership: the Enterprise Foundation provided the training; the Baltimore Neighborhood Indicators Alliance (BNIA) provided the PDAs with software developed by the Enterprise Foundation. The Enterprise Foundation is a nationally known, Maryland-based, highly skilled housing and community development corporation. BNIA is a new nonprofit group dedicated to empowering grass roots community associations with knowledge from data sources, then mapping it through geographic information systems (GIS) for access on its website. BNIA also conducted a formal three-hour session on neighborhood indicators and GIS mapping in the School of Social Work Social Planning class, a relationship that continues to this day.

In the Hampstead Hill neighborhood, the Hampstead Hill Improvement Association asked for university assistance in developing its association. A survey of neighborhood residents was conducted to learn more about the demographics of the neighborhood and to ascertain strengths and weaknesses (1200 surveys were distributed and 100 returned and analyzed). Then focus groups were conducted, and a neighborhood workshop planned and held that covered topics identified by residents. Community strengths, needs, and resources were identified that helped residents move toward development of plans for a new community organization. The outcomes of this phase of civic engagement assisted partner organizations to advance their neighborhood planning goals with new knowledge, technology, and skills.

EVALUATION

The extent to which each university was able to deliver what this diverse group of nonprofit organizations wanted was found to be a function of five factors: (1) geographic proximity to a target low-income neighborhood, (2) leadership for institutional social commitment, (3) use of community based research, (4) external funding as social strategy, and (5) a flexible curriculum. Each factor will be analyzed next.

Geographic Proximity to Poverty

Proximity to a very low-income community may intensify a university's commitment to civic engagement that, in turn, influences the nature and extent of the vertical linkages it brings to participating agencies and through them to the low-income community. The dense, large, urban campus that houses Maryland's graduate professional schools and medical school/hospital complex is located in West Baltimore, one of the city's lowest-income census tracts, an area that over the years received large investments of federal dollars for urban renewal, neighborhood revitalization, public housing demolition, and Empowerment Zone funds.

This inner city Baltimore campus differs sharply from the location of University of Hawaii-Manoa where the flagship campus is geographically located in one of the wealthiest census tracts in Honolulu. This University of Hawaii campus is about 7 miles from the city's low-income census tract where the case study took place. The case study site is in an area with high rates of crime, substance abuse, child abuse and neglect, concentration of high-rise public housing projects, rising immigrant populations, and gang activity. These were neither conditions faculty saw every day, nor an area students requested for internships. While faculty from several university departments had long-standing working relationships with indigenous Native Hawaiians and the rural poor, there appeared to be less campus familiarity with the urban poor. The extent to which university administrators, faculty, and students know and understand the target community of change and the community-based organizations that serve these residents, the more motivated they may be to develop and sustain vertical ties.

Leadership for Institutional Social Commitment

A research university's institutional commitment to civic engagement is an important motivator in developing faculty interest. Executive leadership within the university facilitates institutional social commitment by role modeling the values and behaviors that are most conducive to local-level community participation. A history of being an institutional actor in the formal community builds a foundation on which to extend the nature and type of vertical linkages to community-based organizations.

Differences can be seen in these cases between a *coordinated* and a *dispersed* model of engagement. First, a commitment to serve Baltimore's urban poor was in place among top university leaders long before the current funding for this case study was received. Even though town/gown tensions were historic, the University President at the Baltimore campus made a social commitment to work in partnership–that is, as a *coordinated* process–with neighborhood organizations and leaders toward community betterment using university resources. The President's Office was known to be active in multisector Empowerment Zone development and in the implementation of a much-coveted Community Outreach Partnership Center (COPC) grant funded by HUD and administered by the School of Social Work. The President's Office was the location of monthly COPC meetings attended by participating faculty, leaders of community-based organizations, students, and facilitated by the President's Executive Assistant. This was visible evidence of sustained university civic engagement and long-term relationship building.

Hawaii's model was informal and *dispersed*, that is not targeted to specific communities, goals, or coordinated faculty purposes. Dispersed models of university-community partnerships are difficult to adequately capture and document on paper. For example, the University executive leadership participated in state level task forces with powerful and influential political and business leaders–important ties for the university to cultivate among power centers in the formal community in depressed economic times. To faculty "on-the-ground," however, concrete actions that might role model institutional civic engagement with community-based organizations were not visible.

In both case studies, the role of Graduate School Deans helped to generate faculty interest in civic engagement and facilitate the development of community linkages. At Maryland the Dean of the Graduate School of Social Work created a Social Work Community Outreach Service (SWCOS) to fulfill his own social commitment to use the School's resources and student training power to help address some of the conditions faced by people living in urban poverty. Its mission was "to create innovative models of social work education and service that strengthen under-served individuals, families, and communities in Baltimore and Maryland. Students, faculty, agency, and community representatives join forces in the design, implementation, and evaluation of those models" (SWCOS Annual Report, 2001-2002, p. 1). In sum, commitment to poor communities by university leaders may facilitate civic engagement, irrespective of the model as coordinated or dispersed.

Funding As Social Strategy

A funding stream for university-community engagement that explicitly supports the use of coordinated university resources among several departments, as in the Maryland case, can serve as a vehicle for *social strategy*–the prescient selection of methods needed to change a social condition or to achieve a desired end state. According to Bourdieu (quoted in Portes, 1998) social networks are not a natural given; they must be constructed through investment strategies intended to institutionalize group relations that will be used as a source of other benefits.

Community building, then, benefits from multiple investment strategies to increase social capacity.

A core issue is the extent to which university participants can forge collaborative behaviors in order to represent the university as an institutional community "partner." In the Hawaii case the *dispersed* entrepreneurial approach avoided this element of the engagement process. In the Maryland case, the funder wanted faculty to work with community-based organizations as a *coordinated* entity. Could faculty and administrators from different departments, some known to each other and others not, quickly forge collaborative relationships based on respect and trust? As challenging as these processes were, faculty from a range of university departments ultimately figured out how to work together administratively. They coordinated their respective faculty projects, cooperated at team meetings, and students from different departments worked together in the community on joint projects. The social strategy for a *coordinated* university endeavor generated faculty commitment to the community organizations and residents. All faculty continued their involvement in the East Baltimore community with the same community organizations after the Fannie Mae grant terminated. However, they disbanded the *coordinated* approach in favor of the *dispersed* approach that permitted them more flexibility and autonomy. This approach will make data collection in a future outcome evaluation more difficult.

Community-Based Research

In both case examples faculty linked university resources, including students, to community organizations through community based research. The requested research projects required flexibility and competency in a range of research approaches; multiple methods were used depending on the needs expressed by the community partners. In the Maryland case, action research facilitated the ability of community organizations to better control their own destinies over time (Greenwood & Levin, 1998). In the Hawaii case, an evaluation examined the process of intervention in a complex social situation (Weiss, 2000) and determined program outcomes. A surprising finding related to process revealed that the Family Center that managed Hawaii's Homeless Prevention Program was able to implement its multiple interventions with a small staff of four full-time people because it partnered with 18 different agencies–nonprofit, public, and for-profit–that co-produced its services. In effect, multiple yet invisible interorganizational community partnerships were embedded in every component of the program.

These worked in concert to create an on-site social support network for vulnerable families as long as funding for them lasted. Awareness of the scope and density of such interorganizational and interpersonal relationships helped agency management and funders better understand how and why the program's interventions were as complex and labor intensive to administer as staff experienced them to be. It also illuminated the importance of identifying and measuring interim outcomes within a strategy for the evaluation of community based projects.

Challenges in both case studies included meeting community requests on a very tight time line. Four main issues emerged: (1) the need to quickly make decisions concerning theoretically-based research designs that inside the academy are given careful consideration and time; (2) monitoring the imperative for the triangulation of data; (3) the mismatch of organizational structure, culture, and time between the faculty and student-driven semester system and a community's process-oriented deliberations; and (4) the difficulty of conducting a systematic study in a rapidly changing, and frequently unstable organizational and community environments. Community-based research required faculty to take on multiple roles and to shift gears frequently in a researcher/practitioner relationship (Quinn-Patton, 1997). As data was collected in the field, faculty role modeled for students the ethics of research as codified in the NASW Code of Ethics, how to build and sustain collaborative relationships with practitioners in participatory research, and demonstrated the technical skills required of multi-method research.

There was a lot that faculty could not do in both projects because of budget, time, and funder constraints. For example, grants terminated just as provocative questions emerged. University semester calendars ended student involvement just as community participants learned to work as co-producers with them. Residents re-scheduled community building celebrations to summer months when students and faculty were typically not available to celebrate, bring closure, or collect data. Finally, some penetrating research questions emerged: What is the role of these partnerships in building community capacity? To what extent is the university, as a formal institution, changed by its own participation in civic engagement? A future research agenda has clearly been set.

Flexible Curriculum: From Practice to Theory

Students were key participants in both case studies and a flexible curriculum and innovative classroom approaches helped give them the academic/knowledge support they needed to meet agency requests. There was evidence of Boyer's (1990) scholarship of *application*. While Schools of Social Work have an educational objective to apply knowledge to practice, both cases illustrate a two-way relationship in which practice informed theory. Educational offerings were established to intentionally make that happen. The model was designed to generate student learning from the field–to facilitate student understanding of community building and the central role that community-based research can have on organizational improvement and community development.

New courses were developed to merge material traditionally taught in separate courses. One example drew from human services management, strategic planning, and qualitative research methods. Another drew from community development, housing policy, and qualitative research methods. Half of the weekly three-hour contact sessions were spent in seminars on campus and half at the respective organizations and in the community neighborhoods. Faculty and students became acquainted with the organizations and the neighborhoods by taking guided tours with the organizations' employees and "hanging out" at a few local eateries. In the end, students reported that they valued their participation in all phases of the civic engagement experiences. They reported learning more about the travails of community organizations and their real-world conflicts than they would have in a traditional classroom-bound course. In turn, community organizations valued student involvement. Curriculum change was facilitated when administrators remained flexible, encouraged innovations in course development that overlapped with year-long field internships, and when faculty leadership on such projects was rewarded for departing from the status quo.

CONCLUSION

This article has investigated the potential of university civic engagement as a contributor to community building through university partnerships with nonprofit community organizations. Two case studies were presented and analyzed in which the university partners were large public research institutions and the community partners were typically small, under-capitalized nonprofit community organizations that served very poor urban communities. There is preliminary evidence that civic engagement provided opportunity for bridging differences in the informal community–opportunities for civic participation, the development of exchange networks and formal ways to affect change (Wacquant & Wilson,

1989; Putnam, 1993). Helping to build stronger and more stable community organizations were windows of opportunity for that to happen. University civic engagement brought in more social leverage (deSouza Briggs, 1997) from those in the power structure of the formal community, but the case studies point out that the scope, structure, and intensity can differ in several ways. The extent to which each of the universities developed these links was influenced by five factors: geographic proximity to poverty, leadership for institutional social commitment to community change, external funding as a social strategy, application of community-based research methods, and a flexible curriculum structure. Universities need executive leadership to strategically thread together all these factors when opportunities arise.

Many questions remain unanswered. First, future research is needed to measure specific outcomes so that more can be learned about the longer-term effects of the engagement process on universities, community organizations, residents, and the community itself. Also, there is evidence from this study that a university community partnership as a unit of analysis appears to contain several multi-layered, multi-sector partnerships within it—an important area for future research on the structure of complex social networks. Second, policy makers and funders need to know which investment strategies (Portes, 1998) can institutionalize group relations among those involved in the civic engagement process. And third, in these difficult fiscal times, community organizations are waiting to learn when, if, and in what form university civic engagement will continue.

REFERENCES

Alter, C., & Murty, S. (1997). Logic modeling: A tool for teaching critical thinking in social work practice. *Journal of Social Work Education, 33,* 103-117.

Benson, L., Harkavy, I., & Puckett, J. (2000). An implementation revolution as a strategy for fulfilling the democratic promise of university-community partnerships: Penn-West Philadelphia as an experiment in progress. *Nonprofit and Voluntary Sector Quarterly, 29*(1), 24-45.

Berry, B. (2000). *Strategic planning workbook.* St. Paul, MN: Amherst Wilder Foundation.

Bourdieu, P. (1985). The forms of capital. In J.G. Richardson, (Ed.), *Handbook of theory and research for the sociology of education* (pp. 241-258). New York: Greenwood.

Boyer, E. (1990). *Scholarship reconsidered: Priorities of the professorate.* Princeton: The Carnegie Foundation for the Advancement of Teaching.

Bryson, J. (1995). *Strategic planning for public and nonprofit organizations.* New York: John Wiley.

Connell, J., Kubish, A., Schorr, L., & Weiss, C. (1995). *New approaches to evaluating community initiatives.* Washington, DC: Aspen Institute.

de Souza Briggs, X. (1997). Social capital and the cities: Advice to change agents. *National Civic Review, 86*(2), 167-174.

Fabricant, M., & Fisher, R. (2002). *Settlement houses under siege: The struggle to sustain community organizations in New York City.* New York: Columbia University Press.

Fetterman, D., Kaftarian, S., & Watersman, A. (1996). *Empowerment evaluation: Knowledge and tools for self-assessment and accountability.* Thousand Oaks: Sage.

Gibelman, M., & Demone, H. Jr. (2002). The commercialization of health and human services: National phenomena or cause for concern? *Families in Society, 83*(4), 387-397.

Greenwood, D., & Levin, M. (1998). *Introduction to action research.* Thousand Oaks: Sage.

Marquart, J., & Konrad, E. (Eds.). (1996). *Evaluating initiatives to integrate human services.* San Francisco: Jossey-Bass

Matsuoka, J., Mulroy, E., & Umemoto, K. (2002). Conflicting cultures: Linking agency, university, and community in a community building endeavor. *Social Thought, 21*(2), 3-15.

Maurrasse, D. (2002). Higher education-community partnerships: Assessing progress in the field. *Nonprofit and Voluntary Sector Quarterly, 31*(1), 131-139.

Miles, M., & Huberman, M. (1994). *Qualitative data analysis.* Thousand Oaks: Sage.

Mulroy, E., & Lauber, H. (2002). Community building in hard times: A post-welfare view from the streets. *Journal of Community Practice, 10*(1), 1-16.

Mulroy, E., & Lauber, H. (in press). An approach to user friendly evaluation and effective community interventions for families at-risk of homelessness. *Social Work.*

Naparstek, A., & Dooley, D. (1997). Countering urban disinvestment through community building activities. *Social Work, 42*(5), 506-513.

Portes, A. (1998). Social capital: Its origins and applications in modern sociology. *Annual Review of Sociology, 24*(1), 1-24.

Putnam, R.J. (1993). What makes democracy work? *National Civic Review, 82*(2), 101-108.

Quinn-Patton, M. (1997). *Utilization-focused evaluation* (3rd Ed.). Thousand Oaks: Sage.

Salamon, L. (2001, June). An "associational" revolution. *UNESCO Courier,* p. 36.

Skocpol, T. (1996). Unraveling from above. *The American Prospect, 25,* 20-25.

Stevenson, J., Mitchell, R., & Florian, P. (1996). Evaluation and self-direction in community prevention coalitions. In D. Fetterman, S. Kaftarian, & A. Watersman, (Eds.) *Empowerment evaluation* (pp. 208-233). Thousand Oaks: Sage.

Wacquant, LJD, & Wilson, WJ. (1989). The cost of racial and class exclusion in the inner city. *American Academy of Political Science, 501,* 8-26.

Weiss, C. (1995). Nothing as practical as good theory: Exploring theory-based evaluation for comprehensive community initiatives for children and families. In J. Connell, A. Kubisch, L. Schorr, & C. Weiss (Eds.) *New approaches to evaluating community initiatives* (pp. 65-92). Washington DC: Aspen Institute.

Weiss, J. (2000). From research to social improvement: Understanding theories of intervention. *Nonprofit and Voluntary Sector Quarterly, 29* (1), 81-110.

Yin, R. (1994). *Case study research.* Thousand Oaks: Sage.

Yin, R., Kaftarian, S., & Jacobs, N. (1996). Empowerment evaluation at state and local levels: dealing with quality. In D. Fetterman, S. Kaftarian, & A. Watersman (Eds.) *Empowerment evaluation* (pp. 188-207). Thousand Oaks: Sage.

COMMUNITY OUTREACH PARTNERSHIP CENTER (COPS) PROGRAMS

Connecting a University to a Distant Neighborhood: Three Stages of Learning and Adaptation

Margaret Bourdeaux Arbuckle, PhD
Ruth Hoogland DeHoog, PhD

SUMMARY. The willingness on the part of university participants to listen attentively to community representatives is of great importance to successful collaborations. This article presents three phases of a university-community partnership between the Macedonia neighborhood in

Margaret Bourdeaux Arbuckle is Director, Center for Youth, Family and Community Partnerships, and Ruth Hoogland DeHoog is Professor, Department of Political Science, University of North Carolina at Greensboro.

Address correspondence to: Margaret Bourdeaux Arbuckle, PhD, University of North Carolina at Greensboro, 41 McNutt, UNCG, Greensboro, NC 27401 (E-mail: mbarbuck@uncg.edu).

The analysis and views expressed in this article are those of the authors and are not intended to represent those of the University of North Carolina at Greensboro.

[Haworth co-indexing entry note]: "Connecting a University to a Distant Neighborhood: Three Stages of Learning and Adaptation." Arbuckle, Margaret Bourdeaux, and Ruth Hoogland DeHoog. Co-published simultaneously in *Journal of Community Practice* (The Haworth Social Work Practice Press, an imprint of The Haworth Press, Inc.) Vol. 12. No. 3/4, 2004, pp. 53-70; and: *University-Community Partnerships: Universities in Civic Engagement* (ed: Tracy M. Soska, and Alice K. Johnson Butterfield) The Haworth Social Work Practice Press, an imprint of The Haworth Press, Inc., 2004, pp. 53-70. Single or multiple copies of this article are available for a fee from The Haworth Document Delivery Service [1-800-HAWORTH, 9:00 a.m. - 5:00 p.m. (EST). E-mail address: docdelivery@haworthpress.com].

http://www.haworthpress.com/web/COM
Digital Object Identifier: 10.1300/J125v12n03_04

High Point, North Carolina, and the Center for the Study of Social Issues (CSSI) at the University of North Carolina at Greensboro. Although no professional network and neighborhood contacts were in place prior to this collaboration, the partnership addressed community needs by obtaining federal grant funding and by listening to the residents' concerns. Staff, students, and faculty overcame the challenges of inexperience and the difficulty of working with a neighborhood that was not located near the university. In various phases, the partnership moved away from a technical assistance approach to a self-help model. By actively engaging neighborhood residents through the Community Outreach Partnership Center (COPC), a learning and adaptation process occurred that resulted in successful university-community collaboration. *[Article copies available for a fee from The Haworth Document Delivery Service: 1-800-HAWORTH. E-mail address: <docdelivery@haworthpress.com> Website: <http://www.Haworth Press.com> © 2004 by The Haworth Press, Inc. All rights reserved.]*

KEYWORDS. University-community partnership, Community Outreach Partnership Center, collaboration

INTRODUCTION

The necessary and natural relationships forged by the close proximity of higher education institutions and residential neighborhoods have been the basis for many of the Community Outreach Partnership Center (COPC) projects funded by U.S. Department of Housing and Urban Development (HUD) over the last decade (e.g., Forrant & Silka, 1999). However, one successful project may appear to be an anomaly–a COPC set up in a more distant community about twenty miles away from the university, in a city and neighborhood that historically had no demands or expectations of the university, and where the involved faculty had no long-standing relationships. The collaboration between the Macedonia neighborhood in High Point, NC and the University of North Carolina at Greensboro's Center for the Study of Social Issues (CSSI) is the focus of this article. We will analyze how this kind of collaboration developed and largely succeeded in a fairly unique university-community environment from 1996 to the present.

We analyze the process of collaboration through three developmental stages. In the first stage, CSSI developed a relationship with the City of High Point and its low-income neighborhood through the planning and implementation of a Brownfields Revitalization grant, funded through the Environmental Protection Agency (EPA). In the second stage, the relationship was broadened to include other community partners, and an outreach program was established in a HUD-funded COPC in the neighborhood. The third stage allowed CSSI to step back to a support role of securing small grants for community building efforts. This stage occurred at the time that the community partners constructed a new community center in the neighborhood and the city initiated an affordable housing program.

This analysis of these three stages of the university-community partnership focuses on three questions. How can a university center forge ongoing collaborations with a community at some distance from its campus? How can a university develop collaborations when prior professional networks, trusting neighborhood contacts, and relevant experience are not in place? Finally, how can a university center shift its roles, methodology, and focus as a community changes and develops its own strategies and funding sources? Our analysis suggests the following: (1) the importance of a compelling community need and openness for partnership development; (2) a strong incentive on the part of the university to obtain funding and support for these partnerships; (3) constant attention to changing relationships and opportunities for meeting needs; and, perhaps most importantly (4) a willingness on the part of the university to *listen* to the community in its process of building a collaborative relationship between the neighborhood residents, the city officials, and the university faculty and students. This case also shows how a university-community partnership evolves through an unplanned process, with critical events and stages unfolding to move campus participants to a deeper understanding of the partners and the community. Our practice experience provides insight toward the development of partnerships in geographic areas in which no prior history of community relationships exist.

BACKGROUND TO THE PARTNERSHIP

The University of North Carolina at Greensboro

The University of North Carolina at Greensboro (UNCG) is located near downtown Greensboro, a city of over 223,000. The cities of Greensboro, Winston-Salem, and High Point make up the Piedmont Triad region, one of the three major population centers in the state. Until recently, apart from its longstanding relationship with the public school systems in the region, there were only sporadic or decentralized efforts to work in community outreach or research projects.

To increase UNCG's external research funding, the dean of the Graduate School spearheaded an effort in 1993 to establish a broad, university-wide research center that would assist faculty in the social and behavioral sciences in obtaining large federal grants. With the blessing of the provost, the dean designed a competition among interdisciplinary faculty teams to determine the type and emphasis of such a center. After internal and external reviews of written and oral presentations by three teams, the provost decided to incorporate all three groups and their ideas into the development of a new center. The one condition was that it focus on issues and needs in the Piedmont Triad region. Thus, in 1996, the Center for the Study of Social Issues (CSSI) was born. Its new and energetic director, a tenured faculty member and team member, was a leading grant-funded scholar in the Department of Human Development and Family Studies. Although she had had no experience working with local agencies and communities, her charge was to get the Center off the ground quickly, with limited university funds, and to begin bringing in grant money to sustain its activities.

High Point, North Carolina

High Point lies almost 30 minutes driving time southwest of UNCG. The Macedonia neighborhood, the home of a huge semi-annual international furniture market, is located a few blocks from the downtown. While the downtown is marked by large showrooms, neatly landscaped streets, and many furniture retailers, just a few blocks away lies a blighted commercial/industrial area largely made up of abandoned buildings, former textile mills and factories, marginal small businesses and vacant land. In close proximity is a low-income residential area of primarily small rental homes, neglected properties, and public housing. In 1996, about 15% of the homes were considered neglected, vacant, or in disrepair. The population of the rental area was estimated at 1500 highly transient residents. Approximately 72% were African-American, while only 10% of those in public housing were white (DeHoog, 1998). There was also a small but growing Hispanic population in this neighborhood. Until the mid-1970s, the Macedonia neighborhood had been a thriving community, centered on a close-knit African-American community, and surrounded by white residences, small businesses and several factories. By the 1990s, most of the factories had closed their doors and moved to other locations. As hundreds of jobs left the community, so did the economic and social stability of the neighborhood. Prior to the revitalization planning process, Macedonia residents and business owners had not been organized to combat the deteriorating conditions, and had little record of involvement in community affairs. The city's traditional power structure and culture was one of a mill town–a company town in which a small economic elite made most of the decisions.

STAGE I: COME OVER AND HELP US

EPA Brownfields Project (1996-1999)

Within a few months of starting CSSI, the director accepted an invitation by High Point's mayor to attend a series of meetings on the problem of urban brownfields in the region. Brownfields are economically depressed and blighted areas where former manufacturing plants, abandoned buildings, or other activities have created suspicions of environmental contamination and unsafe conditions. The goal was to determine what policies and programs could lead to the reuse and revitalization of these areas. Although the director and two faculty members from the Departments of Business Administration (DBA) and Political Science (DPS) who attended were unfamiliar with the subject of brownfields and urban redevelopment, the mayor's leadership, city employees, and the technical expertise of several key environmental experts kept the process moving. These meetings led to the city of High Point collaborating with the Center to write a grant proposal to the EPA to study the brownfield area near downtown.

During the grant writing process, the targeted area of commercial and industrial sites was expanded geographically to include the adjacent low-income residential area. This expansion allowed High Point to qualify for the minimum geographic area for the EPA grant and to include the low-income residences and public housing as targets for improvement in the project. Most brownfield projects usually focus on cleaning up soil contamination and removing blighted buildings, but the staff of the city's Department of Community Development and Housing (DCDH) believed that addressing the neighborhood's physical condition, housing blight, and social problems were as important to the economic redevelopment effort as were developing new industries and commercial ventures.

CSSI-City Collaboration. In May 1997, the EPA awarded the City of High Point the $200,000 pilot project grant for the West Macedonia area. A sub-grant for community assistance-needs assessment and project evaluation-was awarded to CSSI. (The term "West Macedonia" was originally used in the EPA grant, but the neighborhood association and residents later encouraged the "West" to be dropped, as it had no meaning for the community.) At the point of submission, neither DBA or DPS faculty nor the CSSI Director had visited the neighborhood. None had substantive expertise in environmental contamination, amelioration, or urban revitalization. They were to provide regional market data for the consultant, the needs assessment instruments and methodology, and a modest summary evaluation. This type of work can be described as traditional technical assistance work for faculty consultants. For their part, the City of High Point staff and elected officials had had no prior connections to the faculty and university administration. Two key city staff involved in writing the proposal with CSSI were the heads of DCDH and the Planning Department (PD), two units that had a history of tension and conflict. CSSI's grant writing experience and leadership offered a way to complete the grant proposal on time and to gain a neutral facilitator to assist the city in developing the brownfield assessment process.

In the fall of 1997, during the first months of the funded EPA project, problems between the two city departments and the PD director surfaced. When the management team was officially formed by the mayor and city manager of High Point, it did not include the planning director, who resigned within a few months of the receipt of funding. As a result of this vacuum of leadership, the Director of the CSSI Center was chosen to lead the team. This gave the Director a prominent role in facilitating the team meetings and setting priorities in a community and subject area in which faculty had no prior history. However, being a quick study, and having a forceful personality, the Center Director took charge and, working with the mayor and city staff, moved the project forward by establishing a steering committee, selecting consultants and getting the residential neighborhood involved. The faculty member who organized the needs assessment offered additional assistance through her two graduate students who interned for the city and CSSI. Both the director and the faculty member saw this project as an opportunity to assist the city and gain a track record in a key community partnership that might lead to future grant funding for UNCG.

Brownfield Research and Evaluation. Over the next two years, a very successful process took place among the leadership of the management team and a community steering committee. In addition to the overall co-ordinating and planning process, an environmental site assessment, a business market study, and the community needs assessment were completed within the first 15 months. While the environmental site assessment was conducted without any university involvement, the marketing study relied on Triad area data supplied by the DBA faculty member. The needs assessment was conducted by the DPS faculty and graduate students in the Master of Public Affairs (MPA) program. It included a residential face-to-face survey, a business survey, four focus groups, a quality of life summary, and a final evaluation of the project (DeHoog, 1999). Participants saw the primary successes of the project as crime abatement, community involvement in the planning process, and the lack of any significant soil contamination. In contrast, the market study did not suggest economic development projects that the steering committee believed were feasible (DeHoog, 1999).

Collaboration Challenges. From CSSI's point of view, the major challenges were organizing the management team, managing conflict among city government officials, engaging the city's economic development leaders, and getting students to complete the door-to-door residential needs assessment. In particular, the needs assessment was a much more difficult task than originally envisioned. With a 30-minute commute to the neighborhood, no public transportation, and no university transportation, the teams of students faced several barriers. Although police were alerted, students were oriented and trained, and city staff volunteered to assist, the dropout rate was significant. One team of undergraduates promptly quit upon driving into the neighborhood and viewing it as unsafe. Other graduate assistants from CSSI failed to complete their interviews due to lack of transportation, time, or incentives. The class of MPA students picked up their assignments, the two graduate assistants coordinated their work, and the surveys were completed.

From the city's perspective, the EPA grant process and revitalization planning were strongly supported by key community leaders, the local newspaper, and more generally, the public. After two decades of neglect, neighborhood organizing in the city was in its early development. Neighborhood residents were beginning to believe that they could have a role in the process. Nonetheless, as collaborations within the community and with CSSI were fairly new to these city departments, tensions about responsibilities, personalities, and leadership were gradually worked out. Ultimately, the public viewed the city's efforts to involve the community through the needs assessment and public participation in planning as a success. As the *High Point Enterprise* editor wrote in February 14, 1999:

> Remarkable progress was made and the project entered 1999 ahead of schedule. The hired guns did their work thoroughly and quickly. Steering committee members who were assigned tasks produced the desired results. West Macedonia neighborhood residents, promised their voices would be heard, enthusiastically joined the party. A neighborhood association has held several meetings-to ask questions, to get answers, to air grievances, to brainstorm. (Blount, 1999, p. A6)

During the second year of the project, the city's staff in the DCDH played the lead role in planning the physical revitalization of the area. This began largely as a straight-forward professional planner-driven process, but soon produced a lesson in neighborhood organizing. In early 1999, a few months after the EPA project consultants' reports were presented to the project steering committee, the High Point Housing Authority (HPHA), an organization outside the city government, presented a plan to build a new community of 34 rental units and a community center in the heart of the neighborhood. It had been carefully and tastefully designed with the plan to convert the units to owner-occupied condominiums after 15 years. The HPHA director had operated very successfully for many years by presenting his finished plans to the city for support, with the promise of federal HUD funding. However, in this case, the newly formed neighborhood association and many Macedonia residents were outraged that this plan would create more rental properties, and mobilized a strong campaign with some city staff support to block the plan. While several steering committee members supported any physical improvements to the area, the vocal residents and their allies won the day with their argument that home ownership was the only way to improve and stabilize the neighborhood. These residents may not have fully represented the younger renting population in the neighborhood or those living in public housing, yet their clearly articulated views convinced the city's leadership that they should not endorse the proposal. Residents now were a force to be reckoned with. Whether it was due to the opposition or other flaws in the HPHA plan, the project did not receive federal funding, and the residents considered that a victory.

STAGE II: LEARNING FROM OUR MISTAKES

The Evolution of COPC and Its Relationships

Even before the first year of the EPA grant was completed, in June 1998, CSSI submitted a proposal to HUD to support a stronger university contribution to the Macedonia neighborhood and bring in new resources for community development. The EPA-funded community needs assessment served as the foundation for the proposal for a Community Outreach Partnership Center (COPC). Overarching goals for the revitalization of the Macedonia neighborhood involved creating a more economically viable and self-sustaining community. The primary expressed needs of the residents were crime reduction, youth recreation and other activities, leadership development, affordable housing, and job training and development. However, in the limited time between analyzing the assessment results and submitting the proposal for the HUD deadline, CSSI staff and faculty failed to consult with the community about the specific programs that would meet these needs. Rather, the writers proposed eight separate programs based on the available resources and willing collaborators with whom they had recently developed relationships within the High Point community and in the university. While in hindsight, this strategy was a flawed one, it illustrates a fairly typical process in university grant writing in which time constraints limit a more comprehensive and thorough review of the options with community feedback.

In October 1998, CSSI was awarded the COPC grant from HUD, and the attention of the director and faculty turned to developing the location and the programs of the COPC. Everyone agreed that the development of the COPC was a direct result of the research and planning work CSSI had done over the course of the prior involvement with the brownfields study. In spring of 1999, the High Point management team disbanded, and the city's community development staff focused on developing a specific land use and housing plan for the area, with a great deal of neighborhood input. At this point, most of the interdepartmental and interpersonal conflicts had been resolved among city employees.

One of the first challenges following the grant announcement was to find the space in the community to house the new COPC. During the needs assessment process the CSSI faculty and staff became increasingly aware of the need for a "place" in the community to host neighborhood meetings, to house new programs, and serve as the visible outreach link between the neighborhood and UNCG. Due to miscommunication and misunderstanding with a local church that had initially offered its facility for the proposal, it was several months before an acceptable location was found. Ultimately, a local community college committed to house the COPC in its High Point campus adjacent to the Macedonia neighborhood as an in-kind contribution to the community efforts. This agreement represented another example of the university connecting in a new way, to expand its relationship with the community college to an outreach partnership in the neighborhood. This office, staffed by a full-time director and two graduate assistants, became the point for information and referral to other city programs, for community meetings such as the Macedonia Neighborhood Association, and for classes for the residents and youth. Another small neighborhood church provided additional space for larger meetings and youth activities.

Once staffed and furnished, the COPC began to focus on social capital development and community building through communication, outreach and neighborhood events. A COPC newsletter and a Macedonia Neighborhood Association newsletter, written by its members were distributed to residents each quarter. A Community Advisory Board (CAB) composed of residents, representatives of community agencies and governmental departments, and UNCG faculty, was organized by the COPC staff to ensure ongoing communication and feedback about COPC programs and community needs. The Macedonia Neighborhood Association, established early on through the EPA project and led by neighborhood residents, had already begun meeting. It became increasingly visible and effective in planning events and activities with COPC support.

Another focus identified through the needs assessment of the EPA grant was crime reduction. This issue had already been addressed somewhat through the High Point Police Department's city-wide "get-tough" approach in response to an escalation of homicides in the mid-1990s. CSSI and COPC staff joined the Violence Task Group (VTG), which was a merger of the Police Department's work on violence with a community based group. VTG developed a local model of the Boston Crime Reduction Program, in which parolees are called in and sternly warned not to commit additional gun crimes or a federal prison sentence would result. Widespread community support for this model, vigorous law enforcement leadership, and strong collaborations among public and nonprofit agencies, combined with the activities of COPC, such as Neighborhood Watch Programs and neighborhood policing. These efforts led to a 13% reduction in violent crime over a five year period (Frabut, 2002).

As a spin off of the Task Force, the Youth Violence Task Group was created. This group initiated a two-pronged approach to addressing youth violence: service coordinators were placed in the Office of Juvenile Justice in High Point to address the needs of adjudicated youth and their families, with particular attention to Macedonia families; and a school-based program developed in one of the local high schools provided wrap-around support services and intervention for at-risk youth. Three other crime prevention programs were also developed as part of COPC with community partners. These included the designation as a "Safe Site" in the Macedonia community to offer education and haven to residents; Macedonia Neighborhood Watch Program, in collaboration with the Neighborhood Association, to increase residential awareness; and the Junior Police Academy, in which neighborhood youth participated in a Police Department summer program.

Changing Strategies to Respond to Resident Interests

As previously noted, the original EPA needs assessment was critical in determining the direction for the COPC grant proposal. Nonetheless, the specifics described in the COPC proposal had to be changed or eliminated upon the involvement of residents. Using the input of the Advisory Committee and the Neighborhood Association members, as well as feedback from community meetings, COPC staff worked with the neighborhood residents to develop programs that more closely met community residents' needs. For example, the original youth and crime prevention project, the Junior Police Academy, became an ongoing program of the High Point Police Department. The COPC youth programs focused on the development of a new project–a youth baseball league. Initiated by a former baseball player and public housing resident who participated in COPC's leadership development program, the youth baseball league became a huge success. Not only have many neighborhood youth ages 8-12 participated in playing baseball, they have also been coached and supported by community residents, civic clubs, and baseball fans from across High Point. Recognizing the significance of the emergence of the Macedonia Baseball Association for the youth and the community, the city donated land and developed a baseball park in the neighborhood in time for the 2003 season. The Director of the COPC with support of neighborhood residents and city leadership nominated the league's creator for state and national awards given to honor community heroes.

A second example of a "change in strategy" in response to resident interests (or lack thereof) was seen in the redirection of the leadership development program. Originally included in the COPC proposal, the eight-week CAN DO leadership program was taught twice by a UNCG faculty member to community residents. Yet when a third class offering resulted in little interest, the COPC staff, in consultation with the Advisory Committee and the Neighborhood Association, decided to design other kinds of leadership programs. In partnership with community-based organizations, COPC offered a pilot proposal writing workshop series that resulted in the award of three city grants for grassroots initiatives, computer training workshops, women's leadership and literacy group, and meetings for job-seeking residents. Macedonia residents and other members of the larger community participated in these opportunities, thus enriching individual lives and bringing additional resources into the community. Two examples of the more innovative efforts were a pilot Music Business Workshop for youth and the Star Achievers program, which awarded school supplies to students returning to school and incentives to those who demonstrated academic improvement. Also, the COPC established and maintained the use of a language line service within a neighborhood school for non-English speaking parents. UNCG's language faculty members, as part of the COPC, conducted research on its use and impact on children and families' lives in their adjustment to school.

In facilitating neighborhood empowerment, COPC recruited and supervised volunteers, graduate assistants, and interns from UNCG to participate in several other programs identified as needed by residents during community meetings: health fairs, youth recreation and activity programs, English as a Second Language (ESOL) tutoring, and opportunities to learn about other community resources and agencies. As the relationship with the Macedonia community developed, the "distance issue" was resolved by involving graduate assistants who viewed their placement as a job and the faculty and staff involved with the community adjusted to the distance as a "commute" to the location.

Additionally, in response to the high dropout rate in the area high schools, the need for job training, and the increased pressure for CSSI to be successful in securing grants, UNCG developed a HUD-funded Youth Build program. The primary recruitment area for participants has been the Macedonia community and the other central city neighborhoods of High Point. Youth Build identifies high school dropouts, aged 16-25, who desire a GED and work skills. Partnering with Guilford Technical Community College, local construction companies, the High Point Housing Authority, and many public and human service agencies,

CSSI again moved into an area without previous expertise with this youth population or in home construction. Now in its third year, the CSSI Youth Build program is considered exemplary by HUD, particularly as an example of excellent community partnerships, and the staff is frequently asked by the regional HUD office to provide information and advice to other Youth Build programs.

The Violence Task Group and the Youth Violence Initiative also exemplified the flexible response and interaction between faculty and members of the High Point community working to address community needs. Having experienced the value of involving citizens at the grassroots level in the program development of the COPC, these initiatives to address community violence utilized the expertise of those directly involved with the neighborhoods to develop programs. Instead of being planned and implemented in a preconceived, structured manner, addressing violence and providing enhanced opportunities for at-risk youth *developed*. While these initiatives were in response to community needs, they led CSSI and faculty who had research interest in areas of violence etiology and prevention, to deep involvement with the community law enforcement and the human service providers.

Meeting Challenges by Adaptation

These partnerships among the university, community residents, and agencies were built upon the previous work in the EPA grant and the development of the COPC. University faculty and staff *listened* to community residents, established working relationships with the leadership in city agencies and nonprofit providers, and, most importantly, did not portray themselves as *the* experts. Throughout this process, strong and trusting relationships grew among the residents of the Macedonia neighborhood, the leaders of community-based organizations, the faith based organizations, the leadership of the DCDH, and the UNCG faculty and staff. The relationships evolved over time, throughout the process of developing the EPA grant to the implementation of the COPC and other grant programs. It happened because there was awareness by the CSSI staff and other UNCG faculty that working with and in community is not the same as being in the classroom or conducting traditional research. These relationships had to be built upon mutual trust. Just as in other meaningful personal relationships, they take time, patience and commitment. Because there was a mutual willingness to "open up," the community and the university could become partners. This result did not occur without challenges, such as the denied expectation that a neighborhood church would house the COPC office, or the fact that Kids Korps USA, an organization that initially agreed to provide a youth program, decided against developing a North Carolina chapter. Additionally, staff changes within the city departments and in the position of the COPC director meant that transitions and relationship building took time and energy away from the program planning, coordination, and implementation. These challenges were met by the persistent involvement of CSSI, the second COPC director, and associated faculty members with the Macedonia neighborhood residents, and the positive results of several COPC program initiatives.

In sum, during this stage, various faculty, staff, and students were involved in projects. Many of these were one-time or one-project types of interactions focused on a particular event or task. As COPC developed, it became clear that the full-time CSSI staff provided the continuity and "glue" to keep the collaborations, relationships, and projects moving along, while the faculty and students were brought in for shorter periods for their expertise and energy when needed. In particular, graduate students in several of the professional programs, not undergraduates, were the most likely to become interested and remain involved as they had their own transportation, greater commitment to community building, and a clearer focus on gaining appropriate professional experience through the COPC projects.

STAGE III: MACEDONIA BECOMES A "PLACE" AGAIN

Family Resource Center and Oral History (2002-2003)

During the development of COPC's programs, the City of High Point's Department of Community Development and Housing had continued to focus on the Macedonia neighborhood in response to the residents' expressed need for safe and affordable housing. Eliminating places that were gathering places for drug sales, dozens of houses in the area were condemned, razed, or rehabbed. A new housing development plan for Macedonia Place, which included new houses rather than the public housing apartments that had been proposed by the Housing Authority years before, was created for the neighborhood by the city's Department of Community Development and Housing. The neighborhood's appearance had improved dramatically and its residents, at community gatherings and meetings of the Neighborhood Association, began to express new pride in their surroundings.

Connected to these plans was the work of the congregation of Wesley Memorial United Methodist Church, the largest and wealthiest white church in the city. Many members of this congregation had a long history in Macedonia because their families had owned the former furniture and textile plants located there. As part of their outreach ministry, the church decided to build a Childcare Center in the neighborhood. In both the city's housing plans and the proposed Childcare Center plans, some residents were wary of what this new construction would mean for their neighborhood. Many feared that the proposed housing would be too expensive for them and many were unsure about whose children would be eligible for the childcare program. Once these concerns were expressed in neighborhood association meetings, the COPC Advisory Committee and the COPC Director worked hard to articulate the residents' concerns to the city and the church. It was important to make certain that issues of fear and distrust were addressed by involving association members in the childcare planning process. Over time, with the residents' input, the plans for the center changed to include not only the childcare program but also, in anticipation of the grant ending, to incorporate the COPC programs. Again, the neutrality of COPC staff and CSSI facilitated communication and began to assuage fears.

As a result of concerns about the imminent changes in the neighborhood, the idea of an oral history project began to take form. During a COPC Community Advisory Board meeting in 2001 that focused on the input of community residents' input into plans for the new Family Resource Center in Macedonia, attendees noted the many changes in the neighborhood over the years. The President of the Neighborhood Association stated that children who live in Macedonia today would not recognize the thriving community in which she grew up decades ago. Nonetheless, community pride and family connections remained part of Macedonia's culture both among some current residents and those who relocated to other parts of the city. She wished this could be captured and passed on to young people growing up in the neighborhood today.

Inspired by this discussion at the CAB meeting, an oral history project was developed to document and celebrate the rich history of the neighborhood. In the last months of COPC funding, thirty interviews with current and former residents were collected by community residents who were trained by an oral historian in interview techniques. Current residents and persons still living in the City of High Point were recruited to participate. A large community culminating event was held to present the highlights of the residents' stories in February 2003. Several current community leaders, such as the mayor and a radio talk show host, came forward to tell their stories of growing up in Macedonia. While they celebrated their memories and relationships, residents of the neighborhood noted that today Macedonia is on the cusp of another great period of change with the planning of the new housing construction, the building of the Family Resource Center, and greater attention to social needs in the area. In addition to being included in a booklet, this collection of stories was also used to develop a social studies curriculum for local public schools focusing on the impact of race relations, economic shifts, and deindustrialization during the mid-1900s. This project exemplified the importance of "listening" to the voices of the community and allowing the residents to set priorities.

DISCUSSION

The literature in community development suggests some ways in which to analyze the process of CSSI's role in Macedonia's revitalization. Christenson's typology (1989) includes three approaches used by community developers: *technical assistance*, *self-help*, and *conflict*. The initial approach used by CSSI in Stage I was clearly the *technical assistance* model where the university faculty and staff saw their role as objective consultants for the city of High Point. However, as staff and faculty became more acquainted with the residents and CSSI became drawn into a leadership role in the growing partnerships, a greater emphasis began to be placed on the *self-help* approach. In Stage II, CSSI staff learned to become facilitators to help the neighborhood identify its goals and strategies and build greater capacity to carry out certain projects. To the extent that some projects included originally in the HUD grant proposal were dropped in favor of those that residents promoted, a process of adaptation to the neighborhood's priorities occurred. Subsequently, in Stage III, CSSI stepped back into a supporting role in community building and accessing funding sources that the neighborhood could not obtain on its own. By this point, CSSI had learned a hard lesson–that planning programs without neighborhood leadership was wasteful and frustrating. Listening to and responding to residents' voices truly educated faculty, staff, and students in what was important to the neighborhood and thus, more likely to be sustained. They also realized that the relationships of trust and cooperation were the glue that held the partnerships together.

This case study of the relationship of UNCG and the Macedonia community in High Point also illuminates ways to overcome geographical barriers and traditional university-community tensions and provides insight into ways to develop trusting relationships between community residents and university personnel. High Point was not in UNCG's backyard and, at the beginning of this partnership, was not a community that had any prior connection to the University or its faculty. CSSI was a new creation, untested, with inexperienced leadership for university-community development collaborations. UNCG faculty and CSSI staff had virtually no connections or networks in place to develop initial collaborative projects. As time went on, staff conflicts and staff turnover in the city and CSSI had the potential to weaken the collaborations. The distance of a 30-minute commute to High Point kept some faculty and students from participating more extensively in the COPC and the neighborhood activities.

So, what made it work? First, the absence of a blueprint or research agenda made for greater openness and responsiveness to the wishes of the city staff and community members. Typically, in offering technical or research assistance, university or academic advice does not always prove to be tailored to the specific needs or expressed concerns of a local area. In the Macedonia case, the lack of topical expertise turned out to be a strength of the project. Listening and adapting to community needs emerged as a primary value of the project. CSSI also was forced to face its mistakes in writing the COPC proposal and develop a self-help approach as the neighborhood residents became more involved. Second, for High Point's city staff and residents, the University was seen as a welcome partner in this revitalization effort initially because of the successful writing of grants that brought resources into the city. Both the city department heads were outside professional planners who had been trained to try to engage the broader community more directly. The CSSI partners' involvement helped to assure that this process developed, and as a neutral player the university partners helped diminish the importance of the political road-blocks and egos. While some personality conflicts arose in the process, both sides became committed to moving the project forward with a clear focus on the revitalization goal. In particular, the city's community development staff recognized an opportunity to have a successful project that demonstrated broader public interest in improving low-income communities in High Point and worked to make this happen.

Third, the philosophy of resident self-help and engagement in the process developed as a key principle in the partnership and the revitalization project. The new housing proposal by the HPHA halfway through the brownfields project proved to be a critical event. It illustrated for both the academic and government partners that the community wanted to be involved in key decisions, rather than being left on the sidelines to ratify the decisions of elites. City staff, steering committee members, and the university participants learned from this event that although the residents might not want to be involved in large numbers in every decision about the neighborhood, they would demand participation in the plans when their interests and needs were directly affected. A neighborhood-based planning approach was even more visible in the COPC program over time as it created and implemented new activities that were more responsive to the Macedonia residents. In Stage III, the church's building plans were greatly influenced by the improved understanding of the role of the neighborhood in directing the plans. As a result the Family Resource Center was built to meet the community's wishes. Also, through the oral history project the neighborhood residents, other city residents and officials, and the University shared joy in recounting the pride in Macedonia as *a neighborhood*. All understood the importance of being in relationship with each other.

In summary, university faculty and CSSI staff, along with those involved with the COPC, learned the importance of openness in becoming engaged with the residents of a distant community. The self-help approach took time to learn, but it developed much greater trust among the partners as residents began making more decisions. This experience taught the university personnel the importance of the development of genuine partnerships that transcend traditional ways of interacting among grassroots citizens, city leadership and university academics. Through this experience, as well as other community partnerships, CSSI developed the basic principle that, order to be effective, community collaborations have to include everyone affected in the decision making process.

REFERENCES

Blount, T. (1999, February 14). Often, medicine is bitter. *High Point Enterprise*, p. A6.

Christenson, J.A. (1989). Themes of community development. In J.A. Christenson & J. Robinson (Eds.), *Community development in perspective* (pp. 26-47). Ames, IA: Iowa State University Press.

DeHoog, R.H. (1998). *West Macedonia needs assessment*. City of High Point. Unpublished report.

DeHoog, R.H. (1999). *West Macedonia Brownfields Revitalization Evaluation Report*. City of High Point. Unpublished report.

Forrant, R., & Silka, L. (1999). Thinking and doing–doing and thinking: The University of Massachusetts Lowell and the community development process. *American Behavioral Scientist, 42,* 814-27.

Frabut, J. (2002). Community safety begins with the High Point violent crime task group: Report to the community. Center for the Study of Social Issues, University of North Carolina at Greensboro. Unpublished document.

The Role of Evaluation in Developing Community-Based Interventions: A COPC Project

Sondra SeungJa Doe, PhD
Daniel Lowery, PhD

SUMMARY. The Community Outreach Partnership Center (COPC) program sponsored by the US Department of Housing and Urban Development (HUD) is designed to support the development of partnerships between universities and colleges and the communities in which they reside. This manuscript reports on the initial stages of the evaluation of a COPC initiative in an impoverished neighborhood surrounding Indiana University Northwest (IUN) in Gary, Indiana. Four distinct projects of the initiative are described, including education, neighborhood revitalization, community organizing, and economic development. The paper shows how logic models and baseline telephone surveys can be used to evaluate broad-scale capacity-building initiatives that are expected to evolve and change over time as a result of participation from community members. *[Article copies available for a fee from The Haworth Document Delivery*

Sondra SeungJa Doe is Director and Associate Professor, Social Work Program, LaSierra University, 4700 Pierce Street, Riverside, CA 92515-8247. Daniel Lowery is Assistant Professor, School of Public and Environmental Affairs, Indiana University Northwest, Gary, IN.

Address correspondence to: Sondra SeungJa Doe, PhD (E-mail: sdoe@lasierra.edu).

[Haworth co-indexing entry note]: "The Role of Evaluation in Developing Community-Based Interventions: A COPC Project." Doe, Sondra SeungJa, and Daniel Lowery. Co-published simultaneously in *Journal of Community Practice* (The Haworth Social Work Practice Press, an imprint of The Haworth Press, Inc.) Vol. 12, No. 3/4, 2004, pp. 71-88; and: *University-Community Partnerships: Universities in Civic Engagement* (ed: Tracy M. Soska, and Alice K. Johnson Butterfield) The Haworth Social Work Practice Press, an imprint of The Haworth Press, Inc., 2004, pp. 71-88. Single or multiple copies of this article are available for a fee from The Haworth Document Delivery Service [1-800-HAWORTH, 9:00 a.m. - 5:00 p.m. (EST). E-mail address: docdelivery@haworthpress.com].

Service: 1-800-HAWORTH. E-mail address: <docdelivery@haworthpress.com> Website: <http://www.HaworthPress.com> © 2004 by The Haworth Press, Inc. All rights reserved.]

KEYWORDS. Community Outreach Partnership Center, university-community partnership, evaluation, community assessment, logic model

INTRODUCTION

There has been a growing national trend toward the promotion of more positive relationships between institutions of higher education and the communities in which they are located. Urban universities, in particular, are being challenged to become "better citizens," and it is believed that this can best be accomplished by connecting in positive ways with the neighborhoods in which they are located. Falling under the umbrella of what has been termed the "scholarship of engagement" (Boyer, 1990; Bringle, Games, & Malloy, 1999; Glassick, 1999; Maurrasse, 2001; Rubin, 1998), faculty members and staff are expected to integrate and apply their expertise for the purpose of community building.

Community Outreach Partnership Center (COPC) programs are unique in several respects. Created as a demonstration project in 1994 by the US Department of Housing and Urban Development (HUD), COPC is designed to facilitate the development of partnerships between universities and colleges and communities. COPC funds can be used to address a broad range of issues, including housing, education, community empowerment, leadership development, and economic development. Ideally, COPC funds are used as seed money to promote the establishment of relationships and initiatives that will be self-sustaining after the grants have been exhausted (Office of University Partnerships, 2000). COPC grants are further distinguished by their malleable design. Unlike other government programs, COPC initiatives are expected to evolve over time as opportunities present themselves, as barriers are encountered, and as learning occurs. It is anticipated that community input will guide the ongoing development of COPC-sponsored initiatives. As noted by Brueggemann (2002, p. 183), "the central theme of community building is to obliterate feelings of dependency and to replace them with self-reliance, self-confidence, and responsibility." With the caveat that each COPC program is unique, these defining characteristics are consistent with the evolving understanding of the university's role as a partner institution.

At the same time, COPC programs present certain challenges both to HUD and to those who administer local COPC programs. In particular, the program's generally flexible approaches to design poses problems to evaluators who like to use consistent sets of outcome criteria. COPC programs may not lend themselves to traditional evaluation methodologies, which tend to focus on concrete objectives that have been clearly defined early on in the planning process. This does not mean, however, that the assessment of programs of this kind should be restricted exclusively to process and effort analyses. The need for capacity-building programs like COPC is promoted on the basis of outcomes pertaining to the development of social capital, the empowerment of neighborhood residents, and social learning. Moreover, the ongoing funding of COPC programs and their local development depends on evaluations that can document links between the different kinds of initiatives that are undertaken and various kinds of tangible and intangible outcomes.

This article reports on the results of a baseline community assessment survey and the implications such methods hold for validating the intervention design and the ongoing development of a COPC initiative. Three following questions are addressed. Can the techniques associated with summative evaluation be used to test the designs of broad-based social interventions like COPC? Can data gathered in a baseline assessment be used effectively to guide community choices in partnership-oriented interventions of this kind? And can survey data be used to address social interventions that focus on such intangible concepts as social capital, community's sense of self-efficacy and empowerment, and awareness of community life?

COPC AT INDIANA UNIVERSITY NORTHWEST

Indiana University Northwest (IUN) in Gary, Indiana was awarded a COPC grant from the HUD in late 1999. The three-year grant committed the University to various activities designed to engender the expansion of social capital in the target community of Glen Park and its collective sense of ownership over its intangible and tangible assets. The Glen Park neighborhood has been in serious decline for over 25 years. The ten-block neighborhood abuts IUN, a regional campus of the Indiana University system. Located to the immediate south of downtown Gary, Indiana, Glen Park has experienced an increasing concentration of poverty, racial segregation, a severe loss of jobs and population, and a high level of gang activity and violence in recent years. Glen Park has the highest murder rate in the city. According to the 1990 Census data, the neighborhood is home to approximately 8,000 residents, 75% of whom are African-American. Approximately 16% are White, and 9% are Latino.

Shared Vision

The University's historic relationship with the target community can best be described as benign neglect. It has not experienced any serious manifestations of town-gown conflict. Any outreach that has occurred has tended to be driven by the research agendas of individual faculty members rather than the institution as a whole. Nevertheless, the University helped create a Community Development Corporation (CDC) in 1996, and has maintained a close link with the organization through a faculty member who serves on its board of directors. The CDC's goals have been twofold: to engender a greater sense of self-efficacy among community members (Rosenberger, 1997; Silverman, 2001), and to channel that renewed sense of empowerment toward neighborhood revitalization initiatives (Rohe, 1998; Stoecker, 1997). Over time, IUN has partnered with the CDC in focusing on various issues pertaining to housing and business development. The University has assigned a part-time employee to the CDC to assist in the implementation of project-related activities. Other forms of community involvement include a teacher development program located in a local grade school and representation on the board of a community-oriented policing program.

From the University's perspective, the COPC initiative is consistent with its recently adopted "shared vision" statement, which was developed alongside the installation of a new chancellor in 1999. As shown in Figure 1, this "shared vision" commits the university to the ongoing support of "individual and community aspirations and growth." The shared vision also endorses the establishment of various kinds of collaborations, which are proven components of successful university-community partnerships (Casto, Harsh, & Cunningham, 1998; Homan, 1999; Krzyowski, Checkoway, & Gutierrez, 2001). At IUN, the COPC initiative has engendered the active engagement of faculty across several disciplines, including public administration, business administration, social work, and education. The concept of the "mutual learning partnership" between university and the community (Sandmann &

FIGURE 1. IUN's Vision Statement

Share the Vision
Indiana University Northwest

Indiana University Northwest

We, the students, faculty, staff, and alumni of IUN, take pride in our unique identity as Indiana University serving the seven-county region of northwest Indiana.

As a student-centered campus, we commit ourselves to academic excellence characterized by a love of ideas and achievement in learning, discovery, creativity, and engagement.

Because we value the complete richness of the human family, we embrace diversity in all its facets and aspire to the full nobility of our shared humanity.

We interact in caring and competent ways to support individual and community aspirations and growth.

We honor and value the contributions of all our members.

We promote well-being through an attractive and convenient environment conducive to learning. Our graduates are prepared for life-long learning, ethical practices, successful careers, and effective citizenship.

Indiana University Northwest collaborates and cooperates with other educational institutions, external partners, and the surrounding communities to enhance our overall quality of life.

Baker-Clark, 1997; Thomas, 1999) is embodied in several of the projects associated with the initiative. Furthermore, the COPC grant has complemented the University's shared vision. Under the new chancellor's leadership, community members have been recruited to participate in campus events and open forums of various kinds dealing with a broad range of community concerns. Thus, the COPC initiative is believed to have contributed to the achievement of IUN's expressed desire to serve the community in various ways as a true partner. It is grounded on the University's newly established commitment to develop a "mutual learning partnership" that involves the entire academic community and the neighborhood.

Four Distinct COPC Projects

IUN's COPC program encompassed four distinct projects in its original plan. These include education, neighborhood revitalization, community organizing, and economic development. *The Education Project* called for the development of a teacher education program, a tutoring program for grade school students, and an adult education program. It also called for the adoption of a year-round academic calendar in the local grade school. A partnership was established with the local school system, and a team was formed comprised of the dean and a full-time faculty member from the University's School of Education, the principal and several teachers from Franklin School, and parents from the neighborhood. COPC funds were used to underwrite an assessment of the grade school's performance and the examination of several alternative programs. The team has developed a formal proposal that calls for the implementation of a new curriculum based on the micro-society model and a year-round academic calendar. A preliminary commitment has been secured from the City of Gary to build a new school on the Franklin School site by 2004. Undergraduate students from the School of Education have been engaged in various ways at Franklin School, including tutoring and the development and direction of small-group learning projects during lunch periods. However, no activities have been undertaken with respect to teacher and adult education, the first and fourth projects in the HUD proposal.

The Neighborhood Revitalization Project envisioned the mapping of various tangible (e.g., community facilities, resources, etc.) and intangible assets (e.g., values, leadership qualities, etc.) in the community and the development of the Geographic Information System (GIS) for a visual presentation of community resources. It also included the further development of a housing rehabilitation initiative in partnership with the Glen Park CDC, the analysis of certain environmental factors that are believed to contribute to criminal activity in the neighborhood (e.g., lighting, landscaping, etc.), and the development of a new park.

The GIS initiative is underway, but has not yet produced results that can be used in any meaningful way. Several steps have been taken to underwrite the activities of the Glen Park CDC, including the development of a strategic plan and board governance documents and the indirect provision of staffing support. Despite these efforts, the CDC continues to struggle with funding and leadership issues. To further support its efforts, a property swap that involved another nonprofit organization was brokered and a partnership was subsequently established with the local Habitat for Humanity organization. As a result, four houses will soon be built on the property formally controlled by the CDC. The CDC has secured two more properties that it may develop in exchange. The project involving the analysis of environmental factors and criminal activity in the neighborhood was subsumed under a cooperative planning initiative that has been undertaken by the City of Gary, IUN, and IVY Tech State College, a technical school also located in the community. The nearly complete "University Park" plan calls for the significant redesign of traffic flow, lighting, and landscaping along 35th Avenue, the thoroughfare that links IUN, IVY Tech, and Franklin School. Finally, preliminary discussions with the City pertaining to the development of a new park have been initiated as part of the Franklin School project.

The Community Organizing Project focused on the University's promise that steps would be taken toward the creation of a community center. Programs and services, including a new police substation, would be co-located in the center. The center would facilitate linkages between various departments of municipal government and the University's several partners, including the Glen Park CDC and the Glen Park Community Oriented Policing (COP) organization. The establishment of a community resources center and a police substation on the Franklin School site necessitated the co-occupancy of a nonprofit organization that would provide before- and after-school programming for students. A model for this kind of cooperative enterprise has been identified and promising conversations have been initiated with the school system and the board of directors of a social services agency in the City that has the capacity to develop and deliver this kind of programming. A "casework management" team has been formed, which includes representatives of the Glen Park CDC and the COP organization and officials from various departments of City government, including the Police Department, Code Enforcement, General Services, and the Department of Parks and Recreation. The team meets every two weeks and "troubleshoots" issues of concern to the community. Priorities are established and expedited interventions are sanctioned. As a result, more than 70 actions have been taken over the course of the last year, including several house demolitions, the replacement of stolen street signs, the cleanup of several dumping sites, and an increase in police patrols in areas in which criminal activity is suspected. The casework management team has also sponsored the development of a draft ordinance designed to help stabilize home ownership in the neighborhood. The draft has been well-received by the two councilmen who represent the Glen Park community, and it now seems likely that a City-wide ordinance will be brought to a vote in the City Council.

The Economic Development Project called for an assessment of the local business community's strengths and weaknesses, and the development of a collective business plan for merchants located along Broadway, the thoroughfare that bisects Glen Park. Less has been accomplished with respect to this element of the grant than the other three. Although the Glen Park Merchants Association has been legally reestablished, it has yet to coalesce as a viable organization. Additionally, the development of specific initiatives has been suspended pending the completion of the City's University Park plan, which focuses on commercial development along Broadway.

In all four of these COPC initiatives, the community has played a significant role in the ongoing development of the COPC initiative. The Franklin School planning team, the Glen Park CDC, and the casework management team have all been actively involved in deciding which activities are undertaken and when they should be pursued. It is anticipated that the Glen Park Merchants Association will eventually play this same role with respect to business development. Several activities that were not envisioned in the original proposal have taken on great importance. The nature of the education program being developed for Franklin School was not anticipated by the academics involved in writing the proposal. Municipal funding for the building of a new school was not a priority until the Franklin School team was formed. The model for a co-located grade school and community center was only recently identified and the broader University Park initiative was not unveiled until after the grant was received. In this sense, the COPC initiative has been opportunistic as well as responsive to the community's desires.

A LOGIC DIAGRAM AND COMMUNITY ASSESSMENT

This analysis of the COPC program at IUN describes how the concepts of social capital (Putnam, 1993; Putnam, 1995; Taylor, 2000), community empowerment (Checkoway, 1997; Keating & Krumholz, 1999; Sirianni & Friedland, 2001), and awareness of community life (Sirgy, Rahtz, Cicic, & Underwood, 2000) are incorporated into the initial stages of a community assessment. First, the team developed a logic diagram to further parse the initiative's objectives. Second, it developed and administered a baseline survey of community residents. A framework was thus established for the ongoing evaluation of the several initiatives noted above.

Logic Diagram

As illustrated in Figure 2, a logic diagram is a graphical representation of the relationships that exist between and among various conceptual elements of a program, including inputs, activities, outputs, immediate outcomes, intermediate outcomes, and long-term outcomes. In the COPC program, inputs can be defined as the financial, human, social, technological, programmatic, and informational capacities that can be brought to bear in addressing an identified problem. Activities represent the tangible tasks that are undertaken as part of a program. Outputs generally refer to units of service, which are often measured in terms of quantity, quality, and timeliness. Immediate outcomes include cognitive and affective changes that accrue from an intervention. Intermediate outcomes include behavioral changes and other kinds of tangible impacts. And long-term outcomes encompass broader concepts such as improved life chances and improved quality of life.

For COPC-like programs, the three-fold specification of outcomes that logic diagrams require is useful. For example, the immediate outcomes pertinent to the education initiatives not only include an increase in the recognition of the importance of education among residents, but also an enhanced appreciation of the need for collaborative efforts to improve educational outcomes. The initiative's intermediate outcomes also include the achievement of learning objectives as well as high levels of participation. With respect to the grant's community organizing initiatives, the immediate outcomes include the recognition of and an increased appreciation for an expanded array of social and governmental services as well as cognitive and affective changes and an increase in the use of new services by the community. The logic diagram also codifies the synergistic impact that is envisioned for the various activities undertaken as part of the initiative. For example, the immediate outcomes go beyond the mere recognition of the importance of education and an enhanced appreciation for collaborative efforts to improve educational outcomes to include the achievement of learning objectives and high levels of participation as well. Similarly, with respect to the grant's community organizing initiatives, knowledge about an expanded array of social and governmental services are tied to increased access and other outcomes.

Baseline Telephone Survey

Based, in part, on the outcomes identified in the logic diagram, the evaluation team developed and administered a community survey. Its

FIGURE 2. LOGIC DIAGRAM

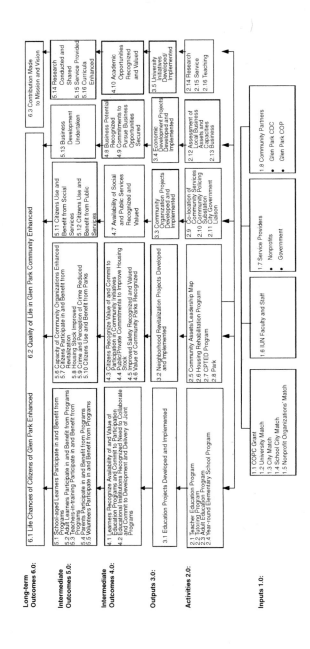

80

design also drew more generally on such broad-based concepts as social capital, empowerment, and social learning. The 107-item survey included both open-ended questions and Likert scales. A number of questions solicited basic demographic and economic information. The survey also focused on respondents' values, community assets, and various quality of life dimensions. The unique characteristics of the COPC program must be kept in mind in assessing this initial step in the evaluation process. Survey data were needed to test the design of the interventions proposed in the grant application. Data are also needed to inform the community's choices about various changes in the initiative's priorities over the three-year life of the grant. Finally, baseline data is necessary to accommodate a more traditional summative evaluation at a later point in time. This poses a particularly difficult challenge given the intangible nature of the outcomes identified in IUN's proposal to HUD–that is, an increase in the amount of social capital available to the community, an increase in the community's sense of self-efficacy and empowerment, and the successful promotion of social learning. Focus group interviews for collecting qualitative data are planned to complement the quantitative survey method. At this early point in the ongoing development of the initiative, the available quantitative evaluation should be assessed against these three criteria.

During the summer of 2001, IUN contracted with ten high school students from the Glen Park neighborhood to conduct telephone surveys over a two-week period. Local students who were trained to conduct telephone surveys were gainfully employed to promote awareness of the COPC initiative in the community. Letters describing the survey were also mailed to all residents in the target area. A newsletter featuring a story about the survey was included in the mailing as well. Residents were advised that students trained by the University would be making calls to randomly selected homes in Glen Park during the following week. They were also informed that anyone who agreed to participate in the survey would be eligible to receive a $20 check.

Using a systematic random sampling method, approximately 400 households were drawn from a telephone user list provided by the local telephone company. A total of 249 residents completed surveys and a 60% response rate was thus achieved. The telephone interviews averaged approximately 30 minutes in length. Sixty-seven percent of the respondents were African-American, 23% were white, and 10% other, a distribution that approximates the makeup of the Glen Park community in the 1990 Census. Since few Latino residents were included in the survey due to the failure to develop a Spanish language survey form

(Batsche, Hernandez, & Montenegro, 1999), the data are not fully generalizable because minorities are underrepresented. Reflecting a slightly higher percentage than was recorded in 1990, 92% of the respondents reported that they had graduated from high school. The survey participants' ages ranged from 18 to 84 with a median age of 49 years. With respect both to age and employment levels, the participants again mirror the Glen Park community as it is reflected in the 1990 Census.

FINDINGS

The findings accruing from the survey can be grouped into six categories (see Table 1). Values and community assets are key elements of social capital. The recognition of community needs and perceptions pertaining to quality of life reflect the residents' awareness of community life. Community ownership and leadership are clearly related to a community's sense of self-efficacy and empowerment.

Social Capital

Values. "Family and home" was rank-ordered as the respondents' most important collective value. "My faith in God" was identified by respondents as the second most important source of help in times of crisis.

Intangible Community Assets. Glen Park residents tend to have lived in the community for long periods of time. A majority of residents had a strong feeling of connectedness with the community and enjoyed solid networks of mutual support. For example, they cited "family and relatives," and "friends, neighborhood, and the community" as potential sources of help. Most notably, residents utilized church-based programs and services much more frequently than other community resources.

Awareness of Community Life

Recognition of Community Needs. The survey results confirmed a high unemployment rate (12.5%), which goes a long way toward explaining the high incidence of poverty in Glen Park. Over 85% of the respondents pointed to the need for economic development in the community. In open-ended questions, the residents noted that neighborhood schools, the public library, playgrounds, and other recreational fa-

TABLE 1. Glen Park Community Assessment Results

Social Capital	**Values** (High importance placed in family, friends & relatives; High level of religiosity and faith in God; Employment security and income). **Community Assets** (Median 19 years of long-term residency; High level of assistance received from (80%) and provided to (95%) family members and friends; High level of trust (87%) toward and positive opinions (85%) about their neighbors; High level of utilization of church-based programs and services (74%) compared to other community resources such as recreational facilities (43%), health care clinics (21%), etc.).
Awareness of Community Life	**Recognition of Community Needs** (Needs for jobs, economic development, businesses such as grocery and restaurants, physical infrastructure, playgrounds, home improvement, and public transportation). **Perceptions of Quality of Life** (Serious concerns over safety and street crime, violence, gang activity, drug dealing; Relatively positive perceptions about the quality of life in the neighborhood; Contrasting opinions about the recent change in the quality of life in the community; High desire to relocate to other areas; Varying degrees of satisfaction about the existing services in the community).
Community's Sense of Self-Efficacy and Empowerment	**Community Ownership** (Sense of high efficacy as good neighbors; Positive perceptions about neighbors; Sense of connection to the community; Positive self-perceptions about one's role in improving community life; A gap between residents' interest in joining community organizations and the actual memberships). **Leadership** (Positive opinions about church leaders and church-based services and programs; A high level of self awareness about the importance of community involvement such as community meetings and elections; Identification of community residents as the chief advocates for community improvements).

cilities were greatly in need of improvement. A great need for grocery stores was expressed by the majority (52%) of respondents.

Perceptions of Quality of Life. An overwhelming majority (81%) of the respondents reported serious concerns about gang activity. Additionally, "neighborhood, families, and friends" together with "safety and street crime" were rank-ordered as the most important factors to be considered in choosing a neighborhood in which to live. Despite their serious concerns over safety issues, a high percentage of the respondents (77.4%) concluded that they felt somewhat good or very good about living in Glen Park. A high percentage of the respondents characterized the overall quality of life in the Glen Park community as very good (9%) or somewhat good (69%). On the other hand, 60% of the respondents reported that they had thought about moving out of the community more than a few times over the course of the preceding 12 months. Most residents (91%) rated the quality of church-based services as good whereas other community-based services provided by other types of nonprofit organizations were less well thought of by the residents.

Community's Sense of Self-Efficacy and Empowerment

Community Ownership. Over 50% of the respondents reported that they believe they can play an important role in making Glen Park a better place to live; another 43% agreed that they can play a somewhat important role. Over 97% of the respondents characterized themselves as "responsible, pleasant, cooperative, friendly," or "helpful" members of the community. Approximately 73% of those who participated in the survey reported that they would be either somewhat or very interested in joining the Glen Park CDC or the COP organization. However, the membership rate was much higher for church organizations (44%) compared to parents' organizations (16%) and neighborhood associations (4%). The wide gap between the residents' interest in joining community organizations and the actual membership may be explained after scheduled focus group interviews have been conducted and resulting data have been analyzed.

Leadership. Churches and church leaders were described as working hard to make the Glen Park community a better place to live. Over 96% of the respondents agreed that residents should attend community meetings in order to improve Glen Park's quality of life. Approximately 85% of those who participated reported that it is very important to vote in local and other elections. The respondents also identified other "Glen Park residents" as the chief advocates for positive change in the community. This was followed by "the Mayor and City government" category. The rank-order of community priorities was led by "community involvement," and this was followed by the need for a more significant focus on public safety issues.

DISCUSSION AND IMPLICATIONS

Can the techniques associated with summative evaluation be used to test the designs of broad-based social interventions? The kind of "true partnership" that is called for in the COPC program requires collaborations that are generally recommended to be in place prior to the onset of planning. In the case of the COPC at IUN, faculty and staff developed a multi-dimensional grant proposal with little input from community residents. In fact, several elements of the original proposal provided for the development of the kind of partnerships promoted by the COPC program. In part, the grant writing team was motivated by the conviction that the University's relationship with the Glen Park community was civil but tenuous in nature. Consequently, they developed a proposal designed to more fully and positively engage the University in the life of its neighbors. The results of the baseline assessment demonstrate that key elements of the original proposal are consistent with the views of many residents. The community agrees that there is a need for economic development, a more intense focus on education and job training, gang interventions programs, and an improvement in the housing stock of the community. The COPC initiative's efforts pertaining to education, neighborhood revitalization, community organizing, and business development thus appear to be in sync with the perceived needs of the community.

At the same time, the grant proposal missed certain concerns that are broadly shared by residents of the Glen Park community. Jobs and employment-related services were not featured as prominently in the grant proposal as the baseline survey outcomes indicate they should have been. In hindsight, this is not surprising given the entrenched poverty of the Glen Park community. Further, residents' concerns about the poor quality of the community's physical and commercial infrastructure were not fully appreciated. Nonetheless, the techniques of summative evaluation were used effectively to test the design of a broad-based social intervention. In this instance, the overall design of the initiative's several programs was generally affirmed. This summative evaluation method was also helpful in promoting learning with respect to the community. In particular, two significant gaps in the grant proposal were exposed through the use of a participatory research method (Alvarez & Gutierrez, 2001) that facilitated residents' input.

Can information of this kind effectively inform subsequent programmatic choices? Again, it is important to remember that COPC interventions are not controlled experiments. But they are expected to evolve over time based on input and participation from the community. For example, as the focus of the COPC program shifted to the financing and construction of a new grade school co-located with a prominent non-profit organization to provide an array of before- and after-school programming. This reprioritization addresses the perceived need for a dramatic improvement in the physical and institutional infrastructure of the Glen Park community. Furthermore, the University Park initiative, under which several aspects of the University's COPC proposal have been subsumed, focuses intensively on the commercial development of the Glen Park community. In each of these ways, the University's COPC program is evolving in a way that is responsive to the priorities voiced by the community in the baseline survey.

At the same time, it appears that IUN's COPC intervention did not effectively leverage certain assets that were under-valued in the original proposal. Glen Park, for example, has solid social capital such as high family values, a strong sense of community, religious faith, effective informal support networks, and a feeling of connectedness within the community. Moreover, the several projects undertaken to date have failed to leverage the deep sense of religiosity and sense of community that are quite apparent in the results of the baseline assessment. Few efforts have yet been made to partner with local churches that provide services which are highly appreciated by Glen Park residents. Thus, the techniques of summative evaluation can inform the choices that must be made as an open-ended social intervention like COPC evolves over time, as evidenced by the shift in priorities that occurred from year one of the grant to year two. The baseline assessment identified a community strength that can be built upon over the course of the next year.

Can a baseline survey be used effectively to address social interventions that focus on such intangible concepts as social capital, community empowerment, and social learning? The techniques of summative evaluation can be employed effectively even when the outcomes desired include intangible concepts such as social capital, community empowerment, and awareness of community life. The use of a logic diagram effectively parsed these concepts—even if it did not "operationalize" them in the conventional sense of the term—and proved instrumental in this regard. A baseline has thus been established against which subsequent surveys can be compared. Focus groups are being conducted to further define the cognitive and affective variables that are most important to residents of the Glen Park community and their relationship to cognitive and behavioral changes and other tangible outcomes specified in the logic diagram.

In summary, the open-ended design of the COPC program appears to be a promising one. Although there is a clear need for rigorous evaluation, the tried-and-true techniques of summative and process evaluation may need to be readjusted in order to more completely account for the kind of approaches that are embodied in programs like COPC. Some evaluative control may have to be sacrificed for improving community participation. If the community is going to be engaged as a full partner, it should be expected that its representatives will, on occasion, recommend or even insist on a change in a program or intervention. Further, it should not be surprising that they will often be much more interested in an initiative's impact than the rigor of the evaluation method. This means that, if the university accepts the community as a full partner, it will, on occasion, be necessary to sacrifice a measure of evaluative control for the sake of program effectiveness.

CONCLUSION

In too many instances, university and college partnerships with neighboring communities are dominated by the educational institution. The COPC program tries to address this imbalance. Indeed, given its holistic approach to the multifaceted problems that impacted communities face, the COPC program underscores the importance of true collaborations between institutions of higher learning and the communities in which they reside as mutually learning partners. This case analysis has demonstrated how a partnership-oriented evaluation method can effectively facilitate a university's engagement in community building efforts as a true learning partner. When an educational institution meets the community as its equal partner, it can discover new knowledge of the community's hidden assets and strengths. A community-centered evaluation method can lead to the maximum utilization of tangible and intangible community resources that are often overlooked in preplanned community interventions.

REFERENCES

Alvarez, A.R., & Gutierrez, L.M. (2001). Choosing to do participatory research: An example and issues of fit to consider. *Journal of Community Practice, 9(1)*, 1-20.

Batsche, C., Hernandez, M., & Montenegro, M.C. (1999). Community needs assessment with Hispanic, Spanish-monolingual residents. *Evaluation and Program Planning, 22(1)*, 13-20.

Boyer, E. (1990). *Scholarship reconsidered: Priorities of the professorate.* Princeton, NJ: Princeton University Press.

Bringle, R., Games, R., & Malloy, E. (1999). *Colleges and universities as citizens.* Needham Heights, MA: Allyn and Bacon.

Brueggemann, W. (2002). *The practice of macro social work* (2nd ed.). Brooks/Cole.

Casto, R., Harsh, S., & Cunningham, L. (1998). Shifting the paradigm for interprofessional education at the Ohio state university and beyond. In J. McCroskey, & S. Einbinder (Eds.). *Universities and communities: Remaking professional and inter-professional education for the next century* (pp. 54-64). Westport, CT: Praeger.

Checkoway, B. (1997). Core concepts for community change. In M. Weil (Ed.). *Community practice: Models in action* (pp. 11-29). NY: The Haworth Press, Inc.

Glassick, C. (1999). Ernest L. Boyer: Colleges and universities as citizens. In R. Bringle et al., *Colleges and universities as citizens* (pp. 17-30). Needham Heights, MA: Allyn & Bacon.

Homan, M.S. (1999). *Promoting community change: Making it happen in the real world* (2nd ed.). Brooks/Cole.

Keating, W.D., & Krumholz, N. (Eds.). (1999). *Rebuilding urban neighborhoods: Achievements, opportunities, and limits.* Thousand Oaks, CA: Sage.

Krzyowski, M., Checkoway, B., & Gutierrez, L. (2001, March). *Educating community workers for collaborative practice: The Michigan neighborhood AmeriCorps Program.* Paper presented at the APM of the Council on Social Work Education, Dallas, TX.

Maurrasse, D.J. (2001). *Beyond the campus: How colleges and universities form partnerships with their communities.* NY: Routledge.

Office of University Partnerships. (2000). *Gateway to the American dream: The state of the community outreach partnership centers program.* Office of Policy Development and Research, U.S. Department of Housing and Urban Development.

Putnam, R.D. (1993). The prosperous community: Social capital and economic growth. *The American Prospect, Spring,* 35-42.

Putnam, R.D. (1995). Bowling alone: America's declining social capital. *Journal of Democracy, 6*(1), 65-78.

Rohe, W. M. (1998). Do community development corporations live up to their billing? A review and critique of the research findings. In C.T. Koebel (Ed.), *Shelter and society: Theory, research, and policy for nonprofit housing* (pp. 177-201). Albany: SUNY Press.

Rosenberger, R. (1997). Spiritual capital for the capital city. *Policy Review, 82,* 19-20.

Rubin, V. (1998). *The roles of universities in community-building initiatives.* RP-1998-01. Institute of Urban & Regional Development, University of California, Berkeley.

Sandmann, L.R., & Baker-Clark, C.A. (1997, October). *Characteristics and principles of university-community partnerships: A Delphi study.* Paper presented at the Midwest Research-to-Practice Conference and Community Education, Michigan Sate University.

Silverman, R.M. (2001). CDCs and charitable organizations in the urban south. *Journal of Contemporary Ethnography, 30*(2), 240-269.

Sirgy, M.J., Rahtz, D.R., Cicic, M., & Underwood, R. (2000). A method for assessing residents' satisfaction with community-based services: A quality-of-life perspective. *Social Indicators Research, 49*(3), 279-316.

Sirianni, C., & Friedland, L. (2001). *Civic innovation in America: Community empowerment, public policy, and the movement for civic renewal.* Berkeley, CA: University of California Press.

Stoecker, R. (1997). The CDC model of urban redevelopment: A critique and alternative. *Journal of Urban Affairs, 19*(1), 1-22.

Taylor, M. (2000). Communities in the lead: Power, organizational capacity and social capital. *Urban Studies, 37*(5/6), 1019-1036.

Thomas, N.L. (1999, June). *Community perceptions: What higher education can learn by listening to communities.* Paper presented at the New Roles, New Skills, and Stronger Partnership Conference sponsored by the American Council on Education. Tallahassee, Florida State University.

Seven Ways of Teaching and Learning: University-Community Partnerships at Baccalaureate Institutions

Steven R. Timmermans, PhD
Jeffrey P. Bouman, PhD

SUMMARY. The vast majority of Community Outreach Partnership Center (COPC) grantees are institutions with both undergraduate and graduate programs. Consequently, baccalaureate institutions are underrepresented in university-community partnerships. Although the current emphasis on partnership and engagement arose out of an examination of the scholarly direction of higher education, this history should not preclude institutions with primary teaching-learning activities. Results from one baccalaureate insti-

Steven R. Timmermans is President, Trinity Christian College, Palos Heights, IL, and was formerly a Professor in the Department of Education, Calvin College. Jeffrey P. Bouman is Director, Service Learning Center, Calvin College, Grand Rapids, MI 49546.

Address correspondence to: Jeffrey P. Bouman, PhD (E-mail: jpb4@calvin.edu).

The authors would like to thank students and colleagues at Calvin College and partners in the community whose work contributed to this project.

The work that provided the basis for this publication was supported by funding under an award with the U.S. Department of Housing and Urban Development.

The authors are solely responsible for the accuracy of the statements and interpretations contained in this article. Such interpretations do not necessarily reflect the views of the government.

[Haworth co-indexing entry note]: "Seven Ways of Teaching and Learning: University-Community Partnerships at Baccalaureate Institutions." Timmermans, Steven R., and Jeffrey P. Bouman. Co-published simultaneously in *Journal of Community Practice* (The Haworth Social Work Practice Press, an imprint of The Haworth Press, Inc.) Vol. 12, No. 3/4, 2004, pp. 89-101; and: *University-Community Partnerships: Universities in Civic Engagement* (ed: Tracy M. Soska, and Alice K. Johnson Butterfield) The Haworth Social Work Practice Press, an imprint of The Haworth Press, Inc., 2004, pp. 89-101. Single or multiple copies of this article are available for a fee from The Haworth Document Delivery Service [1-800-HAWORTH, 9:00 a.m. - 5:00 p.m. (EST). E-mail address: docdelivery@haworthpress.com].

tution show a range of activities appropriate for the involvement of undergraduate institutions in university-community partnerships. This article reviews recent thought and vision to demonstrate the potential advantages of partnership. Seven methods of engagement that can be used by baccalaureate institutions are described. Two important ways include service-learning courses and academically-based service-learning. This article provides examples of these approaches for helping baccalaureate educational institutions become engaged with their communities through their teaching missions. *[Article copies available for a fee from The Haworth Document Delivery Service: 1-800-HAWORTH. E-mail address: <docdelivery@haworthpress.com> Website: <http://www.HaworthPress.com> © 2004 by The Haworth Press, Inc. All rights reserved.]*

KEYWORDS. Service learning, university-community partnerships, baccalaureate education, Community Outreach Partnership Center, teaching models

INTRODUCTION

University-community partnerships are developing rapidly and the concomitant engagement involved in partnership is the subject of much analysis and review. Because the impetus for engagement arose out of an examination of scholarship, research institutions have led the way in developing these partnerships. Thus, a review of recent thought and vision is required to demonstrate the potential advantages of engagement and partnership, and to illustrate their linkages to undergraduate institutions. Three threads, briefly examined, illustrate the relevance of university-community partnerships for baccalaureate education. These include engagement, partnership, and the activities of higher education.

In *Scholarship Reconsidered*, Ernest Boyer (1990) was particularly concerned about the connection of campuses to communities and gave special focus to the scholarship of application, which he later called, the scholarship of engagement. Two months before his death, Boyer spoke to the American Academy of Arts and Sciences. He expressed his hope that through partnership, colleges and universities would continue to contribute to the intellectual and civic progress of the nation by addressing social, civic, economic and moral problems through the scholarship of engagement (cited in Bringle, Games, & Malloy, 1999, p. 28). Other calls for *engagement* have also been issued. The *Presidents' Declara-*

tion on the Civic Responsibility of Higher Education begins with a statement challenging higher education "to become engaged through actions and teaching, with its communities" (Campus Compact, 2000, p. 3). Likewise, a report by The Association of American Colleges and Universities (2002, p. 25) suggests that "quality liberal education prepares students for active participation in the private and public sectors, in a diverse democracy, and in an even more diverse global community."

A second thread, *partnership*, is a needed companion to this call for action. According to Saltmarsh (1998), community is not only a place, but also a set of relationships. Committed to engagement, higher education may understand community as place, yet fail to understand the complexity of relationships between the community and the institution of higher education from which partnership should emerge. Partnership arises out of shared community interests, thereby requiring institutions of higher education to shed their authoritarian stance and become part of the community. After studying the effects of its decade-long community development program, The National Society for Experiential Education suggests that the elements of sustainable partnership are "Thinking, caring, active people within organizations who form a bond with other groups based on trust and open dialogue to arrive at shared values, goals, responsibilities, action and reflection; and to celebrate with style and grieve with passion when called for by accomplishment or loss" (Sigmon, 1998, p. 4).

Two other recent evaluations have occurred. First, the Engaging Communities and Campuses program of Council of Independent Colleges/Consortium for the Advancement of Private Higher Education, gathered community partners of higher education together. Three understandings–from the perspective of community partners–emerged. Good partnerships are characterized by careful preparation, excellent implementation, and meticulous follow-through. Community partners carefully weigh the ratio of benefits to risks and costs in deciding to enter into or continue in a community-campus partnership. Issues of parity–actual and perceived–are always part of a partnership and campuses must recognize and address these issues (Leiderman, Furco, Zapf, & Goss, 2002). An evaluation of the Community Outreach Partnership Center (COPC) program of the U.S. Office of Housing and Urban Development (HUD) identified three factors that impact the quality of partnership. First, both partners–the community and campus–need sufficient organizational capacity. Second, the activities of the partnership are key–that is, the inherent difficulty of chosen activities directly impacts outcomes. And third, partnerships are influenced by the number of partners and the relationships among partners (Urban Institute, 2002).

If *engagement* is the calling of higher education and *partnership*, its posture, then a third thread, the *activities* of higher education, must be examined in order to illustrate the relevance of university-community partnership for baccalaureate education. The literature includes numerous examples of engagement leading to productive scholarship. Recent articles in *The Chronicle of Higher Education* give testimonial to the impact that the scholarship of community engagement can have on academic careers (Cordes, 1998a), and in developing public support for research (Cordes, 1998b). But importantly, the call to engagement and the posture of partnership have sometimes dramatically, and at other times quietly, begun to change the nature of teaching and learning. Saltmarsh (1998, p. 7) suggests that "partnership changes the educational paradigm, first in validating experiential education and second, in providing students with an opportunity to connect their classroom learning with experiences that help them learn what it means to be part of a community." Chickering (2001) suggests that only through major changes in curriculum and pedagogy that implement the comprehensive use of experiential learning in both academic programs and extracurricular activities will civic learning and social responsibility be fully actualized for students. One such form of experiential education, service-learning, is being used as a tool to engage institutions of higher education with local communities (Jacoby, 2003). Service-learning is simultaneously program, philosophy, and pedagogy. Through service learning, students engage in activities that address community issues and, at the same time, learn and develop from participating in these structured activities. Campus Compact leaders conclude that service learning helps students, faculty, and community partners in a wealth of interactive ways (Reed, 2000).

AN ASSESSMENT OF COPC GRANTEES

The call to engagement, the posture of partnership, and the activities of higher education are key to HUD's Community Outreach Partnership Center (COPC) program. Within the context of structured partnerships between communities and academic institutions, HUD includes both research and teaching as areas the COPC grant program is designed to address (The Urban Institute, 2002). This pairing is better understood when the contours of the COPC program are reviewed. Research activities are limited to 25% of a project and 75% of a project should be outreach activities. Given these parameters and the confluence of vision, posture, and the activities of higher education, the goal of this analysis is to suggest that the COPC model or any interdisciplinary partnership effort can be accomplished via an institution's teaching mission. Nonetheless, although university-community partnerships are appropriate for baccalaureate institutions, the majority of COPC programs (77%) are public institutions and universities (81%), and two-year community colleges constitute only 6%. This statement and our experience have led us to undertake to a careful review of the history of COPC grantees according to their Carnegie Classification.

The Carnegie Classification System

The Carnegie Classification system (McCormick, 2001) categorizes institutions based on their degree granting activities from 1995-96 through 1997-98. For purposes of this review, nine categories are relevant. The categories of Doctoral/Research Universities-Extensive and Doctoral/Research Universities-Intensive include schools with many baccalaureate programs and graduate education through the doctorate. The difference between the two categories relates to number of doctoral degrees awarded and the range of disciplines. Master's Colleges and Universities I and II provide many baccalaureate programs and graduate education through the master's level. There are three types of baccalaureate colleges: Baccalaureate Colleges-Liberal Arts, Baccalaureate Colleges-General, and Baccalaureate/Associate's Colleges. All are primarily focused on undergraduate education. Those in the first subcategory award at least 50% of their baccalaureate degrees in liberal arts areas, while those in the second subcategory award less than half of their baccalaureate degrees in the liberal arts. The third subcategory includes those schools where baccalaureate degrees represent at least 10% of undergraduate degrees award. Finally, Associate's Colleges award nearly no bachelor's degrees; Specialized Institutions range from bachelor's to doctoral degrees.

From 1994 to 2002, 141 institutions received COPC grants. This number does not count twice those who received *New Directions* grants which enable previously funded COPCs to undertake new activities in applied research and outreach. Fifty-six percent of grantees were either Doctoral/Research Universities-Extensive (n = 58) or Doctoral/Research Universities-Intensive (n = 21) institutions. Forty-four percent were Master's Colleges and Universities I or II (n = 41). No Baccalaureate/Associate's Colleges were included in the list of grantees and only six of COPC grants went to Baccalaureate Institutions (Liberal Arts: 1; General: 5). Ten colleges were Associate's Colleges, most often these schools identified themselves as community colleges. Finally, there were five Specialized Institutions. Given that 85% of the grantees have graduate education programs (doctoral or masters) as well as undergraduate programs, baccalaureate-only institutions are underrepresented in the list, perhaps even more so than community colleges.

Calvin College, Grand Rapids, Michigan

Calvin College is one of the six Baccalaureate Colleges (General and Liberal Arts) that received a COPC grant in the period from 1994 to 2002. As a private institution of over 4,000 students, Calvin College is classified Baccalaureate-General. The College has an extensive liberal arts core curriculum required of all students, and has worked extensively to translate its undergraduate mission for teaching and learning into COPC outreach activities. Although our COPC experiences are not necessarily generalizable, due to the extremely small number of baccalaureate institutions who have received COPC grants, a quantitative, collective study of these institutions is premature. We do not attempt to address the role of COPC projects situated within undergraduate units of doctoral or masters institutions, nor those with undergraduate links to community colleges. Yet, our encouragement remains: baccalaureate institutions should consider COPC or COPC-like projects to enrich and further their teaching-learning missions.

SEVEN WAYS OF TEACHING AND LEARNING

What forms of engagement for university-community partnership are appropriate for baccalaureate institutions? In this section of the paper, we identify seven different types of teaching and service learning activities–that is, a full spectrum of teaching-learning that is appropriate for partnership and engagement. Our evaluation suggests that some forms are better suited to partnership where the service can arise out of the needs of both the college and the community. These we identify as *partnership driven*. One-time service, work study, residence hall partnership, service learning courses, and academically-based service learning all have the potential to allow community partners–along with the college–to decide which activities are appropriate and needed for student involvement.

Conversely, practicum/internships and independent studies are often, but not always, driven by the needs of the curriculum and requirements of the area of study. These *curriculum-linked* forms of engagement are directly linked to specific courses or programs of study. When both dimensions are considered–partnership and curriculum linkage–service-learning courses and academically-based service learning are important and significant means by which undergraduate institutions can be faithful to their teaching-learning missions *and* establish partnerships that are meaningful and productive for all involved.

One-Time Service refers to one-time activities in which students become engaged in a university-community partnership. During the year of analysis, 53 students participated in *one-time service* activities in our COPC neighborhood. Each year, first-year student orientation begins with a day of community service. Forty-four students provided service to Calvin's COPC partners in the forms of assistance at a neighborhood event in the park, alley clean-up, and other such activities. Once or twice a year a number of partners put on a housing fair in the community. In an introductory sociology course, 9 students were given credit towards a service requirement when they assisted with the housing fair. Although one-time service can be of great, immediate benefit to the neighborhood, it often fails to provide significant contributions toward lasting change or development and it fails to promote extensive learning on the part of the student. Nevertheless, teachable moments and eye-opening awareness can result.

Work Study refers to payment for work as part of a student's financial aid. However, instead of working on campus, work takes place in a community setting and, thereby, meets the requirement that colleges and universities spend 7% of their federally-supplied work study dollars for paid community service. Three work study students were involved in the COPC project during the year of analysis. One work-study student assisted in the office of a nonprofit community development organization; two other students gathered data and provided community organizing activities for the same organization. Although the number is small, partnership is an ideal way to meet the federal requirement.

Residence Hall Partnerships involve specific residence halls that partner with a community agency or nonprofit service provider. In this arrangement, dorm residents provide service on a regular basis. Each residence hall at Calvin College is linked with a community partner. For the COPC project, one of the residence halls was paired with a school in the COPC neighborhood. In this way, the school benefited from the volunteerism of the dorm residents and the dorm residents found that their collective activism was beneficial to the community. Admittedly, guided reflection and subsequent learning from this form of engagement are not integral to the service learning experience because of its disconnection from the academic curriculum. However, given that residence life programming reflects goals for student development, this option holds great promise for other important forms of learning.

Practicum and Internships are typical forms of experiential education and, at times, these experiential activities can be arranged because of partnership and goals for engagement. Community engagement, often in the form of *practicum or internships*, is needed by professional programs such as teacher education, nursing, social work, and the like. Because the desire for placements originates with the university, university program requirements or rigorous accreditation standards sometimes trump community needs. For example, a social work intern was scheduled to be placed in a nonprofit, faith-based health clinic in the neighborhood. Because of the large number of Spanish-speaking clients, a bilingual student social work intern had been selected. However, just prior to the start of the academic year, the only certified social worker at the clinic resigned. This made it impossible for the intern to start work without appropriate supervision. Although the clinic later found a new social worker, by that time the student had been reassigned.

Two additional experiences demonstrate how uneven partnership can be avoided. First, 6 students were involved in traditional student teacher and pre-student teacher placements. From the outset, the partner school's principal immediately understood that traditional model and accommodated our requests. However, in terms of true partnership, he brought other needs to Calvin College and the partners worked out ways to together address needs apart from the practicum model by using the academically-based service-learning model. The need for nursing students to have community health experiences developed differently. Together, community residents, service providers, and faculty designed the community health practicum. This led to a convergence of community need, as well as college and accreditation requirements. Community health experiences were gained in neighborhood clinics, senior citizen complexes, church- or school-based health fairs, clinics, homes, and schools.

Independent Studies are not always tied to a specific curriculum, but with the guidance and mentorship of a faculty member, may be a vehicle for engaging students as an outgrowth of their major or from a specific course. As Calvin College began its COPC project, it was immediately apparent that community groups–particularly nonprofit service providers–expected engagement to be in the form of specialized help for specific projects. They had worked with other colleges and universities before, and they were expecting masters-level interns who would come and take on a specific project such as a community assets map, a community survey, or the like. Masters-level institutions may generate many of these types of experiences, but baccalaureate institutions typically provide limited opportunities for independent studies. Although only five projects occurred, Calvin College was able to meet this expectation. By means of an independent study, a senior photography student chronicled the hopes and dreams of the residents in images and another student used the independent study opportunity to organize the photographs into an exhibit for the college gallery and, later, a neighborhood show. The result was a bilingual booklet of stories with pictures of the community taken from the art exhibit. One limitation of COPC work may be the small number of such activities within baccalaureate institutions.

Service Learning

The last two activities relate to service-learning. In a *Service-Learning Course*, much of the learning activity is experiential. Often, an infrequent (once a week or less) seminar provides opportunity for reflection and evaluation. Rather than pairing community engagement with a course that meets with a professor three to four hours a week on campus or in the community, students may meet formally only an hour every week or bi-monthly. The majority of the "course time" is the experience.

Many students engaged in the COPC project were enrolled in a service-learning course to gain experience in schools prior to entering the teacher education program. Like many of the other activities reviewed above, college requirements tend to drive this form of engagement. However, because the course is primarily "experience" as opposed to "content," community partners can use students in a variety of ways to address their needs, thereby tipping the balance toward equal partnership. Further, because it exists within an established course, orientation, reflection, and evaluation are included. For example, college students were assigned to an after-school web-based science enrichment program that the principal had requested. College students grew in confidence and skill with using technology in teaching, and the fourth graders improved in science and in technology skills. In addition, the majority (57%) of college students indicated they had become more knowledgeable about Hispanic culture as a result of the service.

Academically-Based Service-Learning most often occurs when the service activities are integral to a linked course for which the conceptual content relates to those activities. At Calvin College, academically-based service learning has been the primary means for linking the undergraduate teaching-learning mission to partnership and engagement. For instance, in the teacher education program, the need expressed by the school was to develop stronger Spanish reading skills of Spanish-speaking first and second graders. Faculty responded by situating within core Spanish courses a requirement that college students read to these first and second grade students. This addressed the need of the children and school as well as furthering the speaking, listening, and reading comprehension goals for students.

In the area of business and economic development, the local business association expressed a number of needs. Many of the local business owners needed to improve their English speaking and comprehension skills. Many of the newly founded Latino businesses needed more exposure, and the entire business district needed to work together to create a more welcoming district. An upper-level Spanish course created a tutorial series for the business owners. Students carried out research to better understand the owner's ethnicity and nationality, wrote a news release featuring the owner and his/her business, and submitted it to a local Spanish newspaper. This second need was also addressed by an upper-level marketing class that worked with the restaurants. They developed a coupon program to build a better customer base while working on market differentiation. Another marketing class addressed the third need by doing the research and proposing a holiday lighting approach. Because the partner neighborhood is in an older section of the city, issues of narrow streets, congested traffic, and the safety of children and other pedestrians have been important. A geography class collected data to study volume and patterns. A sociology class became engaged with a local PTA. Together, they pursued community organizing as a way to capture the attention of the city traffic engineer, police, and other community resources and solve some of the more pressing traffic problems. As a way to celebrate a neighborhood that over ten years had shifted from one fourth (26%) Hispanic to nearly two-thirds (63%) Hispanic, 22 students in an English composition class partnered with residents, and elicited their stories and their vision for their neighborhood.

Qualitative indices from college students remind us of the value-added benefits. Students from the upper-level Spanish course engaged in ESL tutorial efforts with business owners reported becoming friends with the owners and were invited into their homes. The value was not limited, however, only to the college students. Aside from the task accomplishments of the COPC efforts, perceptions changed. The Hispanic business woman who chaired the neighborhood planning group told us that even though she had been in the neighborhood for six years, this project by faculty and students marked the first time she felt truly accepted.

In these examples, as well as in all academically-based service learning efforts, the college course and the community were equal partners in shaping these experiences. Student activities were begun only after many conversations that occurred well in advance of the semester's start. COPC leaders, both from the community and the college, sought to identify community issues for which a possible college course connection could be made. Then, those directly involved in a given community issue were approached by the project leadership to explore the issue and envision how college faculty and students could become involved. Simultaneously, another conversation was initiated by the project leadership with a faculty member whose course might relate to the given community issue. If positive indication was received from both parties, project leadership introduced the community members and faculty member. Ultimately, the project leader stepped out of the middle and community members and professor talk and plan directly.

DISCUSSION

Our work has illustrated the benefit of administrative staff dedicated to community partnership and curricular linkage. The COPC model requires leaders with a foot in each world of community and college. Without such leaders, achieving partnership and curricular linkage would be difficult–that is, it could pull already busy faculty members into extensive community involvement or result in ill-conceived and disconnected facultyled projects. In contrast, service activities that are linked to the teaching and learning mission of the university benefits students, community members and organizations, and the college. As outlined in this case example, Calvin College has been afforded new and compelling models for service learning that are curriculum-linked and rooted in partnership.

Of course, we have uncovered challenges. The skilled masters-level intern, often expected by community organizations, is not available because of the limits of baccalaureate education. Yet, using the spectrum of seven types of teaching and learning, partnership needs can still be met. Another challenge relates to college faculty who often approach this type of project focused on their course aims, with insufficient knowledge of community needs and a paucity of community relationships. Fortunately, the COPC grant involved release time for some faculty to develop these relationships. To engage with the community, additional time and support is required to change pedagogical styles and move out of the traditional classroom. Planning between faculty and community members takes time if true partnership is to be achieved. Then, throughout the experience, faculty members must communicate frequently with their community counterparts. Baccalaureate institutions should understand the increased demands on faculty, and ensure that these forms of experiential education are truly situated within partnership and firmly linked with the curriculum. Faculty should endeavor to meet expectations of teaching, service, and scholarship in interwoven ways and, whenever possible, use their community activities to integrate all three expectations. Otherwise, these expectations vie for the limited time of the faculty, often resulting in incomplete success in all three areas or exclusion of one or two of the goals.

Because service-learning pedagogy is not as tidy as traditional classroom teaching, faculty can also expect more communication from their students as clarification is sought, anxiety can be expressed, and excitement is shared. Students also need orientation to the community in which they serve, as well as guided reflection throughout their service. Guided reflection ensures that the connection to the course remains clear; it also serves to uncover problems before they become severe in the messy world of engagement.

Finally, when a community need is expressed, rather than create service delivery apart from existing structures, it is better to piggy-back, whenever possible, on existing infrastructure. For example, working with the PTA to develop a tutoring program is probably easier than setting up one-on-one tutorials apart from any existing organizational structure. This respects and makes use of existing community assets. If there is a need to create new community structures and/or programs, such efforts, done in partnership, require an even greater commitment of time and energy that goes well beyond the scope of the given course's service-learning dimension.

CONCLUSION

With service-learning courses and academically-based service learning as primary, and with the other forms as helpful additions, baccalaureate colleges should more carefully consider opportunities for community partnership. The COPC program provides an excellent framework for partnership. Within this framework, college staff and faculty who are well acquainted with college and community, help realize the teaching-learning mission of baccalaureate institutions. Baccalaureate institutions should consider COPC or COPC-like projects to enrich and further their teaching-learning missions.

REFERENCES

Association of American Colleges and Universities (2002). *Greater expectations: A new vision for learning as a nation goes to college.* Washington, DC: Author.

Boyer, E. (1990). *Scholarship reconsidered: Priorities of the professoriate.* Princeton, NJ: Carnegie Foundation for the Advancement of Teaching.

Bringle, R., Games, R. & Malloy, E. (1999). *College and universities as citizens.* Boston, MA: Allyn & Bacon.

Campus Compact (2000). *Presidents' declaration on the civic responsibility of higher education.* Providence, RI: Author.

Chickering, A. (2001). *Maximizing civic learning and social responsibility.* Boston, MA: New England Resource Center for Higher Education.

Cordes, C. (1998a, September 18). Community-based projects help scholars build public support. *The Chronicle of Higher Education,* p. A27.

Cordes, C. (1998b, September 18). How community-based research changed a professor's career. *The Chronicle of Higher Education,* p. A39.

Jacoby, B. (2003). *Building partnerships for service-learning.* San Francisco, CA: Jossey-Bass.

Leiderman, S., Furco, A., Zapf, J., & Goss, M. (2002). *Building partnership with college campuses: Community perspectives.* Washington, DC: Council for Independent Colleges.

McCormick, A. (2001). *The Carnegie classification of institutions of higher education, 2000 Edition.* Menlo Park, CA: The Carnegie Foundation for the Advancement of Teaching.

Reed, J. (2000). *Building lasting bridges between campus and communities.* Indiana, Illinois, Michigan, and Ohio: Campus Compacts.

Saltmarsh, J. (1998, Summer). Exploring the meaning of community/university partnerships. *SEE Quarterly,* 6-7, 21-22.

Sigmon, R. (1998). *Building sustainable partnerships: Linking communities and educational institutions.* Raleigh, NC: National Society for Experiential Education.

The Urban Institute. (2002). Lessons *from the community outreach partnership center program.* Washington, DC: Author.

SOCIAL WORK AND UNIVERSITY-COMMUNITY PARTNERSHIPS

University-Community Partnership Centers: An Important Link for Social Work Education

Mary E. Rogge, MSW, PhD
Cynthia J. Rocha, MSW, PhD

SUMMARY. In academic settings, community research, and the service that goes along with it, is often not valued as much as other methods of research. The more qualitative and labor intensive nature of applied research

Mary E. Rogge and Cynthia J. Rocha are Associate Professors, University of Tennessee, College of Social Work.

Address correspondence to: Mary E. Rogge, PhD, University of Tennessee, College of Social Work, 225 Henson Hall, Knoxville, TN 37996-3333 (E-mail: mrogge@utk.edu).

An earlier version of this paper was presented at the Council on Social Work Education's 45th Annual Program Meeting, San Francisco, California, March 10-13, 1999.

[Haworth co-indexing entry note]: "University-Community Partnership Centers: An Important Link for Social Work Education." Rogge, Mary E., and Cynthia J. Rocha. Co-published simultaneously in *Journal of Community Practice* (The Haworth Social Work Practice Press, an imprint of The Haworth Press, Inc.) Vol. 12, No. 3/4, 2004, pp. 103-121; and: *University-Community Partnerships: Universities in Civic Engagement* (ed: Tracy M. Soska, and Alice K. Johnson Butterfield) The Haworth Social Work Practice Press, an imprint of The Haworth Press, Inc., 2004, pp. 103-121. Single or multiple copies of this article are available for a fee from The Haworth Document Delivery Service [1-800-HAWORTH, 9:00 a.m. - 5:00 p.m. (EST). E-mail address: docdelivery@haworthpress.com].

often raises concerns about whether pre-tenured faculty can publish the sufficient quantity and quality of work necessary to achieve tenure. This paper describes successful collaborations through a university-based Community Partnership Center with members of community-based organizations in low-income inner-city neighborhoods, social work students, and faculty. Two case examples illustrate the co-authors' involvement with the Center as pre-tenured faculty. The article outlines the challenges and benefits of involvement with an established center for university-community partnerships. With careful planning and coordination, such centers can be excellent vehicles through which to achieve important mutual benefits for community-based organizations, student learning, and faculty responsibilities in research, teaching and service. *[Article copies available for a fee from The Haworth Document Delivery Service: 1-800-HAWORTH. E-mail address: <docdelivery@haworthpress.com> Website: <http://www.HaworthPress.com> © 2004 by The Haworth Press, Inc. All rights reserved.]*

KEYWORDS. Community Outreach Partnership Center (COPC), participatory research, service learning, tenure, university-community partnerships

INTRODUCTION

Within the ebb and flow of political, economic, and social support for civic engagement and partnership between universities and their neighboring communities, educators are challenged to enact ethical, proactive approaches that underscore knowledge and skills for advocacy and community-focused practice. Collaborations between academic social work programs and community-based organizations hold great promise for meeting this challenge (Bembry, 1995; Harkavy & Puckett, 1994). Social work is among the many professions participating in the paradigm shift toward greater university-community involvement, including public health, planning, psychology, education, law, occupational therapy, and sociology (Ansley & Gaventa, 1997; Casella, 2002; Metzler et al., 2003; Sclove, Scammell, & Holland, 1998; Taylor, Braveman, & Hammel, 2004). Increasingly, this involvement is influenced by a range of federal agencies and funding sources to engage more fully in interdisciplinary, inter-community work (Maclure, 1990; Mizrahi & Rosenthal, 2001; O'Fallon & Dearry, 2002). With the collaboration of grassroots community experts (Abatena, 1997), university resources can be applied to programs and services that strengthen communities, students can receive necessary training, and faculty can study community-specific issues.

The ethical and methodological foundation of the university-based community partnership center described in this article derived directly from the participatory democracy and research approaches of Paulo Friere and Friere's friend and colleague, Miles Horton (Gaventa, Peters, & Bell, 1991). Friere's conceptualizations of conscientization, critical consciousness, dialog and reflection, and the belief that fairness and equity should and can be attained, continue to be core values of participatory processes (Castelloe & Watson, 1999; Friere, 1970). As noted later, Horton co-founded the internationally known Highlander Research and Education Center located in East Tennessee (Highlander Research and Education Center, 2004). Such participatory approaches emphasize mutual exchange between citizens and researchers of personal, popular, and professional education, consciousness-raising, and mutual skill development. Shared power and decision-making, from the outset of social change efforts, are essential (Sarri & Sarri, 1992; McNicoll, 1999).

These approaches also form the cornerstone of the rich interdisciplinary heritage and evolving scientific basis of community-based participatory research (Minkler & Wallerstein, 2003; Trickett, 1991). The Interagency Working Group for Community-Based Participatory Research (2002) defines community-based participatory research as "scientific inquiry conducted in communities in which community members, persons affected by condition or issue under study and other key stakeholders in the community's health have the opportunity to be full participants in each phase of the work (from conception–design–conduct–analysis–interpretation–conclusions–communication of results)." In many communities, however, a significant barrier to expanding the community-focused skills of social work students has been a history of disempowering relationships between academic institutions and communities (Livermore & Midgley, 1998; Rogge, 1998). Researchers have been criticized for garnering funds and building careers without appropriate acknowledgement of–let alone recompense for–community member contributions including time, expertise, and intellectual property. From the standpoint of ethical, robust, valid scientific processes, research that claims to be community-based yet does not fully engage community in the creation and critique of knowledge is flawed at best (Sullivan & Kelly, 2001; Israel, Schulz, Parker, & Becker, 1998).

Grassroots organizations, in particular, view university-community collaborations with caution. Ansley and Gaventa (1997, p. 51) argue, "Many communities long ago gave up on universities as places from which they could expect meaningful assistance." Or, as one leader of a fledging neighborhood association noted: "You've got to realize the university is a lion and we [the association] are just a kitten starting out; you can come out here and nurture us and help us grow, or swat us aside with one blow" (A. Gaston, personal communication, April, 1998). Social work has also been criticized similarly as lacking a genuine commitment to community empowerment and participatory processes (Freeman, 1996).

This paper describes the development of successful university-community collaborations among social work faculty, social work graduate students, and community organizations, connected through a university-based, federally funded center. These collaborations are discussed also in the context of pre-tenured faculty engaged in community-based research. In academic settings, community research is not always valued as much as other research methods because of its more qualitative approach and labor intensive nature that can raise concerns about publishing sufficient material to achieve tenure (Ansley & Gaventa, 1997; Euster & Weinbach, 1994). In this article, factors are discussed that have created functional partnerships for university-community collaborators linked through this center. First, the center's mission and funding during the time of the co-authors' involvement as pre-tenured faculty are summarized. Second, two case examples are used to describe mutual benefits derived from relationships with the center. The co-authors discuss how these relationships challenged and contributed to students, community partners and, at the time, to their experience as pre-tenured faculty.

COMMUNITY PARTNERSHIP CENTER (CPC)

Initiated in 1994, the Community Partnership Center (CPC) at the University of Tennessee (UT) is an interdisciplinary, participatory research-based center that connects researchers, technical experts, students, and other UT resources to groups in low to moderate-income communities. The creation of the CPC was influenced significantly by the rich history of grassroots organizing and social action in the surrounding Appalachian region of East Tennessee in general and, in particular, by the work of Paulo Friere, Miles Horton, and their colleagues through the Highlander Research and Education Center (Ansley & Gaventa, 1997; Beaver, 1986; Cable, 1993; Community Shares, 2004; Fisher, 1993, Gaventa, Peters, & Bell, 1991; Highlander Research and Education Center, 2004; Save Our Cumberland Mountains, 2004;

Southern Empowerment Project, 2004). The CPC provides leadership in developing collaborative methods in research, service learning opportunities for faculty and students, and participatory approaches toward sustainable development. Its governing board was structured from the outset so that community members had majority vote; two thirds of the representatives are from community and one third from the university. As identified in its mission, objectives, and governing structure, the overriding intent of the CPC is to direct resources into the community to build community capacity. Housed in the University's Office of Research, the CPC's focus on community-based participatory research is unique among the University's research centers and central to its mission of collaborating to solve social and economic problems. From the outset, the CPC has served a clearinghouse function to identify community-based needs and solicit UT resources to respond (CPC, 2004).

CPC projects have targeted community-identified needs including economic development, homelessness, public safety, education, environmental justice, at-risk youths, and job training (Ansley & Gaventa, 1997; CPC, 2004). Core funding for the CPC core program has been through the U.S. Housing and Urban Development (HUD) Community Outreach Partnership Centers (COPC) program (University Partnerships Clearinghouse, 1998). CPC received its first HUD/COPC grant, for $500,000, in 1995. In 1997, the CPC received a $100,000 Institutionalization Grant under the HUD/COPC, which addressed five issue areas: planning and legal assistance; institutionalization and curricular development; access to the information highway; strengthening community-based organizations; and applied research on the effects of globalization on East Tennessee. In 2001, the CPC was allocated a portion of Knoxville's HUD Urban Empowerment Zone grant to facilitate the development of "citizen learning teams" within the Zone (see CPC, 2004; Gaventa, Morrissey, & Creed, 1998). HUD-related grants have targeted the "Heart of Knoxville" inner city neighborhoods, which are home to over 48,000 individuals with low and moderate incomes (Partnership for Neighborhood Improvement, 1998). Additional funding and programs of the CPC include the Learning Initiative, first funded in 1994 by the U.S. Department of Agriculture, the Ford Foundation and the Aspen Institute to implement and evaluate citizens' learning teams in 10 rural Empowerment Zone/Enterprise Communities across the United States (Gaventa et al., 1998).

SOCIAL WORK-COMMUNITY EXCHANGES THROUGH THE CPC

The two case examples that follow describe how the co-authors, as pre-tenure faculty, collaborated with the CPC and how those collaborations supported mutually beneficial exchanges among community organizations, social work students, and faculty. Following the case presentations, the challenges, benefits, and lessons learned in terms of teaching, research, and service are discussed.

The TennCare Project

In 1995, the second co-author was invited by CPC to collaborate with a local grassroots organization working to improve access to and quality of health care in East Tennessee. To lend legitimacy to their organizing efforts, the organization wanted to systematically document citizens' reports of effects from TennCare, Tennessee's recently implemented federal Medicaid Waiver and mandatory Medicaid managed care program. The co-author was interested in studying and disseminating information about the effects of managed care on poor populations. The CPC saw the match and connected faculty and organization. This interaction was the beginning of a long, interesting, and sometimes stressful relationship. While both faculty and organization cared about the issue, goals were not always the same. From an academic standpoint, time was needed to approach the project objectively, obtain university approval for human subjects' research, and seek funding for the project. The grassroots organization, on the other hand, wanted documentation of what organization members observed to be happening and needed immediate outcomes to pressure government officials to change the TennCare system.

The first task was to find funding and receive university permission for the TennCare study. Long meetings were held with the co-author, organization, and other players to negotiate the final survey instrument. Community members had significant input in regard to sample selection and the choice of research and survey questions. Each player, including a potential funder from outside of the organization and university, had an investment in what questions should be asked. The funder provided support for the study and the UT Graduate School awarded a small faculty development grant. The next task was to decide who would collect the data. Because the collection process would be house-to-house in the moderate and low-income neighborhoods represented by the grassroots organization, members of the organization were the obvious choice for interviewers. The members were paid to participate and were paired with UT graduate social work students. Training sessions were held, and 164 residents were interviewed.

As the initial TennCare research got underway, the CPC decided to pursue its first HUD/COPC grant, subsequently funded in 1995. Because the TennCare team had an established relationship, the CPC asked members of the grassroots organization and faculty to collaborate on a portion of the grant that would focus on community economic development. The team's project was one of twelve community economic development projects funded. The goal was to remove barriers to health care in the Heart of Knoxville inner city neighborhoods. Project objectives and outcomes included: meeting with community residents to discuss research outcomes; developing and implementing empowerment and leadership workshops; networking with local groups and residents to monitor health care programs; organizing and holding an annual community health fair; and conducting process evaluations of the project objectives and a follow-up survey on barriers to health care. In 1997, the HUD/COPC grant funded another TennCare research project with the faculty-grassroots organization team. Paid community members and students paired again to conduct interviews with forty managed care clients who had reported problems with TennCare. Whereas the first TennCare project identified the extent of the problems faced by TennCare recipients, this study produced a more in-depth understanding of those problems and their effects on the lives of the people experiencing them. Many meetings were held with community members to frame the qualitative survey instrument in regard to existing barriers to health care in the community. Members of the grassroots organization also participated in the use of content analysis to interpret the qualitative findings.

The grassroots organization took the results of the study to local media, organized a protest march in the city's downtown area, and held a press conference. Because of this publicity, the Tennessee State Oversight Committee invited the co-author and the organization to testify about the findings of both studies before the Committee. These events point to an important mutual benefit from this university-community relationship. Before the research, the grassroots organization had tried unsuccessfully to testify before the Committee. The involvement of university research lent the legitimacy that the organization needed to be heard by the Committee. On the other hand, the results of these two studies would not have been publicized through the media nor reached state legislators in this way if the organization had not taken to the streets in protest.

Coursework Integration. The co-author integrated this research into her advanced social work policy class that uses experiential techniques to teach policy practice to social work students (Rocha & Johnson, 1997). In this class, students work in semester-long task groups to analyze an issue, develop a purposeful change campaign in response to a community need, and implement a change strategy at the organizational or community level. Depending on the issue, students often have very little or extensive contact with community groups. If there are community groups already working on the issue of choice, the student task group consults with the community groups to assess how the students can be most helpful. Some class projects, such as assisting in the development of a community health fair, came directly from projects created by the HUD/COPC grant. Other projects, such as changing bus routes to better serve a city area comprised primarily of people who are elderly and have low income, were connected through the CPC clearinghouse.

The task group assignment continues to be a core component of the advanced policy course. Each semester, two or three community groups usually request student assistance to work on local or state level issues. Student groups have lobbied successfully for change in state spousal rape laws; assisted grassroots organizations in training welfare advocates to work with families affected by welfare reform; carried out a local awareness campaign promoting the public's help with homeless children; created a resource guide on health care for uninsured persons; developed sex education curricula for public schools; and lobbied, with some success to increase accessibility for students with physical challenges at UT. In addition, student assignments and reflective comments indicate that they also benefit through service learning as a method to increase citizen participation in a democratic society (Bringle & Hatcher, 1996).

Morningside Heights Homeowners' Association (MHHA)

Community Fellows in the Classroom. In response to community requests for help with grant writing, the first co-author initiated a "community fellows" project in 1997. Community Fellows are members of community-based organizations who participate, on a tuition-free, non-credit basis, in a graduate course on financial management and resource development. In the first year, three community fellows associated with CPC-partner groups participated: the executive director of the Morningside Heights Homeowners Association (MHHA), a community organizer with an anti-drug initiative for youth, and the grant writer for a faith-based community development group. In exchange for attending the course, fellows share their experiences in getting financial resources for their organizations. Because the major course assignment is to develop an actual grant proposal based on real agency needs, the Community Fellows also produce a grant proposal relative to their organization's program. Two of the three inaugural fellows' grant proposals were funded. The fellows contributed to lively class discussions on building relationships with potential funders, collecting and organizing assessment information, matching program design to social problems and target population, and budget with program scope. Evaluations from students and fellows have been very encouraging. Students note that, despite initial misgivings, the fellows' sharing of their experiences enriches rather than detracts from learning. One fellow wrote that the experience was "both intense and extremely beneficial . . . I am grateful . . . to learn with you all, and for the tools you have given me to use to good effect in the community in which I work."

The CPC benefited from the community fellow project in that part of the co-author's teaching time and fellow's project time counted toward the CPC's HUD/COPC grant match. One unanticipated benefit was the establishment of a new health clinic in the neighborhood served by the MHHA. During a discussion of organizational best practices among class members and a panel of social work agency leaders, the MHHA fellow described the need for such a clinic. Both the fellow and the panelist from the facility that established the clinic attribute this action directly to their connection during the course (G. Winfrey & B. Dodson, personal communication, December, 1998).

Student Task Groups in the Neighborhoods. A second exchange occurred in a subsequent semester and different course. In a graduate foundation course on practice with organizations and communities, the first co-author piloted an experiential community-based assignment, which was a new experience for most of the students. Groups of three to six students worked with pre-selected representatives of community-based organizations on projects structured by the organizations. Each student worked a maximum of 20 field hours; each organization received from 60-120 volunteer hours. Projects emphasized community assessment or participation in social change efforts. Presentations and discussion of the projects over the semester exposed students to each other's projects.

Organizations were selected primarily because of their social change efforts. Another characteristic of many of the organizations was that they did *not* employ professional social workers (c.f., Johnson, 2000). Such organizations were targeted so that social work students experienced grassroots change efforts in organizations generally unfamiliar to them; organizations experienced the benefits of working with social work students; and groundwork was laid for future university-community collaborations through field practica and community-based research. In good faith with the concept of mutual exchange (i.e., "the what's-in-it-for-you/what's-in-it-for-me," WIFFY/WIFFM principle), tasks with short learning curves were designed to meet concrete organizational needs. Again, the CPC benefited by using part of the co-author's teaching time and student task group time as HUD/COPC grant match. The CPC was the introductory link for over half of the organizations with which students worked, including the MHHA. The co-author, in turn, connected several of the organizations to CPC. The CPC was important in this assignment because of CPC's staff knowledge of local low- and moderate-income community social change organizations and actors.

Variations of the assignment continue to be a core component of this course. During the first semester that the assignment was used, 51 students worked in 12 task groups with 11 organizations, for a total of about 1,051 hours. Projects have included:

- *Neighborhood organizing:* conducting and analyzing a door-to-door neighborhood survey for a local community development center and presenting data at the first meeting of that neighborhood's new association;
- *Local/international political action:* producing an article on international debt burden and the local economy in a regional newspaper, sponsoring a Peruvian speaker on campus, and collecting over 600 signatures for an international petition to forgive the debt of poor developing countries;
- *Environmental justice:* researching funding opportunities and organizing materials in a citizen's library jointly used by a group of workers, an African-American neighborhood, and environmental activists concerned nuclear radiation and associated chemicals;
- *Community violence:* collecting and analyzing police data for a citizen's group concerned about law enforcement violence and creating a guide to public referendum processes; and,
- *Economic development:* for MHHA, helping to implement aspects of the neighborhood's revitalization plan.

Student evaluations indicate that the diversity of organizations, issues, leadership styles, and political contexts helps translate theory about practice with organizations and communities to reality. For exam-

ple, in an in-class exercise using Weil and Gamble's (1995) community-based practice models, students discovered that each of the eight
models was represented by at least one organization with which the
class worked.

BENEFITS, CHALLENGES, AND LESSONS LEARNED

The situations, relationships, benefits, and barriers discussed in the
two cases have challenged and contributed the learning of students,
community partners, and faculty in a number of ways. Although the
cases illustrate partnerships primarily between social workers and community, many of the experiences and lessons learned are applicable in
cross-disciplinary applications. These are summarized in the context of
the triad of academic responsibilities in teaching, research, and service.

Teaching

Over time, the co-authors have adapted the experiential learning
components of the foundation practice and advanced policy practice
classes to build sequentially. The foundation course involves students
in time-limited, pre-selected tasks with supervision from task leaders in
community organizations. In the advanced course, students identify,
shape and carry out semester-long projects, often in coordination with
community organizations. Both courses emphasize experiential learning and reflective processes as important pedagogical tools for making
course materials relevant and "real."

As described in the two case examples, there have been multiple benefits for community partners, social work students and faculty from the
relationship with the CPC and associated community organizations.
Students have experienced organizing and other aspects of grassroots
work, applied participatory practice, advocacy and social action skills,
and observed diverse organizations and leaders in action. The skills that
students have acquired derive from applying sound community intervention techniques including finding creative uses for slim resources;
customizing and carrying out community assessments; building relationships with stakeholders; and presenting one's case to citizens'
groups, city council, transit boards, neighborhood associations, faculty
committees, public forums, and nonprofit organizations. Students report having learned to use the media to bring important issues to the
public's attention through creating public service announcements, writ-

ing editorials, discussing issues on television talk shows, and using the Internet. They have integrated experiences with readings on task force organization, and the translation of mission to measurable outcome. In project evaluations, students note having shared, with each other and their community partners, the challenges of time management and coordination and the frustrations of delayed outcomes, power plays and political intrigue. Students have shared also the excitement of successful local and state lobbying efforts and the gratification of achieving concrete change such as improved transportation in low-income communities and the birth of a new neighborhood association.

Students have learned firsthand about the political nature of organizational control and information management and about the tenacity of citizens dedicated to a cause. Most importantly, students report new insights in understanding social problems from citizens' perspectives and the mutuality of building social capital (Brzuzy & Segal, 1996; McNicoll, 1999). Through partnering with citizens to solve local problems, students experience the challenges and celebrations of how community members come together around an issue to make a difference. After the projects are over, some students have maintained relationships and become volunteers for the organizations with which they worked. Participatory approaches emphasized through these courses move students out of familiar social and professional networks to work with new, diverse groups of people and approaches to social change. A number of relationships formed through the actions described here paved the way for what have become excellent, mutually beneficial field placement opportunities for students to extend service to organizations including the Highlander, Solutions, a member-directed grassroots organization (Solutions, 2004), and the fair economy-focused Tennessee Industrial Renewal Network (TIRN, 2004). Finally, students have reported that the interactions deriving from these assignments have helped them, often for the first time, "get" the relevance of macro social work practice and participatory processes for their own practice.

Research

The case studies illustrate some of the research-related benefits of connecting to community through entities such as the CPC. There are important challenges for both university and community folk associated with collaborative research in neighborhoods and communities (Cordes, 1998; Rogge & Winfrey, 1998). First and foremost, the richness of community-based research and its potential to influence positive change with citizens have been, in the co-authors' experience, well worth undertaking such challenges. Other research-related benefits have included expanded networks within and external to the university, grant opportunities and awards, access to data, and participation in national HUD/COPC grant application reviews. As pre-tenured faculty, community-based associations provided rich material for dissemination through publications and conference presentations (e.g., Rocha, 1999; Rocha, 2000; Rocha & Johnson, 1997; Rocha & Kabalka, 1999; Rogge, Hicks, Stucky, & Conner, 2000; Rogge & Rocha, 1999; Rogge & Winfrey, 1998). The challenges and benefits of enacting a true participatory practice model are inherent in these exchanges. As described in the TennCare project, what would have been most efficient for the community organization was not necessarily what best served immediate interests as a researcher, and vice versa. Researcher and organization members spend more time, engage in more training, and make more concessions than would be made with other, more "traditional" models.

Although no large scale funding was sought or emerged directly from either of the case studies described here, the CPC incorporated materials from both in its successful bid for renewal of the HUD Community Outreach Partnership Center grant that it received originally in 1995 (CPC, 2004). Both co-authors have infused participatory research processes into other large-scale proposals that reflect their substantive interests. The second author used participatory approaches to engage individuals in a National Institute of Mental Health grant to examine the effects of plant closure on former workers. The first author is developing the education and outreach component of an interdisciplinary proposal to the National Institute of Environmental Health Sciences to study chemical contaminants in Tennessee's Chattanooga Creek (see Rogge, 1998).

Organizations such as the CPC provide important clearinghouse and gateway functions that can help the university realize the potential of university-community partnerships. In today's political and economic climate, the academy's acceptance of community-based research continues to be tenuous. CPC-type organizations and their associates must maintain strong leadership to secure resources and standing as "real" researchers. Strategies for broadening academic acceptance of participatory democracy approaches include training more faculty, students, and staff in participatory approaches; providing technical support for locating and securing funding; consulting with faculty and community members regarding project implementation and evaluation; and supporting the production of publications and conference presentations. Such strategies accommodate the best of participatory democracy, research methods and academic requirements. University-community partnership centers can be valuable points of leverage, exchange, and re-sources for social workers and their constituents. Participatory processes can ground faculty and students in understanding the genuine application of em-powerment and "kitten–lion" power differential between community and university.

Service

Overall, a more systematic and deliberate plan to collect community out-come and impact data in short, intermediate, and longitudinal timeframes would have been useful in evaluating service. End-of-project evaluations by community partners and students, however, provide some indicators of the actual service outcomes experienced and perceived by community partners. Community partners report receiving help to achieve work in progress and on organizational work "wish lists" that needed extra person power to tackle. Community members used the hands-on support from students and faculty in a variety of community-generated and defined areas, such as garnering lo-cal media and state legislators' attention and expanding their grant writing knowledge and skills. These areas included the implementation of an annual neighborhood health fair; the extension of public bus routes to underserved populations; changes in state spousal rape laws; the door-to-door collection, analysis, and presentation of neighbors' voices on local issues; greater under-standing of public data regarding law enforcement violence; and, in the con-text of local actors as international citizens, the collection of over 600 signatures advocating debt forgiveness for developing countries.

Certainly, not all service experiences have been uniformly positive from community partners' perspectives. Defining common goals and managing different timeframes for action can be stressful and requires dedicated, mutual communication and flexibility. Community members (and students) at times experience frustration and delay in carrying out project activities as busy project team members try to coordinate sched-ules or as students move "up the learning curve" to a point at which they can contribute directly to the service aspects of the project. Additional learning over time has included how to help both community partners and students assess at the outset their mutual knowledge, skills, and interests to shape service project activities. Together, the two case studies describe a range of measurable and intangible service outcomes for the actors en-gaged in this university-community partnership. Community-based net-works nurtured through MHHA and the CPC greatly enhanced the rapid mobilization of the Youth, Environment and Service (YES) Coalition, also comprised of community and university representatives, which was invited to be lead entity for one component of Knoxville's Urban Empowerment Zone grant (PNI, 1998).

In this pre-tenure work, the co-authors sought to minimize the tenure-related risk of participating too extensively in community service by maximizing the research and teaching components. The CPC and University of Tennessee College of Social Work supported these efforts in important ways. Associations with the CPC resulted in service to the university community in roles on advisory teams for HUD/COPC grants, a university-wide Service Learning Team, the university-community CPC Advisory Council, and an Environmental Justice Research Team. CPC acknowledged faculty involvement in tenure-facilitating ways such as co-nominating the co-authors for a university award for excellence in teaching and leadership.

Two final points regarding the connection between CPC-type approaches to university-community linkage and academic service requirements should be noted. First, financial incentives for universities engaging in community partnering and participatory approaches should be implemented to lend greater weight and value to community service (Maclure, 1990; Reardon, 1998). Second, Sclove, Scammell, & Holland (1998) and others argue that, as participatory and other community-based research approaches become more widely accepted, universities should acknowledge, nurture, and publicize the academic value-added enhancement of community service through such research.

CONCLUSION

Associations with the CPC and community-based organizations continue to be sources of learning about similarities and differences between social work practice and participatory research processes; the nature of personal biases and perceptions; the complex history, culture, and dynamics of community; and the dedication, creativity, and wisdom with which citizens fight for justice. By working with the Community Partnership Center, students, community partners, and faculty continue to exchange learning about the strengths, limitations, and at times the debilitating influences of professional practice and language. When, for example, a community member gently reflects to an academically trained professional that "our community is like a woven cloth; we see the threads and spaces between, you only see the holes," one must rethink the power of familiar phrases such as "community *needs* assessment" (see also Minkler & Wallerstein, 2003; Ansley & Gaventa,

1997). As the science of community-based participatory research continues to evolve and inform, so must we advance in designing, implementing, and systematically evaluating university-community interactions and outcomes. Centers such as the CPC can help to create and sustain the crucial dynamic of trust in long-term, exchange-based university-community relationships. As conduits for student training about the warp and weave–the threads and the holes–in the cloth of community, there can be a high degree of fit among the activities of university-community partnership centers, the mission of social work education, and the wants and desires of communities. For these reasons, and with careful coordination and planning, they can be excellent vehicles through which to achieve important mutual benefits for actors in all aspects of the university-community relationship.

REFERENCES

Abatena, H. (1997). The significance of planned community participation in problem solving and developing a viable community capability. *Journal of Community Practice*, *4*(2), 13-34.

Ansley, F., & Gaventa, J. (1997). Researching for democracy & democratizing research. *Change*, *29*(1), 46-53.

Beaver, P.C. (1986). *Rural community in the Appalachian South*. Lexington, KY: University Press of Kentucky.

Bembry, J.X. (1995). Project SUCCESS: A model for university-school community partnerships. *Social Work in Education*, *17*(4), 256-262.

Bringle, R.C., & Hatcher, J.A. (1996). Implementing service learning in higher education. *Journal of Higher Education*, *67*(2), 221-239.

Brzuzy, S., & Segal, E.A. (1996). Community-based research strategies for social work education. *Journal of Community Practice*, *3*(1), 59-69.

Cable, S. (1993). From fussin' to organizing: Individual and collective resistance at Yellow Creek. In. S.L. Fisher (Ed.) *Fighting back in Appalachia: Traditions of resistance and change* (pp. 69-84). Philadelphia, PA: Temple University.

Casella, R. (2002). Where policy meets the pavement: Stages of public involvement in the prevention of school violence. *International Journal of Qualitative Studies in Education*, *15*(3), 349-373.

Castelloe, P., & Watson, T. (1999). Participatory education as a community practice model: A case example from a comprehensive Head Start program. *Journal of Community Practice*, *6*(1), 71-89.

Community Partnership Center. (2004). Retrieved February 9, 2004 from: *http://sunsite.utk.edu/cpc/*

Community Shares. (2004). Retrieved February 8, 2004 from: *http://www.korrnet.org/cshares/*

Cordes, C. (1998, September 18). Community-based projects help scholars build public support. *The Chronicle of Higher Education*, *45*(17).

Euster, G.L., & Weinbach, R.W. (1994). Faculty reward for community service activities: An update. *Journal of Social Work Education, 30*(3), 317-324.

Fisher, S.L. (1993). *Fighting back in Appalachia: Traditions of resistance and change.* Philadelphia, PA: Temple University.

Freeman, E.M. (1996). Welfare reforms and services for children and families: Setting a new practice, research and policy agenda. *Social Work, 41*(5), 521-532.

Friere, P. (1970). *Pedagogy of the oppressed.* New York: Seabury.

Gaventa, J., Morrissey, J., & Creed, V. (1998). *Rural empowerment zones/enterprise communities: Lessons from the learning initiative.* Knoxville, TN: University of Tennessee Community Partnership Center.

Gaventa, J., Peters, J., & Bell, B. (Eds.). (1991). *We make the road by walking: Conversations between Paulo Freire and Myles Horton.* Philadelphia: Temple University.

Harkavy, I., & Puckett, J.L. (1994). Lessons from Hull House for the contemporary urban university. *Social Service Review, 68*(3), 299-321.

Highlander Research and Education Center. (2004). Retrieved February 8, 2004 from: *http://www.highlandercenter.org/*

Interagency Working Group for Community-based Participatory Research. (2002). Retrieved February 14, 2003 at *http://www.niehs.nih.gov/translat/IWG/iwghome.htm*

Israel, B., Schulz, A., Parker, E., & Becker, A. (1998). Review of community-based research: Assessing participatory approaches to improve public health. *Annual Review of Public Health, 19,* 173-202.

Johnson, A.K. (2000). The Community Practice Pilot Project: Integrating methods, field, community assessment, and experiential learning. *Journal of Community Practice, 8*(4): 5-25.

Livermore, M., & Midgley, J. (1998). The contribution of universities to building sustainable communities: The community university partnership. In M.D. Hoff (Ed.), *Sustainable community development: Case studies in economic, environmental and cultural revitalization* (pp. 123-138). Boca Raton, FL: CRC/Lewis Publishers.

Maclure, R. (1990). The challenge of participatory research and its implications for funding agencies. *International Journal of Sociology, 10*(3), 1-21.

McNicoll, P. (1999). Issues in teaching participatory action research. *Journal of Social Work Education, 35*(1), 51-62.

Metzler, M.M. et al. (2003). Addressing urban health in Detroit, New York City, and Seattle through community-based participatory research partnerships. *American Journal of Public Health, 93*(5), 803-811.

Minkler, M., & Wallerstein, D. (Eds.). (2003). *Community-based participatory research for health.* Indianapolis, IN: Jossey-Bass.

Mizrahi, T., & Rosenthal, B.B. (2001). Complexities of coalition building: Leaders' successes, struggles, and solutions. *Social Work, 46*(1), 63-79.

O'Fallon, L.R., & Dearry, A. (2002). Community based participatory research as a tool to advanced environmental health sciences. *Environmental Health Perspectives, 110*(2), 151-159.

Partnership for Neighborhood Improvement. (1998). *Knoxville, Tennessee: Prospectus for empowerment.* Knoxville, TN: Partnership for Neighborhood Improvement.

Reardon, K.M. (1998). Enhancing the capacity of community-based organizations in East. St. Louis. *Journal of Planning Education and Research, 17,* 323-333.

Rocha, C. (1999, March). *Quality of care issues under a Medicaid managed care program*. Paper presented at the APM Council on Social Work Education, San Francisco, California.

Rocha, C. (2000). Evaluating the use of experiential teaching methods in an advanced policy practice course. *Journal of Social Work Education, 36*(1), 53-64.

Rocha, C., & Johnson, A.K. (1997). Teaching family policy through a policy practice framework. *Journal of Social Work Education, 33(3)*, 433-444.

Rocha, C. & Kabalka, L. (1999). A comparison study of access to health care under a Medicaid managed care program. *Health and Social Work, 24*(3), 169-179.

Rogge, M.E. (1998). Toxic risk, resilience and justice in Chattanooga. In M.D. Hoff (Ed.) *Sustainable community development: Case studies in economic, environmental and cultural revitalization* (pp. 105-122). Boca Raton, FL: CRC/Lewis Publishers.

Rogge, M.E. & Rocha, C. (1999, March). *Community partnership centers: An important venue for social work education*. Paper presented at the APM Council on Social Work Education, San Francisco, CA.

Rogge, M.E., & Winfrey, G. (1998, September). *Evaluating neighborhood-university partnerships: Building capacity together*. Paper presented at the National HUD Community Outreach Partnership Centers Cityscape Conference, East St. Louis, Illinois.

Rogge, M.E., Hicks, S., Stucky, J., & Conner, T. (2000, January). *In the (HUD Empowerment) zone: Implementing a youth, environment and service program*. Paper presented at the Society for Social Work and Research, Charleston, SC.

Sarri, R.C., & Sarri, C.M. (1992). Organizational and community change through participatory action. *Administration in Social Work, 16*(3/4), 99-122.

Save Our Cumberland Mountains (SOCM). (2004). Retrieved February 12, 2004 from *http://korrnet.org/socm*

Sclove, R.E., Scammell, M.L., & Holland, B. (1998). *Community-based research in the United States: An introductory reconnaissance, including twelve organizational case studies and comparison with the Dutch Science Shops and the mainstream American research system*. Amherst, MA: Loka Institute.

Solutions. (2004). Retrieved February 8, 2004 from *http://www.korrnet.org/solutions/*

Southern Empowerment Project. (2004). Retrieved February 8, 2004 from *http://www.southernempowerment.org/*

Sullivan, M. and Kelly, J. (Eds.). (2001). *Collaborative Research: University and Community Partnership*. Washington, DC: American Public Health Association.

Taylor R.R., Braveman B., & Hammel, J. (2004). Developing and evaluating community-based services through participatory action research: Two case examples. *American Journal of Occupational Therapy, 58*(1), 73-82.

Tennessee Industrial Renewal Network. (2004). Retrieved February 8, 2004 from *http://www.tirn.org/*

Trickett, E.J. (1991). Paradigms and the research report: Making what actually happens a heuristic for theory. *American Journal of Community Psychology, 19*, 365-370.

University Partnerships Clearinghouse. (March, 1998). *Colleges & communities: Partners in urban revitalization. A report on the Community Outreach Partnership Centers Program.* Rockville, MD: University Partnerships Clearinghouse, HUD Office of University Partnerships.

Weil, M., & Gamble, D.N. (1995). Community practice models. *The encyclopedia of social work* (19th Ed., 1: 577-93). Washington, DC: National Association of Social Workers.

Community Partnerships:
An Innovative Model
of Social Work Education and Practice

Mindy R. Wertheimer, PhD
Elizabeth L. Beck, PhD
Fred Brooks, PhD
James L. Wolk, PhD

SUMMARY. Community challenges force human service agencies to collaborate in providing services. Such collaborations require practitioners to have skills not found in mainstream social work curricula. This paper explores how a new MSW program evolved through dialog with community leaders and resulted in a curriculum with a sole concentration of community partnerships. *[Article copies available for a fee from The Haworth Document Delivery Service: 1-800-HAWORTH. E-mail address: <docdelivery@haworthpress.com> Website: <http://www.HaworthPress.com> © 2004 by The Haworth Press, Inc. All rights reserved.]*

Mindy R. Wertheimer is Director of Field Education, Elizabeth L. Beck is Associate Professor, Fred Brooks is Assistant Professor, and James L. Wolk is Professor and Director, School of Social Work, Georgia State University.

Address correspondence to: Mindy R. Wertheimer, PhD, School of Social Work, Georgia State University, MSC 8L0381, 33 Gilmer Street, SE Unit 8, Atlanta, GA 30303-3088 (E-mail: mwertheimer@gsu.edu).

[Haworth co-indexing entry note]: "Community Partnerships: An Innovative Model of Social Work Education and Practice." Wertheimer, Mindy R. et al. Co-published simultaneously in *Journal of Community Practice* (The Haworth Social Work Practice Press, an imprint of The Haworth Press, Inc.) Vol. 12, No. 3/4, 2004, pp. 123-140; and: *University-Community Partnerships: Universities in Civic Engagement* (ed: Tracy M. Soska, and Alice K. Johnson Butterfield) The Haworth Social Work Practice Press, an imprint of The Haworth Press, Inc., 2004, pp. 123-140. Single or multiple copies of this article are available for a fee from The Haworth Document Delivery Service [1-800-HAWORTH, 9:00 a.m. - 5:00 p.m. (EST). E-mail address: docdelivery@haworthpress.com].

KEYWORDS. Community partnerships, university-community collaborations, social work education, MSW curriculum

INTRODUCTION

The new millennium has brought major changes, challenges, and hardships in human service delivery. With communities confronting rapidly changing demographics, the growing disparities between rich and poor, and reduced human services funding opportunities, human service agencies are no longer able to operate as independent or competitive entities. Rather, they must develop collaborative networks for service delivery in order to survive and thrive. Such collaborations lead to a re-examination of the skills and knowledge applied by professional social workers and, consequently, to a reconsideration of the curriculum in schools of social work particularly with respect to community practice. Against this backdrop, colleges and universities have sought to broaden their mission to become engaged partners in addressing community needs and issues (Boyer, 1996). The American Association of Higher Education promotes the concept of the engaged campus, connecting the critical tasks of teaching, research, and service with the needs of local communities and the larger society (Astin, 1995).

The move by universities to seek out more community collaborations, the human service agencies shift to embrace collaborative service delivery opportunities, and the social work profession's renewed focus on community practice all converged to present an exciting confluence of conditions for Georgia State University to develop a unique MSW program. The planning for the program focused on the principles that: (1) partnership is critical for human service delivery and building communities; (2) challenges facing individuals and communities are interrelated and that solutions must be as well; (3) students should commit themselves to addressing social and economic justice issues that test the spirit of individuals and communities; (4) students should be educated for leadership roles to facilitate partnerships; and (5) the program must continue to be relevant to the professional lives of students and practitioners and to the needs of diverse communities.

This paper will explore how these five principles guided the development of an innovative MSW program with a sole concentration of Community Partnerships. Addressed specifically are the ways in which these principles interact with the historical evolution of the program, the theories and philosophical orientations used in the development of the community partnership concentration, the development of MSW program objectives and skill sets for the concentration, and examination of specific courses integral to the community partnerships concentration. The discussion includes a focus on student outcomes and program self-renewal.

EXAMINING CURRICULUM IN THE AGE OF PARTNERSHIPS

During the last decade, major changes have affected social work education and practice. Primary in this alteration are: (1) changes in the social and economic context; (2) social work's re-examination of its role with respect to its focus on psychotherapy vs. community practice and the movement toward the strengths and empowerment perspectives in social work; (3) the pressure on universities to broaden their mission and become engaged partners in addressing community needs; and (4) the role of partnership in addressing specific social issues. In speaking about this time in history, Mizrahi (2001, p. 181) states that "overall, the social climate is not conducive to meeting human needs or implementing the values of social or economic justice."

Building on the work of Fisher (1994) and Fisher and Karger (1997), Cox (2001) has identified six factors that have implications for community practice and can be seen as affecting social work practice in general. These factors include privatization and cutbacks in public welfare, de-industrialization and globalization, the ascendancy of individualism over collectivism as an American value, increased availability of technology, and the support of multiculturalism and postmodern theory as challenging universal assumptions that often promote oppression (Faubion, 2001). Other factors affecting the context of social work practice include devolution (Mizrahi, 2001; Sanfort, 2000), changing demographics, growing disparities between rich and poor (Fisher & Karger, 1997), and reduced philanthropic funding for the economically disadvantaged (Foundation Center, 2003).

While most of these factors hamper social work practice they also provide important opportunities and a sobering reminder that social work must be involved in policy and advocacy (Weil, 1996). Specifically, social workers must act to contain federal safety net cuts, engage in local efforts to determine service delivery, and respond to the needs of individuals and families in a resource lean environment (Mizrahi, 2001; Weil, 1996). Given these factors, many social work scholars have emphasized that the community needs to be viewed as the context for service delivery and community practitioners (Coulton, 1996; Johnson, 2000; Netting, Kettner, & McMurtry, 1998).

The re-examination of social work with respect to its focus on psychotherapy or community practice, largely promulgated by Specht and Courtney (1994) and Cox (2001), has been followed by a re-examination of skills within the areas of community and direct practice. In 1999, Cloward and Piven spurred a dialogue among community practitioners when they wrote that community-organizing ventures failed to build power for low-income people, rather they effect change by nurturing a subculture among the poor in which the idea of justice is maintained. Definitions of community practice have shifted to embrace forms of practice that have moved away from traditional conflict (or Alinsky-style) organizing. One such practice is community-centered practice, epitomized by Comprehensive Community Initiatives. These initiatives integrate service delivery, neighborhood, economic development, and civic development (Lambert & Black, 2001; Shonkoff & Phillips, 2000). Others are using models of organizing based on consensus building rather than conflict tactics (Beck & Eichler, 2000). In the areas of direct practice, empowerment (Cox & Parsons, 1996; Delgado, 2000; Dietz, 2000; Gutierrez & GlenMaye, 1995; Parsons, 2001), the strengths perspective (Brun & Rapp, 2001; Chapin & Cox, 2001; Saleebey, 1996; Weick, Rapp, Sullivan, & Kisthardt, 1989), and the realization that a client's community context is integral to therapy are significantly altering practice (Rose, 2000).

Outside the schools of social work, universities are also expanding their mission. Taking heed from Peter Drucker's prediction that universities might find themselves irrelevant as a result of their cost and disconnection from society, colleges and universities are seeking to become involved with communities (Overton & Burkhardt, 1999). Taking the lead in defining a new role for universities and colleges, Boyer (1990;1996) argued that the academy needs to become a vigorous partner in the search for answers to pressing social, civic, economic and moral problems. The outcome of such partnerships he termed as the scholarship of engagement. The seriousness of the academy's commitment to engagement is evidenced in the burgeoning literature that examines the effects, processes, and practices of university and community partnerships (see, for example, Fogelman, 2002; Lundquist & Nixon, 1998; Nyden, Figert, Shibley, & Burrows, 1997). More recently, the U.S. Department of Housing and Urban Development (HUD) has weighed in on university-community partnerships through the development of

Community Outreach Partnership Centers (COPC), which channel federal funds to university and community partnerships.

The proliferation of partnerships can be seen as a response to strained resources and to practices that have emanated from the public health approach in which the individual or problem is viewed within a multidimensional context, and as a requirement of private and public money. Successful partnerships are found in the areas of infant, child, and maternal health; primary education; community building and urban planning, and others (Barry & Britt, 2002; Dooley & Naparstek, 1997; McMahon, Browning, & Rose-Colley, 2001; Sanders & Epstein, 1998). However, there are questions surrounding partnerships as well. Mizrahi (2001) cited the role of partnerships as one of the factors that is affecting the practice of social work and indicated both strengths and concerns about the partnership approach. A community's assets, expertise, and resources are being used to create local approaches, but such collaborations may side-step social justice issues and place local leaders in the role of the oppressors. Her solution is the infusion of knowledgeable, skilled, and principled practitioners. This creates a role for schools of social work in retooling the role of the social work practitioner and designing a curriculum that is responsive to community needs.

DEVELOPING A NEW MSW CURRICULUM

Georgia State University has had an accredited BSW program since 1981. However, the only public MSW program in Georgia was at the University of Georgia in Athens. In 1995, the Board of Regents of the University System of Georgia approved the establishment of three additional state-assisted Masters of Social Work programs with Georgia State's program having a *community organization and planning* specialization. This specialization articulated well with the urban research mission of Georgia State University and its goal of becoming an engaged institution of higher education. More importantly, the expanded definition that developed from this original directive was synchronous with the five principles discussed previously that emphasize partnership and community engagement.

The School of Social Work faculty viewed this political decision as an opportunity to take advantage of the strengths available in metropolitan Atlanta to develop a MSW program with a unique community focus and a community partnerships concentration. From the outset of the planning for this program, the faculty embraced the contributions of the

MSW Advisory Committee comprised of social workers and others from across the public and private human service sectors of greater Atlanta. The Advisory Committee was pivotal in collaborating with faculty on the philosophy and mission of the MSW program. As the philosophy and mission became operationalized into a comprehensive curriculum of program objectives, skill sets, and courses, the Advisory Committee continued to serve as a sounding board for maintaining the integrity of the interface between education and practice. Parenthetically, people in the larger social work practice community, but more pointedly in social work education, admired this direction for the School, but had serious doubts about its potential success. Practitioners and educators questioned whether enough students would be interested in a school with this sole community partnerships focus since the overwhelming majority of students wanted clinical concentrations. They questioned whether sufficient field placements could be located to provide internships. They questioned whether research opportunities could be generated within the context of the community focus. They questioned whether there would be jobs when students graduated. All of these questions have been answered.

Community Partnerships Concentration

The community partnerships concentration evolved in a nonlinear style. Lengthy deliberations between and among faculty and community representatives around philosophy, theory, mission, curriculum, the profession, and community needs, produced a philosophy that sought to educate students to advance the needs and capacities of the total community by promoting social and economic justice while maximizing human potential. Students would be educated to commit themselves to addressing the life circumstances, such as poverty, violence, discrimination, and disparities in social and economic justice that fall disproportionately on vulnerable groups and challenge the spirit of the entire community. This focus incorporates multiple entry points for social work practice at any systems level. Hence, addressing direct practice with individuals and families took on the community focus as context for needs assessment and intervention. From this philosophy, the mission of the MSW program was created: To prepare students in advanced social work practice for leadership roles in the effort to solve, in partnerships with others, the existing and developing challenges that confront communities in the United States and internationally.

Community is defined as a social unit based on common location, interest, identification, culture and/or activities–a definition that reaches beyond a geographical community to acknowledge communities not always visible. Community partnerships, defined as the association of principals who contribute resources in a joint venture sharing the benefits and risks of building communities, have the potential to advance the needs and capacities of the total community through strengthening individuals and families; bridging and reinforcing relationships within and among community groups, among community agencies/organizations, and between community groups and community agencies/organizations; and creating new community resources. Community partnerships are predicated upon an empowerment orientation, which acknowledges and develops the strengths and creativity of all members. The importance of community demographics, politics, economics, geography and human service delivery systems is recognized. In this framework, social work practice integrates and applies values, principles and techniques of the profession to bring about planned change in community systems and its sub-systems. From the philosophy, mission, and these definitions, the School of Social Work began the development of a curriculum for a sole concentration in community partnerships.

MSW Program Overview

Figure 1 summarizes the philosophical and theoretical components of the MSW curriculum. Since the School was working towards an accredited MSW program, the Council on Social Work Education (CSWE) became another partner in the creation of the MSW program. Beginning with the purpose statement of social work education (CSWE, 1994), a linear application of all the program components was created in order to articulate a clear rationale for the MSW program. The community focus, supported by the purpose statement, in turn supported the definition of social work practice that was evolving. In support of the community focus, multiple theoretical perspectives are presented including social systems theory, ecological perspective, empowerment theories, social movement theories, organizational behavior and dynamics, group behavior and dynamics, and individual behavior. These theoretical perspectives inform the nine MSW curriculum content areas required by CSWE. These curriculum content areas are added to the diagram to acknowledge the importance of the professional foundation curriculum in providing core knowledge for competent social work practice. The concentration in community partnerships builds on this professional foundation, which establishes the community, rather than the individual, family or small

FIGURE 1. Community Partnerships Concentration

CSWE (1994) Purpose of Social Work Education:
The purpose of social work education is to prepare competent and effective social work professionals who are committed to practice that includes services to the poor and oppressed, and who alleviate poverty, oppression, and discrimination.

Community Focus:
A community is a social unit based on common location, interest, identification, culture and/or activitites. A community focus provides the foundational core of the curriculum.

Theories:
System theory	Ecological theories
Organizational theories	Social movement theories
Empowerment theories	Human behavior theories

CSWE (1994) Curriculum Content Areas:
Diversity	Social & economic justice
Populations-at-risk	Social work values & ethics
Research	Social work practice
Field Education	Social welfare policy & services
	Human behavior & the social environment

Skill Sets:
Critical Thinking	Community/Organizational Communications
Community Assessment & Resource Development	Community/Organizational Development
Leadership and Management	Research, Evaluation & Technology

Community Partnerships Concentration:
Individual ← → Society

Partnerships are defined as the association of principles who contribute resources in a joint venture sharing the benefits and risks of building communities. Community partnerships have the potential to advance the captivities of the total community by promoting social and economic justice and maximizing human potential.

group, as the unit of analysis. The community partnerships concentration is organized around skill sets, taught in the second year, which have been developed for creating student competencies in the assessment, development, maintenance and evaluation of community partnerships.

MSW Program Objectives and Skill Sets

The original five planning principles provided the essential elements in the development of the MSW program objectives and the skill sets. The objectives and the skills sets shaped each other as educators and practitioners conceptualized the essence of community partnerships in social work practice. The concept of organizing around skill sets rather than objectives began as an intriguing concept that ultimately guided curriculum development. The skill sets focus was thought to allow for more flexibility for meshing educational objectives with community needs.

The MSW program objectives for the foundation year conform to the program objectives for the first year of virtually all MSW programs irrespective of the concentration because of the importance of ensuring that students acquire foundation knowledge, skills, and values. It is in the concentration-year objectives that the uniqueness of the community partnerships perspective is outlined and the clarity of the skill sets can be defined. Specifically, the objectives for the community partnerships concentration are:

- Demonstrate communication/facilitation skills in building community partnership structures.
- Conduct community assessments and engage in community resource development.
- Demonstrate skills for influencing necessary organizational and community change to address populations at risk and advance social and economic justice.
- Demonstrate skills for influencing policy formulation and change in communities.
- Apply knowledge and leadership skills in managing projects, and working with community groups and/or organizations.
- Apply advanced information technology skills to community-based practice.
- Demonstrate skills in quantitative/qualitative research design, data analysis, and knowledge dissemination.

The six skill sets operationalize these concentration objectives without mandating a single course to achieve the objective or acquire a particular skill set. On the contrary, courses have been developed because they are institutionally necessary, but the objectives and skill sets permeate several courses in the concentration year. Knowledge and skills may be shifted between courses should evaluations indicate that the knowledge and/or skill set has a better *goodness of fit* in a different course. Although critical thinking is listed as its own skill set, it is infused in the other five. In Figure 2, the examples given are intended to be representative of a specific skill set and not an exhaustive list.

Overview of MSW Courses

Given that the concentration year is community partnerships, the community becomes the lens through which the professional foundation content is analyzed, understood, and experienced. In the first year, MSW students are required to take *SW 7100: Foundations of Community Partnerships*, which introduces students to the concepts of economic and social justice; to community partnerships using social systems theory, ecological perspective, and the empowerment model; and to additional content to support the community as the unit of analysis. The theoretical knowledge is applied in an experiential commu-

FIGURE 2. MSW Community Partnerships Concentration: Skill Sets

CRITICAL THINKING	COMMUNITY/ ORGANIZATIONAL COMMUNICATIONS	COMMUNITY ASSESSMENT AND RESOURCE DEVELOPMENT	COMMUNITY/ ORGANIZATIONAL DEVELOPMENT	LEADERSHIP & MANAGEMENT	RESEARCH EVALUATION & TECHNOLOGY
A process to assess, critique and evaluate modes of practice, beliefs and attitudes, and research while always considering alternative or opposing points of view.	Varying written and oral modes of interaction and relationship building between individuals, groups, organizations and communities.	Collaborative and cooperative methods to develop and interpret agreed upon needs and goals, and to collectively act toward achieving those goals.	An ongoing process of developing, maintaining and strengthening relationships/ partnerships that builds healthy communities.	The use of concepts, skills, & knowledge from organizational theory, management, community social work, & social administration to address problems at mezzo/macro system levels.	The use of evaluative measures, technological processes, & management of information to facilitate healthy communities through neighborhood associations, institutions, and organizations.
EXAMPLES: Analytic skills Problem-solving process Evaluation of practice	**EXAMPLES:** Participatory skills Group facilitation Negotiation and mediation Training and consultation skills Record keeping Project monitoring	**EXAMPLES:** Goal setting Assets mapping Project identification and development Resource identification and development Grant writing Social entrepreneurship	**EXAMPLES:** Capacity building Partnership development Partnership structures Constituency building Grassroots development Community education Policy formulation	**EXAMPLES:** Strategic planning Supervision Human resources Fiscal management Fund raising Marketing & Public relations	**EXAMPLES:** Information technology skills Information management Scientific method Program planning & evaluation

nity-based assignment. As a core course that provides context for the program's community focus, SW 7100 is one of the summer bridge courses required for advanced-standing BSW students entering the MSW program.

The second-year courses were developed from the skill sets in conjunction with the program objectives to provide students with an integrated repertoire of competencies for partnering with individuals, families, small groups and organizations in the community. *SW 8100: Skills and Techniques of Community Partnerships* focuses on communication skills (e.g., assertiveness, public speaking, persuasion, building consensus, facilitating meetings, use of the media) and resource development (e.g., grant writing, fundraising). *SW 8200: Evaluation and Technology* focuses on formative and summative evaluations of community service delivery systems and addresses the application of technology in assessing and improving programs, policies, and community partnerships. *SW 8300: Leadership and Management* explores management theory and practice, strategic planning, power, and personnel management along with the manager's role as leader to initiate and facilitate community partnerships. The final required course, *SW*

8800: Community Projects is experientially designed to have students apply and synthesize content from the overall MSW curriculum, with an emphasis on the skill sets. There is a required field education course each semester. During their first year, students are placed in a field placement (400 hours) that focuses on generalist practice; in the second year, students are placed in a field placement (500 hours) related to the community partnerships concentration. To illustrate the unique community partnerships concentration, three course examples are presented. Each course has an experiential component, which supports the skills-based curriculum.

SW 7100: Foundations of Community Partnerships course has both a didactic and practical component. Students are provided with an overview of community practice through an examination of theories, history, applications and domains. Explored also are the ways in which the social, political, and economic contexts affect practice. The importance of participation and relationship building are two themes that underpin content related specifically to partnership. Arnstein's (1969) ladder of participation serves as reminder that manipulation, therapy, informing, consultation and placation can easily mask as participatory partnership, and further supports that partnership requires vigilance, time, and a dedication to shared power. Consensus organizing, feminist organizing models, and conflict styles of organizing are used to address oppression and explore the importance of true participation and relationship building in community development (Beck & Eichler, 2000; Bradshaw, Soifer, & Gutierrez, 1994; Freire, 1970; Hyde, 1995).

Students gain a sense of the practices necessary to engage individuals in viable partnerships. They have a chance to practice some of what they are being exposed to in class through experiential learning. Each year the class engages in a community-based activity. The instructor works with local community groups to determine a class project. Projects have included the development of assets maps, needs assessments, and the creation of a community profile. Recently, students have been working with a community-based child protective program on developing community capacity. Students who conducted a community assets map uncovered a plethora of religious organizations, and the following group of students organized a meet and greet with religious leaders so that the community-based child protective program and the religious community could share ideas and resources. There are now several flourishing partnerships between religious institutions and the program.

In the second year of the MSW program, students take a two-semester sequence–Skills and Techniques of Community Partnerships course and

SW 8800: Community Projects–taught by the same professor. Rather than completing a research thesis or an exit exam, the students in the community projects capstone course work in groups with local agencies on community projects. Students are free to initiate their own project with one or more agencies or they can select from over twenty-five project proposals submitted by non-profit agencies. From June through August, the School of Social Work solicits proposals in three ways, including a mailing to 2nd-year field placement agencies, a Request For Proposals (RFP) announcement in a statewide newsletter for nonprofit organizations, and an on-line RFP on the School's web site. The majority of proposals arrive electronically.

In the fall semester students divide into groups and begin reviewing project proposals. Students contact agencies to negotiate the community project goals, objectives and timelines. At the end of fall semester, each group turns in a 10-15 page written proposal that includes project goals, objectives, and deliverables; a review of the empirical/theoretical/practice literature pertinent to the project; a description of how the skill sets will be applied to the project; and a timeline of implementation plans. During the spring semester, students are expected to work approximately ten hours a week on the project in lieu of a weekly class meeting. Groups submit weekly progress reports and meet with the professor as needed or a minimum of once a month. Besides completing project objectives, students are required to submit a process evaluation focusing on their group's dynamics and their own role in the group. At the end of the semester, students make two formal presentations of their project. Students present their project findings to their project sponsor(s) in the form of an in-service workshop or to another appropriate audience in the community. Projects are also presented to classmates and School of Social Work faculty. The success of sharing their respective projects outside the school strengthens the linkage between education and practice in community partnerships.

Although the community project course has not been formally evaluated, feedback from both students and project sponsors suggest that most projects are succeeding at both educational and instrumental goals. Many students say the projects required them to apply much of what they have learned. Course evaluation comments like this are common: "The community project was an excellent way to combine the skills we have learned throughout the [MSW] program." Several projects that did feasibility studies have resulted in concrete new programs in the community. For example, one group conducted a feasibility study to establish a residential shelter for adolescent girls who were in the juvenile justice system for prostitution. Today the shelter is open and the project sponsor credits the MSW student project for jump-starting the creation of this shelter. Another project examined the feasibility of establishing after-hours, supervised visitation centers in places of worship for parents who had lost custody of their children but were working toward reunification. Today one center is up-and-running and expansion of the model is currently underway.

In a 1998 editorial in *Social Work*, Stanley Witkin asserted that the academic-practitioner relationship in social work education is an important part of the effort to develop university-community collaboratives. Although *SW 8500/8900: Community Field Education* is designed to meet the objectives of the social work curriculum, at the same time, it can support the University's mission to be an engaged community partner. Establishing field placement sites for the community partnerships concentration is not difficult since the skill sets have relevance for almost every community entity from a small grassroots agency to a formal bureaucratic organization. All agencies and organizations are seeking to increase collaborative opportunities in service delivery and funding, so once the MSW skill sets are shared with potential field supervisors and they understand what our students can accomplish, there is strong interest in supervising a student. Even in more traditional placement settings such as a medical center, students can practice with a community partnerships focus. The organization around skills sets allows for such adaptability in identifying diverse field placement settings.

Most of the field supervisors are executive directors, associate directors, and program managers and many do not hold a MSW degree. The faculty liaison, with a background of community practice, provides the social work supervision to students without on-site social work supervision. The liaison also facilitates a biweekly field seminar. As part of their orientation to field, students are put through a community building exercise. This exercise sensitizes them to diverse perspectives, goal identification, and the challenges of collaboration. Upon starting field placement, the student is responsible for completing a learning contract, labeled an *Individualized Partnership Plan (IPP)*, which operationalizes the partnership between the university and the agency at the level of student and field supervisor. In developing the IPP, equal consideration is given to the educational objectives/skill sets and agency needs. In addition to the IPP, the student is responsible for completing field seminar assignments that focus on the critical analysis and evaluation of one's community partnerships practice. For example, the student is asked to examine the National Association of Social Workers (NASW) Code of Ethics and critique its relevance to community partnerships practice.

The students complete field education with the ability to apply the knowledge, values, and skills of creating and maintaining community partnerships and to apply critical thinking skills in the integration of academic learning with field-based practice. The major comment that students make about the class is that they saw it as invaluable as a foundation for their other MSW program experiences.

EVALUATION AND SELF-RENEWAL

The School of Social Work engages in a number of evaluative measures to assess student outcomes. Two of the measures will be highlighted in this section. First, a follow-up survey with graduates assesses their preparedness to apply, and importance of, the skill sets in their current employment. Second, use of an email listserv allows the School to collect current information on all MSW graduates' employment. Of the 80 follow-up surveys sent to graduates in 2000-2002, 38 usable surveys were returned. There were no significant differences between the year of graduation or full-time or advanced-standing students. On a six-point Likert-type scale with 1 being unimportant and 6 being very important, student responses to the importance of a skill set to job performance ranged from 4.5 to 5.6. With 1 being not prepared to 6 being very prepared, student responses to their job preparedness for a skill set ranged from 4.5 to 5.2. The means for the importance of a community perspective and community partnerships in the success of their work were 5.0 and 5.2 respectively. In short, graduates highly endorsed the importance of the skill sets and their preparation to engage in them.

Through an electronic mailing list, the School keeps in close contact with most of its graduates and maintains a listing of their employment. They are employed in organizations that represent a range of interests such as child welfare, mental health, criminal justice, housing, healthcare, and community empowerment. Within these special interests, graduates are applying their skills of community partnerships. One graduate is the executive director of a county collaborative that has over seventy-five member organizations. Her community partnership field education experience was a factor in being offered this position. A convenience sample of several employers of these graduates indicated that employers were not always necessarily looking for social workers with a community partnerships concentration, but they have found the perspective a benefit. Moreover, they are very pleased with the performance to date and would hire the person again.

In his landmark monograph on self-renewal chastises higher education, Gardner (1964, p. 76) notes that "much innovation goes on at any first-rate university–but it almost never conscious of innovation in the structure or practices of the university itself." He quips, "University people love to innovate away from home." The School of Social Work at Georgia State University has labored diligently to consistently and thoughtfully apply the partnership philosophy of the educational component of the MSW program to overall school change. For example, the MSW Advisory Committee has evolved into an Advisory Council. In this newly defined role, the Advisory Council helps guide the full nature of the School's activities within a community context. Recently, the School undertook a strategic planning process that involved the Advisory Council. Recognizing its own limitations, the Advisory Council concurred that an even broader community hearing was essential to assist the School with its planning. To that end, the School arranged a community dialogue on the future direction of the School that included additional community representatives and current and former students. One change that resulted from this dialogue was shifting continuing education from a service that met the needs of primarily clinical practitioners to a resource that meets the training needs of community-based workers.

CONCLUSION

The faculty and community partners at Georgia State University planned and implemented a new MSW program in an historical and environmental context that fostered a different approach to social work practice and social work education. A confluence of social and economic conditions, an interrelationship of social problems, a renewed recognition in the importance of socially and economically just institutions, the accelerated pace in the needs of diverse communities, and the need for leadership and a collaborative spirit, led the School of Social Work to its sole MSW concentration in community partnerships. Nothing in the intervening years has given pause to alter that position. Even CSWE's (2003) newly approved accreditation standards and modified definition of the purpose of social work education continue to lend support to the program.

This experience has solidified the belief that the social work profession has the responsibility to take on this leadership role as a primary function of graduate education. This role is grounded in *community* as the framework for the School. The community continues to change and the School of Social Work has a responsibility to respond to, as well as influence, those changes. This reinforces and celebrates social work education's longstanding attachment to, not detachment from, the community. As a result, the School of Social Work supports and educates social workers who are community-based practitioners and is a leader in the University's mission to be an engaged community partner.

REFERENCES

Arnstein, S. (1969). A ladder of citizen participation. *Journal of the American Institute of Planners, 35*, 216-224.

Astin, H. (1995). The engaged campus: Organizing to serve society's needs. *AAHE Bulletin, 7*(5), 3.

Barry, K., & Britt, D. (2002). Outreach: Targeting high-risk women through community partnerships. *Women's Health Issues, 12*, 66-79.

Beck, E., & Eichler, M. (2000). Consensus organizing: A practice model for community building. *Journal of Community Practice, 8*(1), 87-102.

Boyer, E.L. (1990). *Scholarship reconsidered: Priorities of the professorate.* Princeton, NJ: Carnegie Foundation for the Advancement of Teaching.

Boyer, E.L. (1996). The scholarship of engagement. *Journal of Public Service & Outreach, 1*(1), 11-20.

Bradshaw, C., Soifer, S., & Gutierrez, L. (1994). Toward a hybrid model for effective organizing in communities of color. *Journal of Community Practice, 1*(1), 25-41.

Brun, C., & Rapp, R. (2001). Strengths-based case management: Individuals' perspectives on strengths and the case manager relationship. *Social Work, 46*, 278-289.

Chapin, R., & Cox, E. (2001). Changing the paradigm: Strengths-based and empowerment-oriented social work with frail elders. *Journal of Gerontological Social Work, 36*, 165-180.

Cloward, R., & Piven, F. (1999). Disruptive dissensus: People and power in the industrial age. In J. Rothman (Ed.). *Reflections on community organization: Enduring themes and critical issues* (pp.165-193). Itasca, IL: F.E. Peacock.

Coulton, C. (1996). Poverty, work, and community: A research agenda for an era of diminishing federal responsibility. *Social Work, 41*, 509-519.

Council on Social Work Education. (1994). *Handbook of accreditation standards and procedures* (4th ed.). Alexandria, VA: CSWE.

Council on Social Work Education. (2003). *Handbook of accreditation standards and procedures* (5th ed.). Alexandria, VA: CSWE.

Cox, E. (2001). Community practice issues in the 21st century: Questions and challenges for empowerment-oriented practitioners. *Journal of Community Practice, 9*(1), 37-55.

Cox, E., & Parsons, R. (1996). Empowerment-oriented social work practice: Impact on late-life relationships of women. *Journal of Women & Aging, 8*(3/4), 129-144.

Delgado, M. (2000). *Community social work practice in an urban context: The potential of a capacity enhancement perspective.* NY: Oxford University Press.

Dietz, C. (2000). Reshaping clinical practice for the new millennium. *Journal of Social Work Education, 36*(3), 503-521.

Dooley, D. & Naparstek, A. (1997). Countering urban disinvestment through community-building initiatives. *Social Work, 42,* 506-515.

Faubion, J.D. (Ed.). (2001). *Power: Essential works of Foucault: 1954-1984, Volume III.* NY: New Press.

Fisher, R. (1994). *Let the people decide: Neighborhood organizing in America.* NY: Twayne.

Fisher, R. & Karger, H.J. (1997). *Social work and community in a private world: Getting out in public.* White Plains, NY: Addison Wesley Longman, Inc.

Fogelman, E. (2002). Civic engagement at the University of Minnesota. *Journal of Public Affairs, 6*(Suppl.1), 103-118.

Foundation Center. (2003). *Foundation giving trends: Update on funding priorities.* NY: Author.

Freire, P. (1970). *Pedagogy of the oppressed.* NY: Continuum.

Gardner, J.W. (1964). *Self-renewal: The individual and the innovative society.* NY: Harper & Row.

Gutierrez, L., & GlenMaye, L. (1995). The organizational context of empowerment practice: Implications for social work administration. *Social Work, 40*(2), 249-258.

Hyde, C. (1995). Experiences of women activists: Implications for community organizing theory and practice. In J. Tropman, J. Erlich, & J. Rothman (Eds.), *Tactics and techniques of community intervention.* (3rd ed., pp. 393-403). Itasca, IL: F.E. Peacock.

Johnson, A. (2000). The community practice pilot project: Integrating methods, field, community assessment, and experiential learning. *Journal of Community Practice, 8*(4), 5-25.

Lambert, S., & Black, M. (2001). Comprehensive community initiatives: Expanded roles for developmental scientists. *Children's Services: Social Policy, Research & Practice, 4,* 25-30.

Lundquist, S., & Nixon, J. (1998). The partnership paradigm: Collaboration and the community college. *New Directions for Community Colleges, 103,* 43-49.

McMahon, B., Browning, S., & Rose-Colley, M. (2001). A school-community partnership for at-risk students in Pennsylvania. *Journal of School Health, 71,* 53-56.

Mizrahi, T. (2001). The status of community organizing in 2001: Community practice context, complexities, contradictions, and contributions. *Research on Social Work Practice, 11,* 176-189.

Netting, F., Kettner, P., & McMurtry, S. (1998). *Social work macro practice.* NY: Longman.

Nyden, P., Figert, A., Shibley, M., & Burrows, D. (1997). *Building community: Social science in action.* Thousand Oaks, CA: Pine Forge Press.

Overton, B., & Burkhardt, J. (1999). Drucker could be right, but. . . .: New leadership models for institutional-community partnerships. *Applied Developmental Science, 3,* 217-228.

Parsons, R. (2001). Specific practice strategies for empowerment-based practice with women: A study of two groups. *Affilia: Journal of Women & Social Work, 16,* 159-180.

Rose, S.M. (2000). Reflections on empowerment-based practice. *Social Work, 45*(5), 403-413.

Saleebey, D. (1996). The strengths perspective in social work practice: Extensions and cautions. *Social Work, 41*(3), 296-306.

Sanders, M.G., & Epstein, J.L. (1998). International perspectives on school-family-community partnerships. *Childhood Education, 74*(6), 340-341.

Sanfort, J. (2000). Developing new skills for community practice in an era of policy devolution. *Journal of Social Work Education, 36*(2) 183-186.

Shonkoff, J.P., & Phillips, D.A. (2000). *From neurons to neighborhoods: The science of early childhood development/committee on integrating the science of early childhood development.* Washington, DC: National Academy Press.

Specht, H. & Courtney, M.E. (1994). *Unfaithful angels: How social work has abandoned its mission.* NY: Free Press.

Weick, A., Rapp, C., Sullivan, W.P., & Kisthardt, W. (1989). A strengths perspective for social work practice. *Social Work, 34*(3), 350-355.

Weil, M. (1996). Community building: Building community practice. *Social Work, 41,* 481-500.

Witkin, S.L. (1998). Mirror, mirror on the wall: Creative tensions, the academy, and the field. *Social Work, 43*(5), 389-391.

The Collaborative Research Education Partnership: Community, Faculty, and Student Partnerships in Practice Evaluation

Marla Berg-Weger, PhD, LCSW
Susan S. Tebb, PhD, LCSW
Cynthia A. Loveland Cook, PhD, RN, ACSW
Mary Beth Gallagher, PhD
Barbara Flory, LCSW
Ashley Cruce, MA, MSW

Marla Berg-Weger, is Associate Provost, Saint Louis University and is Associate Professor, Susan S. Tebb, is Professor and Dean, and Cynthia A. Loveland Cook is Associate Professor, Saint Louis University School of Social Service. Mary Beth Gallagher is Director, VOICES Project, Saint Louis University. Barbara Flory is Program Coordinator, Heritage House, Provident Counseling, St. Louis, MO Ashley Cruce is Director, Emmett J. and Mary Martha Doerr Center for Social Justice Education and Research, Saint Louis University School of Social Service.

Address correspondence to: Marla Berg-Weger, PhD, 221 North Grand, DuBourg Hall, 106, St. Louis, MO 63103 (E-mail: bergwm@slu.edu).

The authors wish to thank the Emmett J. and Mary Martha Doerr Center for Social Justice Education and Research in the School of Social Service at Saint Louis University for their support of the research described here. The authors also extend their appreciation to Adjunct Professor Betsy Slosar and Dr. Margaret Sherraden for their support in the preparation of this manuscript.

Additional information on the Center is available at *http://www.slu.edu/colleges/SOCSVC/*

An earlier version of this article was presented at APM in New York City, February 2000.

[Haworth co-indexing entry note]: "The Collaborative Research Education Partnership: Community, Faculty, and Student Partnerships in Practice Evaluation." Berg-Weger, Marla et al. Co-published simultaneously in *Journal of Community Practice* (The Haworth Social Work Practice Press, an imprint of The Haworth Press, Inc.) Vol. 12, No. 3/4, 2004, pp. 141-162; and: *University-Community Partnerships: Universities in Civic Engagement* (ed: Tracy M. Soska, and Alice K. Johnson Butterfield) The Haworth Social Work Practice Press, an imprint of The Haworth Press, Inc., 2004, pp. 141-162. Single or multiple copies of this article are available for a fee from The Haworth Document Delivery Service [1-800-HAWORTH, 9:00 a.m. - 5:00 p.m. (EST). E-mail address: docdelivery@haworthpress.com].

SUMMARY. This article discusses the founding and operation of the Emmett J. and Mary Martha Doerr Center for Social Justice Education and Research, an endowed nonprofit organization located within the School of Social Service at Saint Louis University. The nonprofit Center provides a creative mechanism for facilitating university-community agency research. The Research Education Partnership (REP) model creates a partnership among students, community agency personnel, and faculty in funded practice research and program evaluation. Four collaborations, their benefits and challenges, are described. Students are prepared to integrate research into practice. The Center promotes and supports faculty-community partnerships for social justice. *[Article copies available for a fee from The Haworth Document Delivery Service: 1-800-HAWORTH. E-mail address: <docdelivery@haworthpress.com> Website: <http://www.HaworthPress.com> © 2004 by The Haworth Press, Inc. All rights reserved.]*

KEYWORDS. University-community partnerships, collaboration, practice research, program evaluation, social justice

INTRODUCTION

The importance of demonstrating service excellence is an increasingly recognized, valued, and expected function in human service agencies. The ethical standards of the social work profession, policy makers, and funding sources all mandate social work practitioners to provide evidence of the effectiveness of social work interventions (Herie & Martin, 2002). For example, research on the efficacy of agency and clinical treatment outcomes offers an empirically informed approach to improving client services (e.g., Dunn, Flory, Berg-Weger, & Milstead, 2004; Flory, & Berg-Weger, 2003; Flory, Dunn, Berg-Weger, & Milstead, 2001; Gallagher, Cook, Tebb, & Berg-Weger, 2003). Yet, higher education in the field of social work has often fallen short of adequately preparing future clinicians and administrators to study and evaluate their practice effectively (Kirk & Penka, 1992; Penka & Kirk, 1991). Consequently, most social service professionals are unprepared to conduct systematic research in the areas of needs assessments and practice evaluations. Some feel inadequate in the role of evaluator or researcher as they lack the necessary training to implement these projects successfully (Collins, Kayser, & Tourse, 1994). Others are not convinced of the value of applying research skills to practice (Cook, Freedman, Evans, Rodell, & Taylor, 1992). Therefore, knowledge and skills are needed to enable practitioners to use and participate in community-based research (Herie & Martin, 2002).

One factor contributing to the shortcomings of practice evaluation is the pedagogical approach to graduate education in research and program evaluation. Didactic courses on research methods and statistics are required. However, the integration of theory, research, and practice is not always emphasized. The Council on Social Work Education Accreditation (CSWE) Commission (2003) specifies that social work programs should provide students with skills "to develop, use and effectively communicate empirically based knowledge, including evidence-based interventions" (p. 36) and further to "evaluate research studies, apply research findings to practice, and evaluate their own practice interventions" (p. 33). Research course assignments are not typically well integrated with practice experiences; thus, social work students may not develop the level of research skills that can later be translated into quality improvement studies, program evaluations, or assessments of treatment effectiveness (Collins et al., 1994). As Proctor (2003) points out, the profession needs research partnerships that are conceptualized from the outset as "trench, to bench, and back to trench" (p. 67).

To promote the research education needs of students, improve professional practice, and better serve the community, Saint Louis University's School of Social Service embarked on a major school fund raising project to establish the Emmett J. and Mary Martha Doerr Center for Social Justice Education and Research. Opened in 1996, the Center is an endowed, nonprofit entity housed within the School of Social Service and governed by an Advisory Board with an Executive Committee that oversees Center activities. Committees comprised of alumni, community agency professionals, faculty, staff, and students carry out the various functions of the Center (i.e., research, education, marketing, and development). A full-time director, a part-time support staff person, and a part-time graduate assistant staff the Center. The director is a voting member of the School of Social Service Assembly, the School's governing body. Through two generous donations from an alumna and her family and contributions from faculty and alumni, the Center's original endowment exceeded $1,200,000. In addition to the endowment and other donations, the Center has obtained contracts to consult with a major foundation and non-profit agencies on organizational development and program evaluation. The Center also seeks external funds to support more university-community agency research partnerships, student scholarships, and educational programs (e.g., annual Social Justice Night, conferences, and lectures).

The Saint Louis School of Social Service (2003) founded the Center based on a definition of social justice that frames the concept as "the creation of just relationships, structures and resources for the equality of opportunity, access to needed information, service and resources and meaningful participation in decision making for all people." In operationalizing this definition of social justice, the Center seeks to promote social justice within social work education; encourage students to become practitioners of social justice; and support faculty-community partnerships for social justice research.

A primary goal of the Center is to create an innovative model of social justice research education to effectively prepare students and practitioners to practice and to evaluate practice in community-based social service agencies. The Center strives to fund educational and research activities that contribute to structural change and increase the opportunities of those who are vulnerable or marginalized in our society. The model is aimed at enhancing the research emphasis of graduate education and promoting practice evaluation. By funding projects that address discrimination, oppression, access, and other systemic inequities and prepare social workers to understand and work effectively to combat social injustices, the Center endeavors to uphold the core social work value of challenging social injustice as framed by the *Code of Ethics* (National Association of Social Workers, 1999) and the Education Policy and Accreditation Standards (CSWE, 2003).

Research proposals are evaluated for funding based on the project's potential to contribute to the mission and goals of the Center. In order to be approved for funding, a project must address social justice issues within the context of social work education and research and promote operational meanings of social justice. The four criteria used for assessing a project proposal include:

- Alleviation of poverty/suffering and improvement of services to vulnerable populations through projects that seek to address the improvement of the availability, accessibility and affordability of services within local communities and within society;
- Development of educational programs and/or policies that lessen discrimination against groups on the basis of race and ethnicity, gender, age, class/socioeconomic status, physical and mental ability, immigrant and/or displaced status and/or sexual orientation;

- Social action efforts for structural change that are aimed at increasing the participation of underserved groups in efforts to improve such areas as services, community structures and legislation;
- Global awareness within the United State or abroad regarding such social justice issues as human rights, immigration, economic development and workers' rights.

This paper describes the educational model used to involve faculty, students, and social work practitioners in research education partnerships (REP) that teach research skills by fostering hands-on student learning environments. These partnerships are based on the combined expertise of social work faculty, students, and community practitioners. Of the twenty projects funded, to date, process evaluations have been conducted on four projects. One process evaluation is described in detail in this paper and three other projects are briefly highlighted. These four projects were selected as they are representative of the typical projects being proposed and conducted by the university-community partners. Preliminary analysis from this pilot evaluation effort suggests that the model may be a potentially useful strategy for promoting university-community research partnerships. Benefits, challenges, and facilitating factors of the partners' experience are discussed along with implications for replication of the model.

RESEARCH AND SOCIAL WORK EDUCATION

The application of research findings in the practice community has become a focus of attention in recent years. Blum and colleagues (1995) suggest that scholars often make assumptions regarding the significance and integration of their research to practice. These assumptions include the idea that community-based research is more meaningful for service delivery than university-based research, research findings are used to develop new programs and services, and engaging practitioners in research strengthens the findings. Dal Santo and colleagues (2002) further suggest that dissemination of research findings has traditionally occurred through the reporting of findings and that application of the findings is assumed to have taken place.

In addition to the assumptions made regarding the dissemination of research findings, the value of research experiences for MSW students has also been assumed. However, exposing students to agency-based research can pose a challenge for social work faculty members. Should agency-based research be included within the practicum experience? Reisch and Jarman-Rohde (2000) question if the increased emphasis on research in social work schools detracts from the importance of the practicum experience for the education of social workers. For that reason, they strongly recommend partnerships, or at least more collaborative relationships, between schools and community agencies in research education for social workers.

Recognizing the existence of assumptions can provide the opportunity for investigation. The Center creates opportunities for faculty-community collaboration that facilitate the teaching of research methodologies, extends field education into the research domain, and strengthens the research and evaluation skills of practitioners. All three constituent groups in the REP model individually experience barriers in conducting research, but together their shared knowledge and resources make these challenges less formidable. Agency staff may have limited research knowledge and lack time to conduct evaluative research (Cook et al., 1992). Faculty members often have difficulty accessing study samples and maintaining awareness of practice innovations (Rabin, Savaya, & Frank, 1994; Turnbull, Saltz, & Gwyther, 1988). The absence of a strong curriculum that encourages the integration of research into practice may impede students from undertaking research in future practice. To address these challenges, the Center maintains a database of agencies, faculty, and students that are interested in practice research.

In the context of the university-community partnerships to be examined in this paper, the concept of university-agency collaboration is defined as "a mutually beneficial and well-defined relationship entered into by two or more organizations to achieve common goals" (Mattessich, Murray-Close, & Monsey, 2001, p. 4). The operationalization of this definition embraces the development of shared goals, responsibilities, resources, and rewards. In a review of the literature addressing factors that contribute to successful agency-university research partnerships facilitated by university-based researchers, an array of strategies are recommended (Blum et al., 1995; Dal Santo et al., 2002; Flocks & Monaghan, 2003; Mattessich et al., 2001):

- The collaborators are perceived as leaders in the area and mutual respect, trust, and understanding exist between the partners.
- The collaborative serves the self-interests of all the partners.
- Communication regarding both shared and divergent objectives for collaboration occurs early, regularly, and with all involved constituents.

- The partners establish familiarity with respective settings and needs, particularly in the case of the researcher learning about the agency.
- The collaborators identify and clarify roles and tasks and maintain adaptability and flexibility in the designated roles and processes throughout the duration of the project, re-visiting these areas on a regular basis.
- Needed resources (e.g., funding, personnel, time, and leadership) are adequate for the scope of the project.
- The strengths and expertise of the agency staff involved is recognized and utilized.
- The project time frame is appropriate for both the agency and the university research.
- A plan is developed for conducting the research project, communicating throughout the project, disseminating findings, and addressing potential conflicts.
- Scholars have noted the many benefits that stem from such collaborations range from student learning to enhanced service delivery. For example, community agency and academic collaborations of this nature can provide innovative opportunities for effective community services (Leon, 1999; Peters, 2002). University-community collaborations enable participants to gain greater access to resources and outcomes related to a common objective (Austin et al., 1999; Bailey & Koney, 1996).

RESEARCH EDUCATION PARTNERSHIP MODEL

A model developed for community psychologists and first described by Seidman and Rappaport (1974) provides the basis for the Research Education Partnership (REP). Originally, they used the pyramid model to aid faculty and student psychologists in an initial examination of community change, while Rapp and colleagues (1989) adapted the model for social work by introducing practice research and strengthening student participation through the provision of financial support. Conceived as a hierarchical transfer of knowledge in which a person who is most learned transfers her/his knowledge to another, the Center adapted the model into a collaborative partnership with each member having different expertise and sharing this knowledge with the partners, thus enabling all to understand and participate in practice research, learn to be responsible consumers of research, and understand and apply research findings in agency-based settings (Gantt, Pinsky, Rock, & Rosenberg, 1990).

The REP model utilized by the Center brings together three groups with unique resources and skills that enhance agency-based research outcomes. Faculty members bring to the project their research expertise, ability to contribute findings to the literature, and interest in providing meaningful community service. Students bring time, energy, and interest in learning to the REP project. Their untutored questions provide valuable challenges to agencies and scholars alike. While fulfilling degree requirements, students receive financial compensation, gain valuable on-the-job research experience, and an opportunity to co-author presentations and publications. Community agencies bring first-hand knowledge and experience about the research needed to benefit clients.

Each funding cycle, the Center distributes a request for proposals (RFP) to approximately 500 community agencies. Interested community agencies respond to the RFP with a Letter of Intent. Using the Center database, Center staff matches interested faculty members and agencies. Together, the community agency and the faculty member write the proposal. If selected as one of the one to three proposals that are funded each cycle, the faculty member recruits the student research assistants. The student may complete the project as a one or two-semester practicum, independent study, or part-time employment. The practicum curriculum includes learning objectives targeted at assessment, research, evaluation of practice, and evidenced-based practice. In this way, the student's field experience is consistent with curricular goals and objectives. Each three-credit practicum requires 240 clock hours in the field. Once the faculty/community agency/student REP team is formed, a plan is created to determine project schedules, roles and responsibilities, particularly related to student supervision. As the community professional typically serves as the principal investigator, she/he oversees the implementation of the work plan. Leadership of the REP is task-oriented and is typically shared by the principal investigator and the faculty member. The faculty member is responsible for developing the Institutional Review Board proposal.

The partnership of agency and School builds on the respective strengths of each, specifically the agency's ability to be on the cutting edge of social work practice and the school's expertise in research methods. Working together allows faculty to incorporate the latest practice innovations and case examples into their teaching, as well as their research related to the effectiveness of innovations. Community agency professionals, in turn, hone needed research skills to guide and evaluate practice. Most important, this type of partnership provides students with a community setting in which to practice classroom learning. Students who work closely with a community agency and the educational institution develop a realistic view about classroom material as it plays out in the lives of clients (Rabin, Savaya, & Frank, 1994). As students apply their academic skills in an agency setting, they gain knowledge on which to build classroom learning (Lucas, 2000).

While other "town and gown" collaborations abound, the Center's REP model is unique in a variety of areas. First and foremost, the research opportunities provided by Center funding enable all three groups, but particularly the community agencies and the students, to obtain resources (i.e., funding and faculty research expertise) they may not otherwise be able to access. The non-hierarchical learning paradigm that is employed results in the faculty member not being the central source of all information and expertise. Instead, the team relies on one another for important information and tasks.

Team members consider the contributions of each REP team member essential. Collaboration models often use the community agency as simply the setting in which the research occurs (Collins et al., 1994). In this case, the agency may or may not be interested or involved in the research. In situations in which agency staff members have ideas for research projects, they may not be able to identify or access researchers who have research agendas compatible with their needs. Moreover, agency staff may feel that existing research teams or centers that have large-scale funding and established research programs are not approachable or interested in their ideas for research projects. In contrast, REP projects address practice questions that are articulated in the Letter of Intent as high priority by practitioners and bring research opportunities to non-researchers. Because the questions are practitioner-generated, the level of the partners' insight and investment in the project is strengthened. Practitioners and individual faculty members unite around the needs of one specific project idea.

Also unique is the concept that REP projects often direct student experience through practicum which serves to complement their research courses. Students consistently identify practicum as the most influential component of their education (Briar, 1990); therefore, REP experiences can be effective in leading them to become evidence-based practitioners. Participation in the REP projects has also afforded MSW students the opportunity to obtain authorship on scholarly publications and presentations.

From the agency perspective, participation in the REP projects allows the agency to conduct assessments, evaluations, and exploratory research that possess a higher level of research rigor not typically a part of an agency's capacity for assessment, evaluation, and research. Oftentimes, to gain research expertise, an agency must engage a consultant to conduct an evaluation, a venture that can be cost-prohibitive. Having the funding, research expertise, human resources, and human subjects oversight through the university's institutional review process to conduct focused projects is often not available in many social service agencies. Some REP faculty collaborators have been new to research at the time of their participation. The Center staff offers mentoring and support for faculty, agency, and student team members. While faculty members are not compensated for their involvement in the REP projects, they can expand their scholarly activities and provide a needed service to the social service community.

The mission of the University and the School of Social Service includes an emphasis on faculty and students providing service to the communities in which they exist. The Center for Social Justice Education and Research was established in an effort to carry out that aspect of the University and School mission and to enable the faculty and students to be in the service of the local, national and international communities. Specifically, the Center endeavors to fulfill this mission by providing service to the social work practice community through conducting research (e.g., the evaluation of programs and/or treatment outcomes), providing faculty members with a setting in which to further their scholarship, and teaching graduate students pragmatic, "real-world" partnering and research skills. Unlike other educational models, the Center accomplishes these goals through the agency grants that propose high quality research and student learning environments. The Center director oversees the grant administration. Since 1997, the amount of the grants has ranged from $6,000-$13,500 each, totaling $196,432. At least half of the award amount must be used for student stipends and remaining funds for general operating expenses.

REP PROJECT DESCRIPTIONS

In the feedback received from faculty, students, and community agencies that have participated in Center-funded REP projects, the projects consistently produce outcomes that are beneficial for the participants. In addition to the valuable learning and collaboration, tangible products that have resulted from the first eighteen projects include: 25

student research assistantships; 27 publications; and 23 presentations. A special issue of the journal, *Social Thought*, published also as a book entitled, *Practicing Justice* (Stretch, Burkemper, Hutchison, & Wilson, 2003), reports on the Center's research projects. As shown in Table 1, these projects represent the breadth and type of social justice issues and the diversity of faculty, practitioner, and student interests.

The REP projects are widely diverse and all address issues of social injustice. However, in analyzing the type of projects funded, to date, five categories are identified: coalition development, program evaluation, baseline assessment, needs assessment, and exploratory research. Despite the diversity of projects aims, the commonality that exists throughout the five project types is the focus on vulnerable populations. The majority of the projects involve evaluation of new or existing agency-based programs. Needs assessments were conducted in three projects, while two projects were designed as exploratory research efforts and two projects combined baseline/needs assessments with program evaluation. The first Center-funded project focused on the development of a coalition. As the project ideas are initiated by the community agencies, this breakdown suggests that program evaluation is of greatest need at this time. Following is a detailed description of the process evaluation from a program evaluation project that typifies the collaborative research-education partnership. This project is an exemplar of community-generated research needs, the partnership among the faculty, student, and practitioners, and outcomes that have been beneficial to the community.

Outcome Study for Heritage House

This collaborative research unites a social work faculty and student with Heritage House, a program housed in a non-profit mental health service agency that provides supervised parent-child visitation and custody exchange. Partnering with this new and innovative program created an opportunity to contribute to the evaluation of community program outcomes, while simultaneously contributing to needed research in this area. This project exemplifies the social justice mission of the Center in that the laws governing divorce and child custody dictate the legal dissolution of marriage, but not child well-being. The program strives to give a voice to vulnerable children; evaluation strengthens the ability to better serve this population.

Heritage House, a public/private partnership, joins the court and community to fill the gap between law and social services. The goal is to

TABLE 1. Projects Funded by the Center for Social Justice Education and Research

Project Title and Community Partners	Project Focus
Women and Families Affected by AIDS. Women United Fighting AIDS.1997	Launch collaborative for education, services, advocacy
Community Economic Development. MASW. 1998	Baseline survey of state community economic development for low-income
Options for Justice. 1998	Evaluate program serving MR/DD offenders
Promoting Client Empowerment in State Hospital. St. Louis Psychiatric Rehabilitation Center.1998.	Program evaluation of client empowerment of state psychiatric facility patients
WomenStart. Women's Let's Start. 1998	Evaluate program for women ex-offenders
Youth Advocacy Project. Missouri Public Defender. 1998	Assess unmet psychological needs of youths on probation and compare recidivism
Outcome Study for Heritage House. Provident Counseling. 1999	Assess impact of custody exchange program intervention on child and parent behaviors
Bridges Across Racial Polarization. FOCUS St. Louis.1999	Evaluate attitudes and behavior in interracial relationships
When is it Worth Working? Independence Center.1999	Assess risks and benefits of employment for adults with psychiatric disabilities
Empowering Certified Nursing Assistants. Alzheimer's Association. 2000	Evaluate dementia training for residential care workers
Outreach to Children Without Health Care. St. Anthony's Health Center. 2000	Identify barriers to child health insurance eligibility
Homeless Adolescent Count & Needs Assessment. Legal Services of Eastern Missouri. 2000	Profile of characteristics & needs of homeless youth
Economic Justice: Empowering Families with Access to Credit/Assets. Justine Petersen Housing & Reinvestment Corporation. 2001	Evaluate intervention to access to credit for low-moderate income persons
Trauma & Acculturation of Bosnian Refugees in St. Louis. Missouri Institute of Mental Health. 2001	Investigate trauma-related psychiatric & social problems of Bosnian refugees
An Evaluation of Choices–A Jail-Based Substance Abuse Treatment. St Louis County Jail. 2001	Evaluate jail-based substance abuse treatment and assess community outcomes
Empowering People with Mental Illness. Barnes-Jewish-Christian Behavioral Health. 2002	Explore limitation & opportunities to empower persons with severe mental illness
Evaluating Circles of Hope. WomanSpirit, Inc. 2002	Evaluate a grassroots model for low income African American women
Assessing Effective Youth Development. Wyman Center, Inc. 2002	Evaluate longitudinal youth development programs
Reconciling Traditional & Modern Values in Kenya and Rwanda. Peacebuilding, Healing & Reconciliation. 2003	Evaluate peacebuilding program aimed at capacity building of local communities

improve and augment current services, insuring the safety of children in high-conflict child custody disputes by providing a neutral, caring environment for supervised access and custody exchange. This "neighbor-to-neighbor" concept helps parents improve co-parenting and children's well-being. The strengths-based intervention differs from traditional deficit-based treatment approaches that often deem divorce a pathological, even deviant, occurrence (Ahrons, 1994). The model allows both parents the opportunity to be competent and involved parents for their children.

Historically, supervised visitation between non-custodial parent and child is judicially ordered when child safety is at risk. The court/community partnership fills the gap between social services and the law by meeting the needs of families, while aiding the Court in crafting meaningful and lasting judicial dispositions. Although viewed as a model program by legislators and court administrators, limited data were available to support its effectiveness. While anecdotal evidence suggested that Heritage House fulfilled a valuable role in resolving high conflict child custody disputes, outcome documentation was needed. The goal of the REP project was to compare pre- and post-adjustment outcomes for children in high conflict child custody disputes in the areas of frequency of visitation, incidence of interparental conflict, changes in children's behaviors, and physical and emotional health.

Data were collected from court-ordered adult parents (custodial, non-custodial, divorced and never married to each other) and their children that volunteered to participate in the study. (For more detailed discussions of the study, see Dunn et al., 2004; Flory & Berg-Weger, 2003; Flory et al., 2001.) As the aim of this project was to assess the effect of increased visitation on interparental conflict and child well-being, pre-study visitation was compared with the rates of non-custodial parent visitation that occurred within six months after entry into the study. Findings indicate that non-custodial parent visitation increased from program entry through the six-month post-test follow-up. A significant decrease in psychological aggression between the parents was noted. Data also suggest decreased use of corporal punishment in child discipline. Along with the increased visitation and reduced conflicts between parents, visitation consistency by the non-custodial parent also improved. Thus, the findings suggest that the strengths-based premise on which the intervention is built enables parents to have increased opportunities for success and improved parenting.

As a result of the REP, several major accomplishments occurred for the agency and the faculty: (1) an important contribution to a lacking body of literature through three publications and numerous presentations; (2) attracting major funding sources to enable the continuation and expansion of Heritage House (a $350,000 grant proposal is currently under review); (3) promoting development of similar programs (program staff consult on program development in other jurisdictions); and (4) informing legislative advocacy efforts on an ongoing basis.

Roles and Responsibilities. The Heritage House Project Coordinator served as the principal investigator, assuming oversight of the project and supervising the student and the research coordinator. Another staff member supervised data collection, analyses, and interpretation. The faculty collaborator consulted on the project and facilitated the Institutional Review Board process, provided expertise in data collection, statistical analyses and interpretation, and assisted in the development of multiple presentations and three publishable manuscripts. Using this project as a practicum, the student conducted participant recruitment and data collection and entry. All partners participated in the writing of articles for presentation and publication.

Benefits. Benefits of this project for the agency, student, and faculty member are numerous. The primary benefit from this collaboration is the outcome evaluation itself. The agency developed a mechanism for the systematic evaluation of program services and is contributing to the sparsely researched area of supervised access and custody exchange. The findings have contributed to legislative and additional fund-raising efforts. The faculty collaborator supported the agency in developing a culture for research and strengthened the bonds between the agency and the School, particularly in field education and was able to participate in a relatively new area of research and publication. The student participated in community agency-based outcome research, strengthening her research skills and observed and participated in an effective collaboration.

Challenges and Obstacles. Challenges identified by the investigators in this study can be categorized as client and collaboration-related. Similar to other REP efforts, challenges related to subject recruitment. Gaining informed consent can be difficult. Parents involved in child custody litigation are reluctant to disclose information that may be introduced into court or place them in an unfavorable light (despite the presence of Confidentiality Orders). In cases of documented or undocumented violence, the alleged perpetrator is often reticent to participate due to the potential self-incrimination that may occur as a result of disclosing violence-related information.

Collaboration-related challenges relate to the tension that exists between expeditiously completing the project and attending to student learning needs. The practicum schedule can limit student availability, a problem in working with a population that involves court delays and parental reluctance to participate due to distrust of the legal and social service systems. The research team worked to reassure parents that the information provided could not be used in court enhanced the comfort level of some, but not all potential participants. Extending the practicum past the designated ending point allowed for all the data to be collected by the student and all the learning objectives to be met, and enabled the student to participate in dissemination of findings.

Facilitating Factors. In reflecting on the experience, members of this REP identified factors that contributed to the success of this project as: (1) early and ongoing clarification of roles, responsibilities, and expectations by all members of the team; (2) acknowledgement of each member's strengths and areas of expertise; (3) development of a realistic time frame for completion of the project with a routine re-evaluation of that time frame; and (4) regular meetings to discuss the project, student progress, and related issues. As the principal investigator served as the field instructor, she met weekly with the student and research coordinator. The faculty member served as the practicum liaison and met regularly with the research team.

Samples of Other REP Projects

Brief summaries of the process evaluations of three additional Center-funded projects are presented here. These three projects were selected as they include examples of a needs assessment (Youth Advocacy Project), a baseline assessment (Community Economic Development Project) and a variation on the program evaluation model (Promoting Client Empowerment in a State Psychiatric Hospital). Interviews were conducted with partners are described here. Table 2 provides a summary of the interviews with the three projects, including participants' perceptions of roles, responsibilities, benefits, challenges, and factors that facilitated the respective partnerships. The benefits are documented only in terms of the collaborative partners. Substantial benefits to the community and to vulnerable populations, in particular, also emerge from the research. Following are highlights from three funded projects.

Youth Advocacy Project. An example of a needs assessment project, this collaboration between the Office of the Public Defender in the City of St. Louis and the School addressed the high rate of recidivism among youth in the juvenile justice system (over 30% re-arrest in three months). The REP identified youths at highest risk of failure to meet the conditions of probation and developed a systematic assessment tool for identifying these high-risk youth. Four presentations have been made using data from this project.

TABLE 2. REP Project Highlights

Project	Managing the Partnership	Benefits/Effects	Challenges/ Difficulties	Facilitating Factors
Youth Advocacy Project	Agency: initiated project and oriented supervised student Faculty: obtained human subjects approval; designed research & method; recruited student Student: conducted interviews, selected research subjects, and entered data All: papers & presentations	Agency: demonstration of the effectiveness of an intervention, allowing more youth to participate in program; and best use of scarce resources Faculty: publication opportunity and community service Student: first publication; public presentations; assessment experience, networking for jobs	Staff turnover at the agency made continuity a challenge Institutional Review delayed the project start	Ongoing dialogue on juvenile court system aided the faculty and student to grasp problems faced by juveniles Student commitment: "The project changed my life…."
Community Economic Development	Agency: analyzed data, made presentations, authored report Faculty: obtained human subjects approval, analyzed data, made presentations, authored report Student: developed, piloted, & disseminated questionnaire	Agency: concrete tool to use in subsequent tracking of economic development in the state Faculty: opportunity for publication and presentation Student: Extensive exposure to community economic development activities; research experience	Survey returns took much longer than planned The delay created problems for students' timetable	Gaining multiple, broader perspectives True teamwork Student stipend Center support from Center Director on methods and Institutional Review
Promoting Client Empowerment	Agency: described research problem; enlisted agency support, determined feasibility, held focus groups Faculty: analyzed data and co-authored articles & reports Student: participated in focus groups, contributed to articles	Agency: evidence of program's effectiveness: participation reduces recidivism Faculty: great satisfaction in meeting a real community need Student: co-author on six publications, learned data collection and entry	Negotiating roles was challenging	Support from hospital administration Obtained input on study design from multiple groups Funders demand such evidence of effective practice

Community Economic Development. To provide comprehensive information on community economic development resources and their access, faculty collaborated with the Missouri Association for Social Welfare (MASW) to establish a baseline measure of asset building activity in the state and identify barriers to community economic development. The data provide support for resource and policy improvements that enable practitioners (from state agency workers to community social workers) to more effectively reach low-income communities. Findings provided a basis for state accountability to local communities and citizens, including two scholarly publications and presentations at local and national conferences (Sherraden, Slosar, & Sherraden, 2002; Sherraden, Slosar, Chastain, & Squillace, 2003).

Promoting Client Empowerment in a State Psychiatric Hospital. Another example of a partnership in program evaluation, this project assumes that empowering persons with mental illness to make decisions about their own lives can address social injustices experienced by this population. The student, faculty, hospital researchers, and persons with mental illness, evaluated the level of empowerment occurring among patients in a state psychiatric hospital and made recommendations for empowerment. Six scholarly publications have resulted from this collaboration (Linhorst & Eckert, 2002; Linhorst & Eckert, 2003; Linhorst, Eckert, & Hamilton, in press; Linhorst, Eckert, Hamilton, & Young, 2003; Linhorst, Hamilton, Young, & Eckert, 2002; Linhorst, Eckert, Hamilton, & Young, 2001).

EVALUATION AND IMPLICATIONS

The qualitative evidence presented here suggests that the REP model may be an effective strategy for bringing agencies and universities together to conduct agency-based research. Potential benefits for agencies include financial support for their practice-based research and the chance to leverage additional funding with pilot data. Faculty research and service goals can be supported. Students can benefit from the hands-on experience of practice research and the possibility of publication. The Center monitors projects through annual and final reports. Utilizing data from two focus groups comprised of faculty members and agency personnel, the Center plans to formalize a comprehensive evaluation of all REP projects, including periodic focus groups with partners and two-year follow-ups to determine if change has occurred.

The first focus group, comprised of eight representatives from funded agencies yielded the following recommendations for enhancing the collaborative process: (1) clarification of appropriate agency/faculty/student roles and responsibilities; (2) training for agency partners in the human subjects approval and budgeting processes; and (3) development of a mentoring process matching previous awardees with applicants. Feedback from the faculty focus group mirrored the agency feedback in terms of the need for clarification of roles and responsibility and further training in the process of conducting university-based research. The faculty focus group members noted that this model of conducting social justice research provides a mechanism for responding to community needs and to connect faculty members with community agencies around research issues. Faculty members voiced concern about the timing of the funding projects and the challenges in balancing the human subjects approval process with student and agency schedules for completing the project. As a result of the feedback received from the two focus groups, the leadership of the Center has determined that the overall funding process will undergo a thorough review in order to devise strategies to better serve the faculty, students, and agency participants. While the suggestions offered by faculty and agency partners are consistent with those recommendations noted in the literature (Blum et al., 1995; Dal Santo et al., 2002; Mattessich et al., 2001), the identification of needs for additional training and mentoring provide Center staff with guidance and direction for enhancing the collaborative experience.

Also emanating from the focus group feedback has been the development of a pre-post assessment of the knowledge, attitudes, and behaviors related to social justice for those students who participated in REP projects. Additional plans are underway for the development of an integrative seminar for REP students aimed at integrating social justice theory with their practice experiences and a joint student/faculty/field instructor publication on social justice education.

The Center's approach to research education is based on its close partnership with the community. With a focus on social justice, a diverse range of special populations characterizes the projects that have been funded. These projects serve needs of the community, students, and faculty, while strengthening the missions of the University, School, and Center to educate students and contribute to the amelioration of social injustice. For example, the findings of the evaluation of the jail-based substance abuse treatment program contributed to the improvement of services to inmates, while data from the baseline and program evaluation of the dementia training program for certified nursing assistants was used in crafting a legislative effort mandating dementia training for health care providers. Students learn about and experience the integration of research and practice (Tsang, 2000) and social work research and practice do go hand-in-hand.

With increasing demands from funding sources for baseline data and program and outcome evaluations, the REP model can serve agencies by providing expertise and assistance. The model can be replicated in social work and other programs. Partnerships that focus on education, faculty development, and community needs are the force that drives the REP. Funding has provided the incentive and resources to maximize the success of these projects. Funding is only one incentive that, for some individuals, may be less important than other benefits, such as having hands-on research education, opportunities to conduct research in new areas, readily available research expertise, and evidence that supports a best-practice approach to service delivery.

With creativity, the REP model can be replicated with less or no funding. For example, a REP project may be incorporated into a course, practicum, or independent study. The essential ingredient is the motivation to work collaboratively as a unit to answer a research question. Drawing from the authors' experience building a research education partnership, other areas for enhancement of the model include:

- Commitment to an equal partnership among the student, faculty member, and practitioner. Proactively striving for a non-hierarchical research team can enhance the student's investment and learning, particularly if she/he feels like an equal partner in the process and participates in the design phase of the project.
- Ongoing commitment to the community agency and its staff-partnering with the practitioner to mentor and support her/his introduction into community-based research and publication can enrich the findings and their implications.
- Compensation for agency staff time, labor, and resources as well as for faculty contribution and involvement.

This three-pronged approach which promotes social work research can be beneficial to all constituents. The possibilities for agency-based research topics become limitless. The necessary ingredient to success is the motivation to work collaboratively. However, the limitations and challenges related to collaboration must be considered. Before launching into a research project, an assessment of such issues as the history of collaboration, motivation, potential outcomes for the student, researcher, and agency, and barriers should be conducted by both researchers and practitioners. While the collaborative approach can result in considerable gains, an evaluation of the associated "costs" is essential.

The projects described herein demonstrate that combining the expertise of social work faculty, students, and community agency professionals can contribute to the development of evidence based practice that may enhance the ability of the social work community to provide effective services. In the case of most of the projects funded, to date, the use of existing evidence based literature and practices contributes to the development of the project designs and methodology. Moreover, in the program evaluation projects, the research being conducted through these projects analyzes program effectiveness, thus contributing to the literature on evidence based practice. Upon completion of the project analyses, the community agencies then have evidence to support their programs as they apply for future funding and agency credentialing.

REFERENCES

Ahrons, C. (1995). *The good divorce.* New York: Harper-Collins.

Austin, M.J., Martin, M., Carnochan, S., Goldberg, S., Berrick, J.D., Weiss, B., & Kelley, J. (1999). Building a comprehensive agency-university partnership: A case study of the Bay Area Social Services Consortium. *Journal of Community Practice, 6*(3), 89-106.

Bailey, D., & Koney, K.M. (1996). Interorganizational community-based collaborations: A strategic response to shape the social work agenda. *Social Work, 41*(6), 602-611.

Blum, A., Biegel, D.E., Tracy, E.M., & Cole, M.J. (1995). Agency-university collaboration. Partnerships for implementing and studying practice innovations. In P.M. Hess, & E.J. Mullen, *Practitioner-researcher partnership: Building knowledge from, in, and for practice.* Washington, DC: NASW Press.

Collins, P., Kayser, K., & Tourse, R.C. (1994). Bridging the gaps: An interdependent model for education accountable practitioners. *Journal of Social Work Education, 30*(2), 241-251.

Cook, C.A.L., Freedman, J.A., Evans, R.L., Rodell, D., & Taylor, R.M. (1992). Research in social work practice: Benefits of and obstacles to implementation in the Department of Veterans Affairs. *Health and Social Work, 17*, 214-221.

Council on Social Work Education. (2003). *Handbook of accreditation standards and procedures (5th edition).* Alexandria, VA: CSWE.

Dal Santo, T., Goldberg, S., Choice, P., & Austin, M.J. (2002). Exploratory research in public social service agencies: As assessment of dissemination and utilization. *Journal of Sociology and Social Welfare, XXIX*(4), 59-81.

Dunn, J. H., Flory, B.E., Berg-Weger, M., & Milstead, M. (2004). An exploratory study of supervised access and custody exchange services: The children's experience. *Family Court Review. An Interdisciplinary Journal, 42*(1), pp. 60-73.

Flocks, J., & Monaghan, P. (2003). Collaborative research with farmworkers in environmental justice. *Practicing Anthropology, 25*(1), pp. 6-9.

Flory, B.E., & Berg-Weger, M. (2003). Children of high-conflict custody disputes: Striving for social justice in adult focused litigation. *Social Thought, 22*(2/3), 205-219.

Flory, B.E., Dunn, J., Berg-Weger, M., & Milstead, M. (2001). An exploratory study of supervised access and custody exchange services: The parental experience. *Family and Reconciliation Court Review. An Interdisciplinary Journal, 39*(4), 469-482.

Gallagher, M.B., Cook, C.A.L., Tebb, S.C., & Berg-Weger, M. (2003). Practicing social justice: Community based research, education, and practice. *Social Thought, 22*(2/3), 27-39.

Gantt, A., Pinsky, S., Rock, B., & Rosenberg, E. (1990). Practice and research: An integrative approach. *Journal of Teaching in Social Work, 4*(1), 129-143.

Herie, M., & Martin, G.W. (2002). Knowledge diffusion in social work: A new approach to bridging the gap. *Social Work, 47*(1), 85-95.

Leon, A.M. (1999). Family support model: Integrating service delivery in the twenty-first century. *Families in Society: The Journal of Contemporary Human Services, 80*, 14-24.

Linhorst, D.M., & Eckert, A. (2002). Involving people with mental illness in evaluation and performance improvement. *Evaluation and the Health Professions, 25*(3), 284-301.

Linhorst, D.M. & Eckert, A. (2003). Conditions for empowering people with severe mental illness. *Social Service Review, 77*(2), 279-305.

Linhorst, D.M., Eckert, A., Hamilton, G., & Young, E. (2001). The involvement of a consumer council in organizational decision making in a public psychiatric hospital. *The Journal of Behavioral Health Services and Research, 28*(4), 427-438.

Linhorst, D.M., Eckert, A., Hamilton, G., & Young, E. (2003). Practicing social justice with persons with mental illness residing in psychiatric hospitals. *Social Thought, 22*(2-3), 177-189.

Linhorst, D.M., Hamilton, G., & Eckert, A. (in press). Promoting participation in organizational decision making by clients with severe mental illness. *Social Work.*

Linhorst, D.M., Hamilton, G., Young, E., & Eckert, A. (2002). Opportunities and limitations to empowering persons with severe mental illness through treatment planning. *Social Work, 47*(4), 425-434.

Lucas, E.T. (2000). Linking social work and service-learning, *The Journal of Baccalaureate Social Work, 5*(2), 167-178.

Mattessich, P.W., Murray-Close, M., & Monsey, B.R. (2001). *Collaboration: What makes it work (2nd edition).* Saint Paul, Minnesota: Amherst H. Wilder Foundation.

National Association of Social Workers. (1999). *Code of Ethics.* Washington, DC: NASW.

Peters, J. (2002). University-school collaboration: Identifying faulty assumptions. *Asia-Pacific Journal of Teacher Education, 30*(3), 229-242.

Proctor, E.K. (2003). Developing knowledge for practice: Working through "trench-bench" partnerships. *Social Work Research, 27*(2), 67-69.

Rabin, C., Savaya, R., & Frank, P. (1994). A joint university-field agency: Toward the integration of classroom and practicum. *Journal of Social Work Education, 30*(1), 107-115.

Rapp, C.A., Chamberlain, R., & Freeman, E. (1989). Practicum: New opportunities for training, research, and service delivery. *Journal of Teaching in Social Work, 3*(1), 3-16.

Reisch, M. & Jarman-Rohde, L. (2000). The future of social work in the United States: Implications for field education. *Journal of Social Work Education, 36*(2), 201-214.

Saint Louis University School of Social Service Emmett J. and Mary Martha Doerr Center for Social Justice Education and Research. (2003). Center mission, goals and social justice criteria. St. Louis, MO.

Seidman, E., & Rappaport, J. (1974). The educational pyramid: A paradigm for training, research, and manpower utilization in community psychology. *American Journal of Community Psychology, 2*(2), 119-130.

Sherraden, M.S., Slosar, B., Chastain, A., & Squillace, J. (2003). "Human-sized" economic development: Innovations in Missouri. *Social Thought, 22*(2/3), 97-117.

Sherraden, M.S., Slosar, B., & Sherraden, M. (2002). Innovation in social policy: Collaborative policy advocacy. *Social Work, 47*(3), 209-221.

Stretch, J.J., Burkemper, E.M., Hutchison, W.J., & Wilson, J. (2003). *Practicing Justice*. NY: The Haworth Press, Inc.

Tsang, A.K.T. (2000). Bridging the gap between clinical practice and research: An integrated practice-oriented model. *Journal of Social Service Research, 26*(4), 69-90.

Turnbull, J.E., Saltz, C., & Gwyther, L.P. (1988). A prescription for promoting social work research in a university hospital. *Health and Social Work, 13*, 97-105.

A University-Community Partnership
to Change Public Policy:
Pre-Conditions and Processes

Roni Kaufman, PhD

SUMMARY. This paper describes a project aimed at promoting major change in government policy toward the growing problem of food insecurity in Israel. The project was initiated by Ben-Gurion University in collaboration with community service and social advocacy organizations. This joint action led to a dramatic change in government activity. The problem of food insecurity moved from a state of obfuscation to the establishment of a special ministerial committee mandated to develop policy guidelines for a national school lunch program. For higher education to contribute to the community, necessary preconditions must exist: Is the faculty committed to promotion of social change? Do the organizational and community environments legitimize university-sponsored activity for such purposes? Is the faculty competent to act effectively in the community and adopt strategies for political influence? Are there organizational mechanisms, action frameworks, and community contacts that enable collaboration for the purposes of social change? This case discussion uses the

Roni Kaufman is Assistant Professor, Social Work Department, Ben-Gurion University, P.O. Box 653, Beer-Sheva, 84105, Israel (E-mail: ronika@bgumail.bgu.ac.il).

[Haworth co-indexing entry note]: "A University-Community Partnership to Change Public Policy: Pre-Conditions and Processes." Kaufman, Roni. Co-published simultaneously in *Journal of Community Practice* (The Haworth Social Work Practice Press, an imprint of The Haworth Press, Inc.) Vol. 12, No. 3/4, 2004, pp. 163-180; and: *University-Community Partnerships: Universities in Civic Engagement* (ed: Tracy M. Soska, and Alice K. Johnson Butterfield) The Haworth Social Work Practice Press, an imprint of The Haworth Press, Inc., 2004, pp. 163-180. Single or multiple copies of this article are available for a fee from The Haworth Document Delivery Service [1-800-HAWORTH, 9:00 a.m. - 5:00 p.m. (EST). E-mail address: docdelivery@haworthpress.com].

http://www.haworthpress.com/web/COM
Digital Object Identifier: 10.1300/J125v12n03_10

163

analytical framework developed by Taylor (1985) to evaluate the preconditions for action and the processes involved in facilitating university-community collaboration for promoting policy change. *[Article copies available for a fee from The Haworth Document Delivery Service: 1-800-HAWORTH. E-mail address: <docdelivery@haworthpress.com> Website: <http://www.HaworthPress. com> © 2004 by The Haworth Press, Inc. All rights reserved.]*

KEYWORDS. University-community partnership, public policy, social change, community organizing, food security, hunger

INTRODUCTION

The decline of the welfare state in Israel, the conservative political climate, the erosion of social services and benefits, and the ongoing economic recession have exacerbated social problems such as unemployment and poverty, and have generated new ones, such as food insecurity and hunger. This situation is not exclusive to Israel, but is a global phenomenon the roots of which lie in economic globalization (Riches, 1997). The moral imperative that the social work profession promote social justice and demand activism (Mary, 2001) is embodied in the social workers' codes of ethics around the world (National Association of Social Workers, 2000; Mansbach, & Kaufman, 2003). In light of this imperative and of changing social conditions, social work organizations, including schools of social work and universities, must adapt their modus operandi to the new reality. One way higher education shows its involvement is through activity designed to solve social problems and promote social justice (Boyer, 1990; Hackney, 1986; Bringle, Games, & Malloy, 1999). Some schools have risen to the challenge by offering specializations in political social work and moral practice (Fisher, 2001) or by training students to work in social-change organizations and political frameworks (Moore & Johnston, 2002). Other institutions combine new curricula with innovative teaching methods, such as social activism, action research, and coalition building (Mizrahi, 2001).

The growing trend toward academic involvement in improving the community, and the imperative to teach community and social change intervention strategies to social work students, have given rise to the development of university-community projects integrating academic and community social change approaches. Through field experience and class work, students experience methods of social activism and contribute to meaningful community change while their teachers act as role models providing past knowledge, skills, and values. This enhances the students' commitment to act as social change agents after completing their studies.

In collaboration with eighteen local community human service agencies and two national social advocacy organizations, a community project for the promotion of social justice was initiated by faculty members and students of the Social Work Department at Ben-Gurion University of the Negev (hereafter: the Department). Aimed at promoting the right to food security in Israel, the project was designed to change the professional and public discourse on the subject, raise awareness, activate university and community agencies and organizations, and pressure policy makers to address the problem.

The project is described based on the experience of the author of this article as observer-participant, on documentation of the activity and publication in university newsletters, local and national newspapers, and on twenty detailed reports by students who took an active part. The experience gained in this project helps answer practical questions regarding higher education mobilization for social change: What conditions favor university-community collaboration for social change? What roles can schools of social work play in promoting community action aimed at influencing public policies? How can the impact of the intervention on the social problem, the community, and the university be evaluated?

PRECONDITIONS FOR ACADEMIC MOBILIZATION

Community-university collaboration for social change, like other collaborations and partnerships, should meet the traditional standards and roles of the university and community organizations. It should also confer benefits such as prestige and legitimacy on the parties involved within the university and the community (Battistoni & Hudson, 1997; Bailey & Koney, 1995; Zlotkowski, 1998).

Schools of social work are involved in the community as part of their traditional missions to train students, promote service and conduct research. Generally, however, they have not been involved in promoting social change because social activism by institutes of higher education can generate conflict. Both dissimilar organizational cultures, as well as power struggles can cause conflicts between university and community agencies (Austin et al., 1999). In addition, the activity requires a considerable investment of resources, and tends to be controversial due to different organizational priorities and agendas within the university and its departments, and even among faculty members (Staudt & Thurlow, 2000). Like universities, community service agencies do not see their main role as social change agents (Specht & Courtney, 1994). In particular, community services that are government-sponsored, as are most Israeli service organizations, traditionally shrink from involvement in social activism (Mansbach & Kaufman, 2003).

What are the conditions and factors conducive to activism by institutes of higher education? Borrowing from an analytical framework developed by Taylor (1985), three main preconditions for the involvement of mainstream social work organizations in social-change activities. These include commitment, legitimacy, and individual and organizational competency. These three preconditions can be applied to universities and communities in the process of their collaboration for social change. First, university administration, dean, faculty members and students must feel a *commitment* to promoting social change, wish to take an active role on social issues, and be prepared to change their priorities to enable the activity to take place. Second, the target community must perceive social activism by the university as *legitimate*, positive (fostering good relations), and innocuous (not endangering the status of organizations that already exist in the community). Legitimacy is particularly important because the university's involvement in social change could disrupt the balance of power within the community. Nonetheless, commitment and legitimacy are not enough for the success of academic social activism. To effectively exploit these factors requires *competency*, including expert knowledge of the issues involved, the processes of social change, and community organizing. In addition, structures must be developed to foster university-community collaboration, and to assume leadership and responsibility (c.f., Austin et al., 1999). The development of these preconditions for action and the way they facilitated university-community collaboration for promoting policy in Israel are described.

BACKGROUND

The Problem of Food Insecurity

By 1999, following reports by students and service agencies that clients were suffering from hunger, faculty members of the Social Work Department at the Ben Gurion University of the Negev became aware of the increasing severity of the problem of food insecurity and hunger. The increase in poverty among low income people in Israel, of which hunger is a new and extreme manifestation, is not surprising. It is the outcome of major cuts in social services and National Insurance allocations in recent years (Swirski, 2002). The Negev area, one of the most socially and economically vulnerable regions in the country, has suffered greatly from these policies. It has the largest number of income-supplement recipients in Israel, and the Bedouin population (25% of the region's population) is the poorest in Israel (Korazim, 2003).

Although hunger in Israel is an unfamiliar problem, the Israeli government responded by ignoring or obfuscating the problem. It made no efforts to measure the extent of the problem, identify populations at risk, or devise solutions and programs to eradicate or reduce the problem. The government's only response was to encourage community and voluntary activity, as demonstrated by then Prime Minster Ehud Barak's request in 1999 to "open their hearts to the needy." The feeling among the public at large and among professionals and policy makers was that this was a passing crisis that could be solved by voluntary activity (Kaufman, 2001a). No community agencies or even social advocacy organizations demanded a change of policy.

In March 2000, the Department sponsored a public conference titled "Is there hunger in Israel?" at which members of the community and experts debated the problem. Following this conference, the problem of food security and hunger became a major focus of investigation in community intervention courses both on the graduate and undergraduate levels. The more the problem was investigated, the clearer it became that something should be done. The problem was increasing and needs were not being met. Since no institutions, agencies, or policy makers were taking action, it became clear that the Department would have to take a leading role to change these dynamics. This conviction reinforced the faculty and student commitment to social justice as a necessary precondition for social action. Faculty also saw this as an opportunity to integrate the theoretical teaching of social change and community organizing with real life practice.

Three developments, two of which were not directly connected to the problem of hunger, also occurred in 2000 and contributed to fulfilling the preconditions that enabled mobilization. These developments were the addition of social change courses to the curriculum and the promotion of action research, the establishment of a faculty-student forum for social justice, and the start of a university-community sponsored soup kitchen. The Department added social change oriented courses to the curriculum to enhance the willingness and competence of the students to engage in social action. Since then, all first-year students are sent for their field placement to voluntary social-change organizations. In addition, courses that compliment field experience, such as "Building Community Coalitions and Partnerships" and "Community Action Research for Social Change" have been added to the BSW and MSW programs. Community action research integrates academic research with activities to promote change (c.f., Stoecker & Beckwith, 1992). Research of this type helps the community to define problems in an operative manner. It provides needed data for action, empowers the participants in the research, establishes foci of power within the community and activates a previously passive community (Rubin & Rubin, 1992). "The Joint Forum of Faculty and Students for Social Justice" (hereafter: the Forum) was also established in 2000. It continues on a voluntary, informal basis, and is headed by a faculty member with experience in the field of community organizing. The Forum initiated a number of community action activities on issues of social justice. In varying degrees, most of the Department's students and faculty participated in these activities. The more active students gained practical experience in community mobilization for social change. In addition, working relations evolved between the Forum and agencies in the community, such as the Union of Social Workers, social services in the Negev, advocacy organizations, clients' organizations, and the local and national media.

The third useful development was the establishment of a soup kitchen in 2000 by the Department faculty and students in collaboration with the university administration and community service agencies. The soup kitchen, the first of its kind in the region, was highly regarded by the community because it provided a needed service (Dafna-Tkoa & Witenberg, 2001). The soup kitchen also provided an opportunity for interested students and faculty to study the problem of hunger. However, an evaluation of the soup kitchen's activity and limitations (Kaufman, 2001a) as well as an assessment of the literature in fighting hunger in the US and other countries (c.f., Eisinger, 1998; Riches, 1997), led faculty and students to believe that voluntary activity can provide only a partial solution. Faculty and students who investigated the issue concluded that a new strategy must be developed to respond to the growing needs in the community. Taken together, these developments strengthened the Department's sense of commitment and sense of the legitimacy, while enhancing individual and organizational competencies.

THE MOBILIZATION PROCESS

Setting Objectives

In 2001, graduate students, most of whom were experienced field workers and directors of welfare agencies in the region, conducted a comprehensive analysis of the problem of hunger as a part of their community field placement. Aimed at changing the public state of inactivity regarding the policy aspects of the food security and hunger, the plan had three main objectives. The first objective was to define food insecurity as a social problem, thereby engendering a commitment to solving it. This meant fostering processes that would lead to a measurement and definition of the problem in a way that would transform the public and professional discourse. It was essential to cease treating food insecurity as a minor, episodic problem that could be handled by volunteers, and begin seeing it as a major growing complex social problem. Hunger needed to be seen as social problem that required a comprehensive public policy response. In order to define food insecurity as a problem, it was necessary first to collect data, to identify the population at risk, and to devise necessary concepts (Eisinger, 1998).

The second objective was to frame solutions based on the principle of social entitlement, thereby legitimizing the effort. According to Riches (1997), existing programs for combating hunger and food insecurity are, to a greater or lesser degree, associated with stigma. For example, programs based on voluntarism, such as soup kitchens, are perceived as stigmatizing. Programs based on social rights, such as income supplement allowances, are perceived as furthering choice and dignity. It was therefore important to develop alternatives to local and national policy, predicated on "the right to food security." By defining food security as a social problem, the Department legitimized the participation of various community organizations in the public discourse regarding alternative solutions and services for victims. The third objective was to mobilize the university and community for policy change. The aim was to identify potential partners within the university and within the community, and to encourage them to collaborate and to take action to promote change.

Researching the Problem

In December 2002, under the supervision of faculty members, students conducted a community survey to measure levels of food security.

This was the first survey of its kind in Israel to use the Food Security Core Survey Module (U.S. Department of Agriculture, 1999), an instrument widely used to measure food insecurity and hunger (Holben, 2002). The students surveyed 953 clients of 23 social services in 11 localities in the Negev, including cities, development towns, and Bedouin settlements. The goal of the survey was to examine the degree of food security among various population groups that are potentially at risk (Kaufman, Slonim-Nevo, & Anson, 2002). The questionnaire, which included the Food Security Core Survey Module and other questions, was developed by Department researchers and a group of students from the Community Action Research course.

A major challenge in conducting the survey was to secure the cooperation of the community services whose clients were the target population. In order to overcome concerns, especially among governmental service agencies, a strategy combining formal and informal tactics was used. The formal tactics included sending a letter from the Dean to all the service agencies in the region that provide field practicum placements for the students. The letter explained the importance of the research and its implications for policy change. It also offered the agencies several forms of assistance. These included the services of students to conduct the research, help with data analysis of the food security situation of the clients of each service, and faculty supervision and consultation for agencies interested in developing projects to promote food security for their clients. Informally, especially in the case of governmental service, graduate students employed in the service suggested to their superiors that the students conduct the survey as part of their academic work. This tactic was very successful and the students formed the bridge that enabled the mobilization and cooperation of eighteen agencies.

The findings of the survey (Table 1) caused tremendous repercussions. They received abundant media attention, including a front page headline article in one of the national newspapers (Sinai, 2002). The findings showed that only 28% of the households surveyed enjoyed food security, and that 50% of the children were at risk. The survey also found that twice as many Bedouin households suffered from food insecurity and hunger as did Jewish households (Kaufman et al., 2002). The report and the research findings were disseminated among community groups, professional agencies, and political institutions.

Strategies for Organizing

In the wake of these findings, a conference titled "The Right to Food Security" was sponsored by the Forum at Ben Gurion University. The

TABLE 1. Food Security Among Welfare Services Clients in the Negev Area

	Food Secure	Children–Not At Risk	Food Insecure– with Hunger Evident	Children–At Risk
All sample	28%	50%	72%	50%
Jewish households	33%	40%	67%	60%
Bedouin households	10%	87%	90%	13%

purpose of the Conference was to discuss the findings and implications of the survey. The Conference was organized in collaboration with the community service organizations that participated in the survey. Speakers at the conference included the President of the University, representatives of service organizations, a representative of food-insecure and hungry families, social policy and public health experts from the university, food pantry heads, and community service organization directors. The conference proposed an alternative to voluntarism in the fight against hunger among disadvantaged populations in Israel (Alush, 2002, December, 26). Following the conference, the Forum launched a public campaign to promote the right to food security. The campaign strategy included the collection of signatures for a petition and the formation of a public lobby of organizations and institutions to campaign for eliminating hunger among schoolchildren. The petition demanded that the government take steps to measure the level of food security in Israel and to develop programs to help the food-insecure and hungry. Signatures were collected from both social services employees and their clients in an attempt transform the professional discourse on the issue and encourage clients to organize. Hundreds of students rallied round the petition drive, and more than five thousand signatures were collected.

The Forum began the formation of a public lobby by convincing the leaders of two major national social change organizations, Yadid (The Association for Community Empowerment in Israel) and Shatil (The Empowerment and Training Center for Social Change Organizations in Israel), to collaborate in promoting the right to food security. The collaboration was established following another conference at the University which focused on child food security. This specific issue was selected because it was evaluated as meaningful for many in the community, widely felt, and potentially winnable (see, for example, Bobo,

Kendall & Max, 2001). The collaboration led to the formulation of the National School Lunch Program Bill, drafted by a lobby of Knesset (parliament) members from both the opposition and the coalition. The lobby was led by Knesset members Yuli Tamir (Labor–opposition) and Eti Livni (Shinui–coalition) (David, 2003; Yadid, 2004b). In addition, a pressure group consisting of parents' groups and professionals was organized for a campaign aimed at mobilizing grass roots support for the bill.

The joint campaign led to impressive results. A three month national petition drive in support of the school lunch bill secured one hundred thousand signatures (Yadid, 2004a). The growing public support for the bill led the Israeli Prime Minster, Arik Sharon, to establish a special task force which includes four ministers, among them the influential Treasury Minister, Bibi Natanyahu. The task force is mandated to develop guidelines for the operation of a national school food program (Alon, 2004). The vote on the bill and the presentation of the recommendations of the Ministerial Committee are expected soon.

Finally, based on collaboration between the services that participated in the research and interested faculty members, a number of community and research projects were developed. Those graduate students who were also agency workers played the role of a bridge between the university and the community. As part of their course work, they developed projects to promote research and food security at the local level and for special populations. One such project was a task force established in the city of Dimona to promote community food security whose recommendations won the support of Dimona's newly elected mayor (Azulai, 2003). Another was a study focused on food security problems among Bedouin populations and on alternative ways of addressing the special needs of this unique population (Bader & Saai'd, 2003).

In summation, the university-community mobilization to promote food security comprised two main stages. The preparatory stage (preconditions) fostered commitment, developed skills, expertise, and community legitimacy, and created the necessary frameworks for intervention. In this stage, initial contacts for contending with the problem were made, and frameworks were established to enable integration between teaching and research on the one hand, and community-based intervention for social change, on the other. Two frameworks were established: an academic framework (the Community Action Research Course and other community practice courses) and an organizational framework (the Forum for Social Justice). The intervention stage fostered research and public action aimed at influencing the professional and public discourse. Through the introduction of new research findings and concepts, community organizations were mobilized to demand concrete solutions.

EVALUATION

The social change project attempted to achieve two different, but interdependent goals. The first was a political goal: to raise community awareness and organize it to pressure the decision makers to change policies. The second was an academic goal: to instill the values and skills associated with social activism and social change in the university community.

Public Policy Goals

With social-change activity, it is hard to prove a direct correlation between effort invested and impact on public policy. Among other constraints, the process is lengthy, comprises many intermediate stages, and involves a variety of players (Dery, 1984). Nevertheless, this evaluation focuses on the attainment of the three objectives outlined in Forum's work plan: redefining hunger as food insecurity, framing solutions based on the principle of social entitlement, and mobilizing the community. The university-community activities helped to redefine the problem of hunger through conducting research and disseminating the findings. As a result of these efforts, the term "food security" has replaced the general term "hunger" in public discourse. "Food security" has become an integral part of the debate on the issue of poverty and deprivation in Israel. The Minister of Welfare, for example, has begun using the phrase "the right to food security" in connection with children (David, 2003). The research findings and the successful use of the food security measurement index have encouraged some major Israeli social research institutions, including the Ministry of Health, to include the Food Security Core Survey Module in their current research (Brookdale Institute, 2003).

The Prime Minister's support and the establishment of the governmental task force represent progress, but as yet the National School Lunch Program Bill has not been passed and no policy guidelines have been developed. The scale and nature of the school lunch program are undetermined. Furthermore, the Finance Minister estimates the cost of the program at 200-500 million American dollars (Alon, 2004). The government, which recently made additional cuts in social budgets, may not allocate the funds necessary to supplement donations and parents' participation in the costs.

It was important to increase community activity in order to promote solutions to the problem. One success in this context was the mobilization of two major social-change organizations to place the struggle for the national school lunch program on their agendas and to work in coordination with the Forum on promoting legislation followed by a grass roots campaign (David, 2003). Another success was the local community food security projects developed by students based on collaboration between the Welfare Service and faculty members. There is also evidence of a change of direction in the public media debate on hunger. The debate, which in the past focused on the major role of voluntarism in solving the problem, now links social policy with food insecurity. It calls for the government to assume responsibility and guarantee food security as a social right, especially for children (Ochayon, Daskal, & Dror, 2003; David, 2003). Nonetheless, the process of formulating policy on food security is still in its infancy, and the real struggle over policy alternatives has yet to take place.

Academic Goals

One of the main academic goals was to instill the values and skills of social activism and social change by offering practical experience in the field to students and the academic community. Most of the students and faculty members in the Department participated in the project to some extent. The students participating in the Community Action Research and in the Forum were the most active. Others were involved through participating in the survey, the petition drive, or by focusing on the problem of hunger in their course work. For most of the students, this was their first experience of organized activity for social change.

The expertise acquired through the project led several faculty members to collaborate in conducting research on various aspects of food security among special populations such as Bedouins, new immigrants, elderly, and drug addicts. Moreover, the extensive publicity the project received in the university newsletters, the Negev regional media, and national media added to the reputation of the Social Work Department and the Ben Gurion University administration as leaders in community involvement and social change activism.

DISCUSSION

The Role of the University

This paper describes the active role played by the Department of Social Work and the University in collaboration with the community in order to promote social change. This role is not a traditional role of a higher education institution. Schools that wish to enhance their contribution to the community must first determine whether the necessary preconditions exist: Is the faculty committed to the social-change activity? Does the organizational and community environment legitimize the university sponsored social-change activity? Is the faculty competent, on both a theoretical and practical level, to act effectively in the community and adopt strategies for political influence relating to the problem at hand? Are there organizational mechanisms, action frameworks, and community contacts that enable involvement for the purposes of social change?

An analysis of the project demonstrates that apart from these prerequisites, other factors such as the academic context and agenda are important. In this particular case, the activity complemented and was consistent with the changes in the curriculum that promote social-change values, and with the university administration's emphasis on community involvement. This facilitated the allocation of necessary resources, especially precious time by both faculty and students. The activity also complemented the research agenda of some faculty members who were exploring various aspects of hunger, poverty, and social change. In order to ease the burden on students and faculty alike, the activity was integrated into existing curricular frameworks, such as courses, field practice, and research.

The university's main function was that of catalyst and organizer. Due to the absence of any organized activity in the outside community to define the problem or devise effective strategies, these functions did not clash with community organizations. The university's role as catalyst found concrete expression in research and public activities designed to expose the extent of the problem, and thereby change the community discourse. The Department played the role of organizer by encouraging various organizations in the community, particularly social-change organizations, to participate in defining the problem, developing alternatives, and demanding solutions from policy-makers. The success of this activity, in the short space of an academic year, indicates that the role of catalyst in conducting initial organizing activities is compatible with higher education institutions, and can be implemented by dedicated faculty leaders. This is because the catalyst role provides a high level of control by the University over the nature of the project, its emphases, and schedule.

In this case, the main challenges were on the intra-organizational level: mobilizing and organizing students, faculty, and university administration for non-traditional university-community collaboration. A useful strategy in gaining support was the emphasis on maintaining high academic standards, particularly in research and community intervention, and the use of traditional academic practices such as research and conferences at the university.

Challenges for University-Community Collaboration

At the inter-organizational level, the challenge was mobilization community organizations to join the efforts of the university. Like the university, service organizations are not traditionally involved in social change activities. A useful tactic for promoting trust and minimizing participation costs was encouraging graduate students who were also workers in the services to act as a bridge between academia and the community. The data and analysis on food security by the university enabled the advocacy organizations, which were not familiar with the problem of food insecurity, to get media exposure. This was a meaningful participation benefit. The ongoing formal and informal relationships of the university and individual faculty members with the community services and the advocacy organizations promoted the collaboration.

The evolving partnership between the university and the advocacy organizations in order to promote the National School Lunch Bill requires changes in the role played by the university with these organizations. Acting as a partner has its own issues and difficulties both for university and community organizations. Conflicts may arise due to differences in organizational culture, pre-existing tensions among community organizations (inter-organizational rivalry, prestige, resources investment), and differences in values and modus operandi (Kaufman, 2001b). Much time is invested in trying to solve these conflicts. Therefore, the development of work procedures, the sharing of responsibility, and setting in place coordination and decision-making mechanisms is imperative (Austin et al., 1999).

Higher education practitioners who are interested in organizing university-community collaborations and partnerships for social change should be aware of the complexity of such activity. Commitment, legitimacy, and competency (Taylor, 1985) are the minimal preconditions. Other prerequisites are prior definition of, and agreement to, clear intervention objectives, and an obligation to continue with the activity until the objectives are met. The intervention creates expectations and elicits cooperation by various groups and organizations in the hope of receiving resources from the community change agent, in this case, the academic institution.

CONCLUSION

Current socio-economic policies in Israel exacerbate social problems and even create new ones, such as food insecurity and hunger. The apathy and ineptitude of the authorities place greater responsibility on social workers, who are forced to seek answers on how to meet growing needs by increasing numbers of clients. Collaboration between the university and community agencies can modify this situation. Influencing social policy and promoting values of social justice are an integral part of the social work profession. It is the task of schools of social work to impart these values to students and to teach them intervention strategies aimed at bringing about social change. The universities' growing recognition of the need for academic intervention in addressing social problems enables faculty and students to promote social change values while conducting their traditional academic work.

Involvement in the community is not the exclusive province of the social work department. Other university departments that have links with the community, in fields such as medicine and public health, education, law, administration, and political science, also have a part to play in promoting social change. Institutions of higher education are not social-change organizations. They are dedicated to research and teaching. However, the involvement of higher education with community agencies related to social policy can result in positive outcome for both community and university.

REFERENCES

Alon, G. (2004, January 13). A special Ministers committee was appointed to established food program to children in the school system. *Ha'Aretz*. (Hebrew).

Alush, Z. (2002, December, 26). "Study: About half the disadvantaged households in the south suffer from hunger." *Yediot Aharonot*. (Hebrew).

Austin, M.J. et al. (1999). Building a comprehensive agency-university partnership: A case study of the Bay Area social services consortium. *Journal of Community Practice*, *6*(3), 89-106.

Azulai, E. (2003). Promoting community food security in Dimona–guidelines for action. Unpublished student paper, practicum in community intervention. (Hebrew).

Bader, A., & Saai'd, A. (2003). Promoting community food security in Bedouin towns–guidelines for action. Unpublished student paper, practicum in community intervention. (Hebrew)

Bailey, D., & Koney, K.M. (1995). Community-based consortia: One model for creation and development. *Journal of Community Practice*, *2*, 1-20.

Battistoni, R., & Hudson, W. (Eds.). (1997). *Practicing democracy: Concepts and models of service learning in political science*. Washington, DC: American Association for Higher Education.

Bobo, K., Kendall, J., & Max, S. (2001). *Organizing for social change: Midwest Academy manual for activists* (3rd Edition). Santa Ana: Seven Locks Press.

Boyer, E. (1990). *Scholarship reconsidered: Priorities of the professorate*. Princeton: The Carnegie Foundation for the Advancement of Teaching.

Bringle, R., Games, R., & Malloy, E. (Eds.). (1999). *Colleges and universities as citizens*. Needham Heights, MA: Allyn & Bacon.

Brookdale Institute. (2003). *Update on food security in Israel: Highlights of the findings*. Jerusalem: JDC-Brookdale Institute.

Dafna-Tkoa, S., & Witenberg, T. (2001). The establishment of "Beer-Sova" food kitchen–A community development perspective. Beer-Sheva: Department of Social Work, Ben-Gurion University, unpublished manuscript. (Hebrew).

David, M. (2003, May 9). "If there's no food, there are food stamps. The state will distribute food stamps to needy families and hot meals to hungry pupils." *Ma'ariv*. (Hebrew).

Dery, D. (1984). *Problem definition in policy analysis*. Kansas: University Press of Kansas.

Eisinger, P.K. (1998). *Towards an end to hunger in America*. Washington, DC: Brooking Institute Press.

Fisher, R., Weedman, A., Alex, G., & Stout, K.D. (2001). Graduate education for social change: A study of political social workers. *Journal of Community Practice*, *9*(4), 43-65

Hackney, S. (1986). The university and its community: Past and present. *Annals of the American Academy of Political and Social Sciences*, 488, 137-147.

Holben, D.H. (2002). An overview of food security and its measurement. *Nutrition Today*, *37*(4), 176-189.

Kaufman, R. (2001a). Who are the "Food organizations" in Israel?–Initial findings. Israeli Center for Third Sector Research, Ben Gurion University, Beer-Sheva, Israel. (Hebrew).

Kaufman, R. (2001b). Coalition activity of social change organizations: Motives, resources and processes. *Journal of Community Practice*, *9*(4), 21-42.

Kaufman, R., Slonim-Nevo, V., & Anson, J. (2002). *Food security in the Negev–Research report*. Beer-Sheva: Department of Social Work, Ben-Gurion University. (Hebrew).

Korazim, Y. (2003). *Children at risk in Bedouin municipalities of the Negev*. Jerusalem: Ministry of Welfare and Labor. (Hebrew).

Mansbach, A., & Kaufman, R. (2003). Ethical decision making of social workers' associations: A case study of the Israeli Social Workers Association's responses to whistle blowing. *International Social Work, 46*(3), 1-12.

Mary, N.L. (2001). Political activism of social work educators. *Journal of Community Practice, 9*(4), 1-20.

Mizrahi, T. (2001). The status of community organizing in social work at the end of the 20th century: Community practice context, complexities, contradictions and contributions. *Research on Social Work Practice, 11*(2), 176-189.

Moore, L.S., & Johnston, L.B. (2002). Involving students in political advocacy and social change. *Journal of Community Practice, 10*(2), 89-101.

National Association of Social Workers. (2000). *A framework for the social work profession in international development*. Washington, DC: National Presidential Initiative Task Force.

Ochayon, K., Daskal, H., & Dror, N. (2003). *Position paper and a program, for the Ministry of Welfare, to fight food insecurity*. Jerusalem: Mandel Institute. (Hebrew).

Riches, G. (1997). Hunger and the welfare state: Comparative perspectives. In G. Riches (Ed.). *First world hunger: Food security and welfare politics* (pp. 1-13). London: McMillan.

Rubin, H.J., & Rubin, I.S. (1992). *Community organizing and development* (2nd.ed.). NY: Macmillan Publishing.

Sinai, R. (2002, December 24). Most clients of the social services are potentially hungry. *Ha'Aretz*, p. 1. (Hebrew).

Specht, H., & Courtney, M. (1994). *Unfaithful angels*. New York: Free Press.

Staudt K., & Thurlow, B.C. (2000). Higher education engages with community: New policies and inevitable political complexities Retrieved October 1, 2003, from *COMM-ORG: The On-Line Conference on Community Organizing and Development*. http://comm-org.utoledo.edu/papers.htm

Stoecker, R., & Beckwith, D. (1992). Advancing Toledo? Neighborhood movement through participatory action research: Integrating activist and academic approaches. *Clinical Sociology Review*, 10, 198-213.

Swirski, S. (2002). *The State of Israel against the Welfare State*. Tel Aviv: Adva Center. (Hebrew).

Taylor, S.H. (1985). Community work and social work: The community liaison approach. In R.W. Roberts & S.H. Taylor (Eds.). *Theory and practice of community social work* (pp. 191-205). NY: Columbia University Press.

U.S. Department of Agriculture (1999). Retrieved October 1, 2002, from http://www.ers.usda.gov/Briefing/Food Security/surveytools/FS_SHORT.doc

Yadid. (2004a, January 12). *Press Release: A call for the Prime Minster: Keep your promise for the school food program and call the coalition to support the bill (to be voted upon on January 25)*. Jerusalem: Yadid, The Association for Community Empowerment in Israel. (Hebrew).

Yadid. (2004b, February 14). *Press Release: A national poll reveals: 87% of the Israeli public support the school food program and 80% are ready to pay if for their child's lunch*. Jerusalem: Yadid, The Association for Community Empowerment in Israel. (Hebrew).

Zlotkowski, E. (1998). *Successful service learning programs: New models of excellence in higher education*. Boston: Anker Publishing.

THE PROCESSES OF CIVIC ENGAGEMENT

Partnerships and Processes of Engagement: Working as Consultants in the US and UK

Jeremy Kearney, MSc, CQSW
Denys M. Candy, MSW

SUMMARY. Government policy in both the United States (US) and United Kingdom (UK) has given increased importance to the concept and practice of partnership. Indeed, partnerships have become a key requirement of most community-based activities. This article explores the nature of partnerships and the need to see partnership as a process committed to engaging all participants. Some examples of partnerships with

---

Jeremy Kearney is Director, Centre for Social Research and Practice, University of Sunderland, England. Denys M. Candy is Managing Partner, Community Partners Institute, Pittsburgh, PA.

Address correspondence to: Jeremy Kearney, MSc, Director, Centre for Social Research and Practice, University of Sunderland, Priestman Building, Green Terrace, Sunderland, SR1 3PZ, England (E-mail: jeremy.kearney@sunderland.ac.uk).

[Haworth co-indexing entry note]: "Partnerships and Processes of Engagement: Working as Consultants in the US and UK." Kearney, Jeremy, and Denys M. Candy. Co-published simultaneously in *Journal of Community Practice* (The Haworth Social Work Practice Press, an imprint of The Haworth Press, Inc.) Vol. 12, No. 3/4, 2004, pp. 181-201; and: *University-Community Partnerships: Universities in Civic Engagement* (ed: Tracy M. Soska, and Alice K. Johnson Butterfield) The Haworth Social Work Practice Press, an imprint of The Haworth Press, Inc., 2004, pp. 181-201. Single or multiple copies of this article are available for a fee from The Haworth Document Delivery Service [1-800-HAWORTH, 9:00 a.m. - 5:00 p.m. (EST). E-mail address: docdelivery@haworthpress.com].

http://www.haworthpress.com/web/COM
Digital Object Identifier: 10.1300/J125v12n03_11

university-community links from both countries demonstrate the use of a range of consulting skills and creative techniques for facilitating effective collaborative action among community organizations and university partners. The article features the role of consultants in planning, developing, and implementing high engagement techniques in the development of community partnerships. *[Article copies available for a fee from The Haworth Document Delivery Service: 1-800-HAWORTH. E-mail address: <docdelivery@haworthpress.com> Website: <http://www.HaworthPress.com> © 2004 by The Haworth Press, Inc. All rights reserved.]*

KEYWORDS: Partnerships, processes of engagement, consultants, engagement techniques, university-community collaboration, international

INTRODUCTION

In both the US and the UK the notion of partnership has become a key focus in many community-based activities (Audit Commission, 1998; Hudson, 1999; Delgado, 2000; Margolis et al., 2000; Maurrasse, 2001; Glendinning, Powell, & Rummery, 2002). Government policy in both countries often assumes that its agencies will form partnerships with local voluntary organizations and not-for-profit groups and local authorities are required to collaborate with the private sector. Most importantly, all of these organizations are expected to involve members of the local communities affected by the partnerships. Although this rhetoric of partnership is not new, what is meant by the term is by no means self-evident. Powell and Glendinning (2002, p. 2) have suggested that "partnership risks becoming a 'Humpty Dumpty' term ('when I call something a partnership, by definition it is one')." In a report on partnership, The Audit Commission (1998), an independent body established in the UK to ensure that public money is spent properly, described it as a "slippery concept" that is difficult to define.

We believe that Murphy and Cunningham's (2003) description of sound planning applies equally to partnering: success depends on "patience, flexibility and the ability to meld disparate interests" (p. 155). This is difficult to attain without paying due attention to the processes of partnership–that is, the factors that are important in establishing and maintaining partnership relationships. Thus, public and private agencies that require partnership as a matter of policy risk constructing top-down relationships that re-enact the very social hierarchies that such collaboration is intended to defuse. In some contexts in the UK, for example, partnership is required as a duty and the Government has powers to take over what it regards as "failing" partnerships (Clarke & Glendinning, 2002).

This article is concerned not so much with the issue of partnership per se or how partnership is defined, but rather with the question: What are some of the processes that enable a partnership to work? How do we align the rhetoric that "we must have a partnership" with actual collaborative practice between different people, organizations and communities? We describe the development of collaborative practice between different people, organizations and communities as "processes of engagement." The processes of engagement are ways that enable people to work together on the basis of trust, reciprocity and shared purpose. In turn, it is these elements that are generally recognized as some of the important aspects of a successful partnership (Hudson & Hardy, 2002). These high engagement processes draw on Spano's treatment of public dialogue (Spano, 2001). He recommends a methodology of facilitation that is "always customised to fit the unique circumstances of each community and each public dialogue event" (p. 37). Such processes must necessarily rely on a practitioner's repertoire of basic methods and skills, as well as the ability to improvise in real time. Often, these engagement processes are ignored, undervalued or taken for granted. This lack of attention can lead to a dilemma which we call the *partnership paradox*. The partnership paradox occurs in situations in which an inherent and often unstable tension exists between the aims of the leading institution or funding organization and the desire to involve the members of local communities in a positive way.

To address the question of how to facilitate a high engagement process between individuals, organizations and local communities, we outline an approach used by the authors as consultants. We detail some of the techniques and tools used in our work as consultants to facilitate processes of engagement and demonstrate these in practice. Three case examples with university-community links from both the US and the UK are used to illustrate various types of high engagement techniques and the methods used to facilitate the development of partnership organizations.

The Partnership Paradox

Partnership is often seen as a "thing" which can be created by bringing a group of people together or by following a fixed series of steps. This approach is consistent with the rational social planning model in which emphasis is placed on convening a group, gathering data, crafting a solution, and moving into action (Rothman, 1995). However, the social planning model does not pay attention to the "spirit and design of the process itself" (Murphy & Cunningham, 2003, p. 155). Process is not seen as a critical component. Though skilled in other areas, people involved in convening may lack abilities in facilitating participation, which, in turn, can lead to misunderstanding and failure (Daley & Marsiglia, 2000). By this way of working, either a great deal of time and energy is spent in trying to deal with difficulties and conflicts that have been brought forth, or alternatively, one of the stronger groups decides to take control and directs the way the partnership should go. Not surprisingly, either scenario can lead to a great deal of dissatisfaction in the partnership and, in the worst cases, to its dissolution.

In contrast, partnership should be seen as a "process" which is formed through collaboration with other groups and which changes and develops over time (Wiewel & Lieber, 1998, p. 2). This view of partnership is especially important if desired change is to emerge in complex systems. This approach is more reflexive. It focuses both on the process of collaborating and on its outcomes, and sees the two as interconnected in a reciprocal relationship. Knowledge about the partnership itself informs each developing stage (Arches, 2001). Thus, how the partnership is set up, resourced and facilitated, and how imbalances of power are dealt with, affect the outcomes achieved. Conversely, if potential outcomes are prescribed in a rigid manner, this will influence the collaboration process.

Health Action Zones

Health Action Zones (HAZ) are multi-agency partnerships established in the UK to bring together all those involved with the health of a local community to work towards improving it. In the initial stages, a key HAZ obligation is the involvement of local people and local communities to devise new ways of facilitating and developing a collaborative process. As a result, many of the Health Action Zones spend a considerable amount of time working on ways to involve local people in deciding the most appropriate health priorities for their particular community (Barnes, Sullivan, & Matka, 2001; Clarke, Carr, Jones, Molyneux, & Procter, 2002). However, mid-way through the HAZ funding cycle, the Government introduced a change of policy and decided that all of the action zones should pursue three national government health priorities–cancer, coronary heart disease and mental health. These new constraints had negative effects on the partnership relationships within some of the HAZ schemes. For example, those who had decided after a local consultation process to concentrate on different areas such as young people's health were told that this was too narrow a focus, and that they needed to concentrate on national priorities (Barnes & Sullivan, 2002). The evaluation report on one particular HAZ described the negative effect of this decision:

> The HAZ "supported a growth in bottom up change that focused most directly onto the needs of the population. It was, therefore, all the more crushing for the work of the HAZ, for the Government to shift the agenda at the mid-point of the HAZ and orient it to the NHS (National Health Service) priorities." (Clarke et al., 2002, p. ii)

One way of understanding this unconstructive process is to see it as what has been called a "strange loop" (Cronen, Johnson, & Lanneman, 1982; Pearce, 1989). "Strange loops" occur when different levels of communication contradict each other and lead to a repeating pattern of unhelpful behaviour (see Figure 1). On the one hand, in the example above, the Government's overall agenda was to tackle health inequalities by achieving national priorities; on the other, it required facilitating local groups to meet their specific health needs. In practice, however, this is framed by an overall political message that the Government be seen as delivering improved health care. Thus, at the level of implementation, there are two contradictory stories within the overall aim of the Government's health policy. One message emphasizes the need to meet national priorities which leads to a specific message at the local level. The other message encourages collaborative partnerships and the involvement of local people in setting their own health agenda. The two stories are incommensurate.

If one follows the implications of the message on the left-hand side of the diagram, it leads to a position (fixed targets) which is at odds with the message on the right-hand side (local decisions). Consequently, there is a repeating loop between the two patterns of incompatible behaviours (Pearce, 1999). These loops are not merely contradictions, but take the form of a paradoxical or polarized pattern which operates like a figure eight rather than a circle (Oliver, 1996). As one story is told–that is, the importance of national priorities and the need to have set targets–it immediately brings forward the other story of community involvement and local decision making. Those involved in the particular context constantly "flip" from one story to the other. This paradox is held in place by the higher level stories of the need to address health in-

FIGURE 1. Different Levels of Communication that Create the "Partnership Paradox"

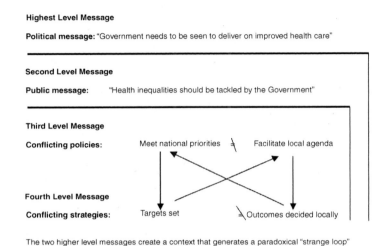

Highest Level Message

Political message: "Government needs to be seen to deliver on improved health care"

Second Level Message

Public message: "Health inequalities should be tackled by the Government"

Third Level Message

Conflicting policies: Meet national priorities   Facilitate local agenda

Fourth Level Message

Conflicting strategies: Targets set   Outcomes decided locally

The two higher level messages create a context that generates a paradoxical "strange loop" at the levels of policy and strategy oscillating between two conflicting agendas

Source: adapted from Pearce, 1989

equalities while at the same time showing that the Government is effective in delivering change.

Getting Out of the "Loop"

One of the ways out of these "loops" is by changing the higher level story which constrains those below it. In this case, for example, if the higher level story were the *importance of partnerships for achieving change*, this would have an impact on the levels below. As consultants, one of our purposes in focusing on the processes of engagement in working with partnerships is to make them (at least initially) a higher level story than that of achieving specific outcomes. In this context, it is interesting to note that while early evaluations of HAZ programs are promising, progress "was in many cases more about putting issues on the agenda and establishing systems and frameworks than actually realizing measurable change" (Bauld & Judge, 2002, p. 288).

In the US context, clarity of roles and expectations and self-awareness are emphasized as crucial components of partnerships (Arches,

2001). Moving from "acting upon" to "acting with" is seen as a valued outcome. For example, one indicator of system change brought about by Community Health Partnerships (CHP) may be the extent to which "legitimacy granting roles" are realigned at the community level (Mitchell & Shortell, 2000). In short, collaboration and partnership require a set of skills, techniques and perspectives that may run counter to the standard practices and routines of individuals and organizations. These skills and techniques are what we describe as high engagement practices.

PROCESSES OF ENGAGEMENT

Based on the discussion above, a process model of constructing partnerships is crucial to achieve long-term change. Particular practices, tools and techniques are effective in building engagement processes. As consultants, our work is influenced by systemic thinking and practice (Senge, 1990; Evans & Kearney, 1996; Pearce & Littlejohn, 1997; Campbell, 2000; Spano, 2001) which pays attention not only to the people who make up any organization, but also to the network of reciprocal relationships between the people. A systemic approach is also useful in that it focuses attention on the wider systems in which any particular group exists and also acknowledges the importance of different levels of context, e.g., economic and social factors and issues of race and gender (Pearce, 1994). At the same, attention to process, rather than content, encourages facilitators and consultants to be very aware that what is happening "in the moment" is highly significant in influencing what the potential outcomes might be (Kearney, 2004).

Drawing on a systemic framework, it is possible to utilize many different techniques and tools–as long as they are applied appropriately in each individual context. Some of the tools that systemic practitioners are using include the *Reflecting Team* (Andersen, 1987; 1990), which was developed in family therapy; *Physical Thinking* (Bryner & Markova; 1996) from group work; *Appreciative Inquiry* (Hammond, 1996; Anderson, Cooperrider, Gergen, Gergen, McNamee, & Whitney, 2001) from organizational consulting work; *Future Search* (Weisbord & Janoff, 1995) and *Open Space Technology* (Owen, 1992). The use of such techniques is illustrated in the case examples below. These examples describe three projects with different levels of university-community links. As an essential step to creating an effective partnership, these examples focus on the importance of taking time and space to engage with all the partners involved in any collaborative enterprise.

WORKING AS CONSULTANTS

Revitalizing the Hill District of Pittsburgh, USA

One of the authors (DMC), who has worked as a community organizer in Pittsburgh for over 20 years, has had a long-term involvement as a consultant with an inner-city area of Pittsburgh known as the Hill District. The Hill is an African American community with a multi-ethnic history of strong economic, social, and familial ties among neighbors. In the pre- and post-WWII era, it was regarded as a hotbed of African American economic and cultural life. One writer has described that period in the Hill as "pound for pound" more creative than its larger New York counterpart, Harlem, during *its* renowned renaissance (Fullilove, 2004, p. 133). However, by the late 1940s, a large area of the Hill was designated as "blighted" and the area suffered the massive demolition of urban renewal. From the 1970s on, the Hill became disconnected both physically and socially from the city–a shadow of its former self with poor housing and high unemployment. Although some strong community groups are active in the neighborhood, its history of failed economic and social policies means that local people can distrust the motivations of outside groups. This case illustrates the consultant's role in creating processes of engagement and use of high engagement techniques in partnership development and trust-building work with local community organizations and institutions.

Renewal Efforts and Rebuilding of Trust: Phase I

In 1993, DMC was invited by the Hill Collaborative, a multi-organization human services partnership serving women and families, to work as a member of a consulting team of four. The team would assist forty-five organizational representatives in addressing critical issues related to the governance and allocation of externally funded resources for the Collaborative. Previous reliance on a rational Social Planning approach had contributed to: (1) varying levels of trust among individual members as well as between local and outside organizations; (2) power imbalances resulting from organizational differences in size and influence over resource allocation decisions; and (3) underlying tension between white and black members manifested in differing perceptions of key issues (Baltimore, 2003). To address these obstacles, DMC and the consultant team facilitated a one-day planning meeting in which high engagement techniques were used.

For the Collaborative's meeting, the team presented an outline of the day's schedule and invited participants to modify it so that it satisfied everyone. Ground rules were established by the entire group, and included a "right to choose" between direct participation in an activity and participation by observation. DMC then led a "physical thinking" facilitation exercise adapted for a river city community from Andy Bryner and Dawna Markova's "telephone pole shuffle" (Bryner & Markova, 1996). Imaginary "river logs" were outlined with tape on the floor, and participants were divided into groups of eight to ten. Each group was then assigned a consultant as facilitator, and asked to position half of its members at each end of a log. The participants then had to begin moving toward the center and to pass each other without "falling off the log." The goal was for participants at one end of the log to switch places with those at the other end. The entire group of participants established two ground rules for the exercise: the goal should be attained, and everyone in each group must be satisfied with the process by which the goal was attained. It was agreed that if anyone stepped off a log, all members of that group had to begin again.

The larger meeting was then reconvened, and DMC facilitated discussion of the stories of encountering racial, gender and size differences on the logs, and remarked on the absence of the usual social tensions. Applied to the larger issues at hand, such experiences suggested to participants that "stepping on toes" might be acceptable if all were clear on the goals, and that organizations seeking to work together toward solving a problem were better off ignoring each other's size. Other applications of lessons gleaned from the exercise were explored and, finally, a set of initial principles were drafted to govern the Collaborative's work. The rest of the day was spent refining operating procedures and clarifying follow-up responsibilities. DMC continued to work with the Collaborative as needed throughout the 1990s.

Renewal Efforts and Rebuilding of Trust: Phase II

In 2000, Carnegie Mellon University sought to engage in dialogue with the Hill community about how the university could further assist in revitalizing the neighborhood. A modicum of trust was already in place as a result of Professor of Architecture David Lewis' Urban Laboratory project, in which Hill community representatives were offered design ideas crafted by students. Due to DMC's work with the Collaborative throughout the 1990s, there was also trust between the Hill Collaborative and the outside consultant. Many Hill residents, however, were still harboring the neighborhood's historical legacy of distrust of urban planners and institutions. This lack of trust had to be addressed before the university could expand its work beyond the smaller rubric of a few organizing community groups.

DMC was asked to design and facilitate a meeting at which a broadly representative group of residents and organization members would be in attendance. Carnegie Mellon University had expressed a willingness to commit to a multi-year partnership with the Hill and was asking the community's permission to proceed. While this gesture was largely symbolic (as no one expected the residents to say no), it was nonetheless intended and received as a respectful one. DMC developed a facilitation strategy that would enable participants to decide whether the university would have an ongoing presence in the Hill and, if so, to identify a set of partnering principles. The Collaborative was concerned that the meeting not get "bogged down in war stories" about various universities' previous use of the neighborhood for their own educational goals without visible reciprocal gain to residents.

The designed meeting began with introductions, establishment of ground rules, and a statement of intent, namely, dialogue with Carnegie Mellon University as to "whether an ongoing relationship would be mutually beneficial and what operating principles might guide such an enterprise" (Baltimore, 2004). Participants were then assigned randomly to mixed teams of faculty and community members and asked to walk over to tables designated for different teams. At each table were large flip charts, or "communal notebooks" (in place of the individual notebooks the Hill residents had noticed were often used by Architecture faculty and students), and colored markers. Members of each team were asked to collaboratively design motor vehicles that depicted effective and ineffective partnerships. A half-hour was allotted for this exercise.

The room was then termed an "art gallery" in which the participants' illustrations of vehicles were displayed for quiet review. In one example, a drawing of a bus depicted effective partnership. The picture featured a diverse group of smiling participants looking out of the bus windows and a clear road ahead. In contrast, another bus represented an ineffective partnership. The bus had multiple steering wheels and drivers, a missing wheel, and was positioned on a bumpy road that seemed to lead nowhere. DMC insisted on silence at this stage to allow participants to concentrate on the images and their implied messages. Having walked through the "gallery" and completed their review, participants were asked to make notes on what they had observed with regard to effective and ineffective university-community partnering in the illustrations. Only then was a more traditional discussion held. Partnering principles were identified and formulated as core components of a partnership of equals. Placing a high value on mutual trust and reciprocity, the principles identified were not unexpected. Their significance lay in a sense of common ownership by all parties based on their shared experience.

In 2002, the university-community partnership between Carnegie Mellon University and the Hill was applied to a larger partnership that expanded to include the Riverlife Task Force, a regional planning entity, and Community Partners Institute, a consulting firm started by DMC in 2000. The goal of this larger partnership was and is to support Western Pennsylvania's regional river development activities by engaging neighborhoods in river-related planning and development projects. *"Find the Rivers!"* has begun work in the Hill District with the aim of expanding the community's economic, social and cultural opportunities by linking its residents and organizations to the economic and recreational development of Pittsburgh's three rivers. Design plans initiated by Hill residents and created by Architecture students are now central to the strategy for re-connecting the Hill to its surroundings. Whereas previous renewal efforts initiated by city planners focused on regenerating the Hill's central corridor and the adjacent business district, the residents' vision seeks to re-establish long severed ties to other neighborhoods and to the rivers. While reviewing the work of students sponsored by *Find the Rivers!*, a Hill resident stated, "They say the demon in the world today is the spirit of hopelessness. I've lived here in the Hill since 1968, and my heart breaks to see it deteriorate. What you've given me today is hope" (Community Partners Institute, 2003, p. 1).

Working with Primary Health Care Providers in the UK

Recently, one of the authors (JK) was invited by a number of UK health care managers to consult with them on a process for managing a restructuring of the primary health care service in their region. These managers were responsible for locally based health care services that included general practitioners (community doctors), nursing services, occupational therapy and physiotherapy services, health promotion work and also technical and administrative staff. In the region in question, there were nine of these area teams and there was a preliminary proposal from the Director of the service to reduce these nine teams to fewer but larger groupings. It was planned to hold a consultation process throughout the organization to discuss what these larger groupings might look like. The managers who made the initial contact with the consultant were from three adjacent primary care teams and they felt that one possible outcome was the merging of their three teams. Therefore, their aim was to see if it was possible to create a workable partnership between the three areas so that they could be proactive in engaging with the consultation process.

In planning the consultation process with the managers, JK decided to draw on some of the ideas of a group called the Public Dialogue Consortium (PDC), a non-for-profit organization which is involved in a number of community projects in the USA. It has developed a way of working it calls the "public dialogue" approach which emphasizes the quality and form of the consultation process rather than focusing on outcomes. In particular, the group has been involved in a multi-year, city-wide collaborative community action project with the city of Cupertino in California (See Spano, 2001). The public dialogue approach seeks to secure as much public involvement as possible at a very early stage and works to create a process which enables all voices to heard (particularly, those of normally excluded groups, e.g., local residents, young people, minority ethnic groups, elders) before any decisions are made or outcomes decided. The group uses the acronym SHEDD to describe the strategic process design underlying its work. This stands for: Getting *S*tarted, *H*earing all the voices, *E*nriching the conversation, *D*eliberating the options, and *D*eciding and moving forward together (Pearce, 2002; Pearce & Pearce, 2000).

The SHEDD design contrasts with the "public education" design described by Yankelovitch (1991) in which governmental or managerial "elite" contemplate and decide on a particular issue, and then attempt to "educate" the public, or the staff of an organization, to agree with them. This approach has been described *decide-advocate-defend* or DAD model, in which a previously made decision is argued for, and then defended against criticism from those not involved in the making of it (Pearce & Pearce, 2000). It is probably fair to say that the cynicism of many staff and community groups towards consultation exercises arises from experiences of such a process. One key difference between the two approaches is the level of involvement in the making of the "decision" and its timing within the overall sequence of events.

In negotiating to facilitate the consultation process, JK first sought agreement with the three managers. Were they were willing to participate in a "dialogue" process as described above? And, most importantly, were they willing to be open about what outcome might emerge from the process–even if it was not their preferred result? With these agreements in place, discussion (Getting Started) took place as to who needed to be involved in the process and who needed to be informed that the process was taking place. It was decided that the process should be as open and transparent as possible, and therefore accessible to all sectors of the three health care teams and local community groups. In relation to the second point, it was agreed to inform the regional director that this process was taking place and to welcome his attendance. The purpose of the initial meeting would be to allow people to discuss ways in which they might respond to the consultation process.

The second stage of the process (*H*earing all the voices) began with the holding of the meeting and the consultant's role was to manage the "conversational architecture" (Pearce & Pearce, 2000) of the day so that the kinds of conversations that took place were managed, and importantly, different from the types of conversations that usually take place in these situations. A number of specific techniques were used to facilitate this. After the usual introductions and having given people the opportunity to say what they would like out of the day, JK used a technique called the *reflecting team* (Andersen, 1987), which was originally developed in family therapy but is now used in organizational and consulting contexts. This can be described as having "private conversations in public" so that the wider group can listen in on what is being said, but not participate directly in the conversation. Using this model, the consultant interviewed the three managers in front of the rest of the group of about 25 people. He asked them to explain why they had initiated the process, what they hoped to achieve and to share their concerns. The wider group was then asked to get into small groups, which mixed together people from different local health areas, and people from different work disciplines (e.g., a general practitioner, health promotion worker and local community representative) to discuss their responses to what the managers had said and to raise any questions they wished. All this material was then collected on flipcharts and displayed around the room but not responded to at that point. The aim was to gather and bring out into the open people's views, questions and concerns but not to debate them. At that early stage in the process, debate can often lead to people "taking sides" or adopting fixed positions before a basis for useful dialogue has been established.

To move the meeting forward, the consultant used a technique from the appreciative inquiry approach (Hammond, 1996; Anderson et al., 2001) that seeks to encourage people faced with change to focus on the positive aspects rather than the disadvantages of such change. Again utilizing small mixed groups, JK asked people to consider what aspects of the current organizational structure they would like to take forward with them into any changed structure. This approach encourages people to identify the positive aspects of their existing organizations and differentiate between the positive parts of their current organization and the less helpful aspects. It avoids the situation where groups faced with change feel the need to defend *all parts* of their existing organizational structure and so opens up a space for potential negotiation. Since three different groups were involved, the exercise identified areas of agreement and areas of difference. For the consultants, this is very important in terms of creating a workable partnership.

The day finished with the participants agreeing to continue the process but not deciding on any particular outcome. In order to check that the process (*H*earing all voices) would continue outside the meeting, the consultant asked the group to consider two questions: Who else needed to be involved? Who needed to be influenced? The aim of these questions was to get the group to think about relationships both downwards through the involvement of local communities, and upwards via the senior managers of their wider organizations. As a result of thinking about these questions, the group decided to circulate details of the day as widely as possible via email, to encourage colleagues in other health areas to attend and to involve outside agencies, such as Social Services, as they would be affected by any changes. It was also decided to try and influence the wider process by feeding ideas from the day into as many formal organizational meetings as possible, i.e., management group meetings, training days, etc. It was agreed to hold a second workshop and to again make it open to as many people as possible.

The second day followed the pattern of the first and again focused on process. By the end of the day, it was clear that some agreement was emerging on how the three health areas might link together. Therefore the consultant decided that it seemed appropriate to think of ways to move to the third stage (*E*nrich the conversation) of the strategic process design. Following discussion of ways to do this, the participants decided to hold "road show" events in the local community areas to involve as many local people as possible who had not been able to attend the meetings, and to gather their views to bring to the next meeting. It was also decided to invite a representative of senior management to attend the next meeting and present senior management thinking on the proposed re-organization. The timing of this invitation was useful to the consultant in understanding the current state of the group process. It was clear that rather than feeling anxious or defensive at this stage, they were interested to hear the senior management's views. It also focused the group members to think about what they agreed on as a partnership so as to present a coherent view to the senior management representative.

With the extra information provided by feedback from local people and the input from senior management, the group members were able to start to plan what needed to be done (*Deliberating the options*) in order to create, in concrete terms, a partnership made up of the three groups. A number of specialist working groups were formed to produce proposals in such areas as clinical services, technical and administrative services and community links. Although the working groups had a coordinator and core members, they were again open to others who wished to attend. Another group worked on a draft proposal for senior management. All working documents continued to be widely circulated by email.

At this stage in the process, people were starting to think about what actions should be taken. This occurred only three months after the initial meeting had taken place. However, the work that had been put into creating an effective partnership, through the processes of engagement, meant that group members felt they had mandates to operate, and, thus, produced their reports quickly and efficiently. A final group meeting was held to consider the reports and decide on a process for producing a final document. Again, since everyone had been involved in the process of creating this material and was aware of the time and energy that had gone into it, there was little that was contentious. Most people felt their views were being fairly reflected. The consultant did not attend this final meeting because the group felt it was strong enough as a partnership to manage it. From the consultant's view, this was a positive outcome in and of itself. The definitive document was produced and presented to senior managers. The managers accepted the overall rationale for linking the three health areas and also adopted many of the detailed operational proposals that were submitted as a blueprint for the overall re-structuring.

Creating a Trans-National University-Community Partnership

Richard Freeman highlights the importance of informal relationships and the process of "translation" of ideas and programs across national boundaries. He notes that frequently, joint work is initiated over coffee or drinks or in informal meetings rather than as a result of formal sessions at conferences and symposia (Freeman, 2002). A hybrid approach, blending formal and informal meeting sessions with the use of high engagement facilitation tools, was taken in an international symposium in April 2003 in Pittsburgh, Pennsylvania. The purpose of the symposium was to connect people from the former industrial powerhouse of the Pittsburgh region with colleagues in post-industrial regions of the United Kingdom. Their task was to explore joint learning and action related to reducing health inequities in both countries.

The Graduate School of Public Health (GSPH) and the University Center for International Studies (UCIS) of the University of Pittsburgh provided seed funding for a Global Academic Partnership (GAP) program to stimulate trans-national faculty to faculty research and collaboration. In a competitive proposal process, a joint faculty-community team proposed a dialogue between community and university actors in post-industrial regions like Pittsburgh. Rather than focus on national issues, the co-chairs, author DMC and a university-based faculty member in the medical and public health schools, deliberately targeted region-to-region dialogue to facilitate the potential for local follow up. A more traditional approach would have focused exclusively on university-to-university links. The symposium was explicitly structured to involve, in addition to faculty, field practitioners and community-based workers. The Pittsburgh region (USA) and Glasgow, Edinburgh, Sunderland and Newcastle (UK) were included. A planning team was recruited comprised of community residents representing Pittsburgh's Hill District along with service providers and university faculty. Thus, a diversity of both university and community perspectives were built in from the start.

Based on an earlier symposium, involving the University of Pittsburgh's School of Social Work and community practitioners from the USA and Europe, the assumption of the planners was that informal networks of colleagues have great potential for joint action (Soska, 2001). They also shared a conviction that substantive involvement of community actors in real partnerships, despite a sometime rocky history, holds potential for accelerating effective strategies to tackle issues, including health inequities. A further shared conviction was the necessity of having these multi-stakeholder gatherings carefully designed and facilitated in a non-traditional manner, which we have referred to as *high engagement* facilitation.

This approach was chosen to overcome three challenges identified by the planners. First, a strategy was needed for the effective convening of multiple actors from two continents, many of whom would not have met before. Some UK participants met for the first time in Pittsburgh; others had actively participated in information sharing through a web page in advance of the symposium (US/UK Dialogue web page: *http://www.ucis. pitt.edu/gap/health_ineq/*). Second, a large amount of complex background information on both countries would be required. Third, there was a wish to move beyond basic information sharing to engaged dialogue. The symposium brought participants together for two and a half days. Participants, through facilitated sessions using high engagement tools, together crafted a common sense of the historical evolution of inequities along with efforts to address them and their respective roles in those efforts.

The tone was set in the opening session. Time for introductions was minimized, basic ground rules were agreed to and participants were encouraged to create relationships over the course of the symposium. To establish how recent history had shaped health inequities in both countries, the historical evolution of university-community partnerships, and the personal stories of the participants, time lines were created. In contrast to a lecture or expert panel format, three large white boards with multiple coloured markers were arranged in the room. Having reflected and made notes on the three issues, participants then constructed time lines in a fairly random fashion, each one adding or amplifying the contribution of others. For example, rises in income and health inequality were plotted along a similar time line in the USA and the UK. Differences in emphasis and language on economic "inequalities" (UK) and racial "disparities" (USA) were self-evident on the charts. What emerged in a reasonably short time was quite a comprehensive overview of all three issues which greatly enhanced the mutual understanding of the participants. The time lines were further refined in constituent groups (US and UK university, community and service provider) to allow colleagues with similar roles an opportunity to further clarify and interpret the data.

The symposium then moved to the Hill District. After lunch, hosted by community organizations, the second working session of the first day refined earlier work. Then a local artist took participants on a walking tour of the Hill. They strolled around the area, met residents and visited taverns before having dinner together. Considerable space was left for the informal networking and relationship building, which was seen as the key to effective follow up. The rest of the symposium followed this format. It ended with Open Space meeting tools, whereby participants self selected issues around which they would commit further time and attention.

Initial results from the Symposium are very promising and significant commitments to further action were made. Several initiatives are already in progress. First, a set of partnering principles to guide further joint action have been defined. Informal networking among colleagues has started and communication has commenced through a listserv and directly between colleagues. This article is the result of such networking. Further trans-national work has commenced. Four US colleagues, academics and practitioners, attended meetings in Newcastle, Sunderland, Edinburgh and Glasgow in February 2004. As a result, a group of residents and practitioners from the UK will visit the USA in October 2004. They will attend the conference of Community/Campus Partnerships for Health and then visit Pittsburgh. Lastly, UK residents and practitioners are collaborating with their US counterparts in Pittsburgh to share experience and learning on current efforts to address heart disease, obesity and diabetes through community-wide exercise and education campaigns in Pittsburgh and Newcastle. Most importantly, this interim work will shape the agenda for further contact and follow-up meetings.

CONCLUSION

These examples illustrate that a close emphasis on process and on engaging all participants in a partnership is a crucial aspect of developing an effective collaboration. By utilizing a consulting model and high engagement techniques which are focused on the process but not concerned with achieving a particular outcome, members of university-community partnerships are given space to decide outcomes which match their particular context. Although such an approach is time consuming and demanding, it can also produce more lasting relationships and more durable results. By managing the processes of partnership, collaborative groups can develop skills which are not only useful for the specific project in question, but also become on-going resources for managing their internal and external relationships in a whole range of different areas. As a Carnegie Mellon faculty member working in the Hill District has noted, "If you spend time creating the right kind of partnership and doing the right things, everything accelerates from this" (Community Partners Institute, 2003, p. 14).

REFERENCES

Andersen, T. (1987). The reflecting team: Dialogue and meta-dialogue in clinical work. *Family Process, 26,* 415-428.

Andersen, T. (Ed.) (1990). *The reflecting team: Dialogues and dialogues about dialogues.* Broadstairs: Borgmann.

Anderson, H., Cooperrider, D., Gergen, K.J., Gergen, M., McNamee, S., & Whitney, D. (2001). *The appreciative organisation.* New Mexico: Taos Institute.

Arches, J. (2001). Powerful partnerships. *Journal of Community Practice, 9* (2), 15-30.

Audit Commission. (1998). *A fruitful partnership: Effective partnership working.* London: Audit Commission.

Baltimore, T.L. (August, 2003 & January, 2004). Author interviews (DMC) with the Director of the Hill District Community Collaborative.

Barnes, M., & Sullivan, H. (2002). Building capacity for collaboration in English Health Action Zones. In C. Glendinning, M. Powell, & K. Rummery (Eds.) *Partnerships, New Labour and the governance of welfare* (pp. 81-96). Bristol: Policy Press.

Barnes, M., Sullivan, H., & Matka, E. (2001). *Building capacity for collaboration: The national evaluation of health action zones.* HAZ strategic overview report July 2001. Birmingham: University of Birmingham.

Bauld, L., & Judge, K. (Eds.) (2002). *Learning from Health Action Zones.* Chichester, UK: Aneas Press.

Bryner, A., & Markova, D. (1996). *An unused intelligence: Physical thinking for 21st century leadership.* Berkeley, CA: Conari Press.

Campbell, D. (2000). *The socially constructed organisation.* London: Karnac.

Clarke, C., Carr, S., Jones, D., Molyneux, J., & Procter, S. (2002). *Tyne and Wear Health Action Zone evaluation: Patterns of engagement and retrenchment.* Final report April 2002. Newcastle upon Tyne: Tyne and Wear Health Action Zone.

Clarke, J. & Glendinning, C. (2002). Partnership and the remaking of welfare governance. In C. Glendinning, M. Powell, & K. Rummery (Eds.) *Partnerships, new labour and the governance of welfare.* Bristol: Policy Press.

Community Partners Institute. (2003). *Find the rivers! Connecting Pittsburgh's neighborhoods to the rivers.* Pittsburgh: Community Partners Institute.

Cronen, V., Johnson, K., & Lannaman, J. (1982). Paradoxes, double binds and reflexive loops: An alternative theoretical perspective. *Family Process, 21,* 91-112.

Daley, J., & Marsiglia, F. (2000). Community participation: Old wine in new bottles? *Journal of Community Practice, 8*(1), 61-86.

Delgado, M, (2000). *Community social work practice in an urban context: The potential of a capacity-enhancing perspective.* NY: Oxford University Press.

Evans, D., & Kearney, J. (1996). *Working in social care: A systemic approach.* Aldershot: Arena.

Freeman, R. (2002). *Public health in translation.* A Fulbright New Century Scholars Program Report. University of Edinburgh.

Fullilove, M. (2004). *Root shock: How tearing up city neighborhoods hurts America and what we can do about it.* NY: Ballantine Books.

Glendinning, C., Powell, M., & Rummery, K. (Eds.) (2002). *Partnerships, New Labour and the governance of welfare.* Bristol: Policy Press.

Hammond, S. (1996). *The thin book of appreciative inquiry.* Plano: Thin Book Publishing Co.

Hudson, B. (1999). Dismantling the Berlin wall: Developments at the health-social care interface. *Social Policy Review, 11,* 187-204. Luton: SPA.

Hudson, B., & Hardy, B. (2002). What is a "successful" partnership and how can it be measured? In C. Glendinning, M. Powell, & K. Rummery (Eds.) *Partnerships, New Labour and the governance of welfare* (pp. 51-66). Bristol: Policy Press.

Kearney, J. (2004). Knowing how to go on: Towards situated practice and emergent theory in social work. In R. Lovelock, K. Lyons, & J. Powell (Eds.) *Reflecting on social work–Discipline and profession* (pp. 163-180). Aldershot: CEDR/Ashgate.

Margolis, L. et al. (2000). Educating students for community-based partnerships. *Journal of Community Practice, 7*(4), 21-34.

Maurrasse, D. (2001). *Beyond the campus: How universities form partnerships with their communities.* NY: Routledge.

Mitchell, S.M., & Shortell, S.M. (2000). The governance and management of effective community health partnerships: A typology for research, policy and practice. *The Milbank Quarterly, 78* (2), 241-290.

Murphy, P.W., & Cunningham, J.V. (2003), *Organizing for community controlled development: Renewing civil society.* Thousand Oaks, CA: Sage.

Oliver, C. (1996). Systemic eloquence. *Human Systems, 7*(4), 247-264.

Owen, H. (1992). *Open space technology: A user's guide.* Potomac, MD: Abbott.

Pearce, K.A. (2002). *Facilitating dialogic communication: A training manual*: California: Public Dialogue Consortium.

Pearce, W.B. (1989). *Communication and the human condition.* Carbondale: Southern Illinois University Press.

Pearce, W.B. (1994). *Interpersonal communication: Making social worlds.* New York: HarperCollins.

Pearce, W.B. (1999). *Using CMM: The coordinated management of meaning.* California: Pearce Associates.

Pearce, W.B., & Littlejohn, S.W. (1997). *Moral conflict: When social worlds collide.* Thousand Oaks, CA: Sage.

Pearce, W.B., & Pearce, K.A. (2000). Extending the theory of coordinated management of meaning (CMM) through a community dialogue programme. *Communication Theory, 10,* 405-423.

Powell, M., & Glendinning, C. (2002). Introduction. In C. Glendinning, M. Powell, & K. Rummery (Eds.) *Partnerships, New Labour and the governance of welfare* (pp. 1-14). Bristol: Policy Press.

Rothman, J, (1995). Approaches to community intervention. In J. Rothman, J. Erlich, & J. Tropman (Eds.) *Strategies of community intervention* (pp. 26-63). Itasca, IL: F.E. Peacock.

Soska, T. (2001). *Building a transatlantic dialogue on community development and social inclusion.* Report of the First EU-US Symposium on Social Policy and Community Practice. In *ACOSA Update, 15*(1), 12-19.

Spano, S. (2001). *Public dialogue and participatory democracy: The Cupertino community project.* Cresskill: Hampton Press.

US/UK Dialogue web page: *http://www.ucis.pitt.edu/gap/health_ineq/*
Weisbord, M.R., & Janoff, S. (1995). *Future search.* San Francisco: Berrett-Koehler.
Wiewel, W., & Lieber, M. (1998). Goal achievement, relationship building and incrementalism: The challenges of university-community partnerships. Great Cities Institute Working Paper. Chicago: University of Illinois at Chicago.
Yankelovitch, D. (1991). *Coming to public judgement: Making democracy work in a complex world.* Syracuse, NY: Syracuse University Press.

Community and University Participation in Disaster-Relief Recovery: An Example from Eastern North Carolina

Stephanie Farquhar, PhD
Noelle Dobson, MPH

SUMMARY. Marginalized groups that are traditionally excluded from policy and decision-making are often also disproportionately affected by the hardships of natural disasters. By including community residents in research and planning, public health practitioners and researchers can create programs that have immediate relevance and policy implications. This article describes a case study of the formation of a community-uni-

Stephanie Farquhar is Assistant Professor, Portland State University, School of Community Health, 450F Urban Center, 506 Mill Street, Portland, OR 97207-0751. At the time of the study, Dr. Farquhar was a W.K. Kellogg Postdoctoral Fellow, University of North Carolina at Chapel Hill. Noelle Dobson is Program Manager, Active Living by Design, American Heart Association, Pacific Mountain Affiliate, Portland, OR.

Address correspondence to: Stephanie Farquhar, PhD (E-mail: farquhar@pdx.edu).

Portions of this article were adapted with permission from a book chapter written by Farquhar, S.A., and Wing, S. (2002). Methodological and ethical considerations of community-driven environmental justice research: Examination of two case studies from rural North Carolina. In M. Minkler & N. Wallerstein (Eds.), *Community-based participatory research for health* (pp. 221-241). New York: Jossey Bass. This material is used by permission of John Wiley & Sons, Inc.

[Haworth co-indexing entry note]: "Community and University Participation in Disaster-Relief Recovery: An Example from Eastern North Carolina." Farquhar, Stephanie, and Noelle Dobson. Co-published simultaneously in *Journal of Community Practice* (The Haworth Social Work Practice Press, an imprint of The Haworth Press, Inc.) Vol. 12, No. 3/4, 2004, pp. 203-217; and: *University-Community Partnerships: Universities in Civic Engagement* (ed: Tracy M. Soska, and Alice K. Johnson Butterfield) The Haworth Social Work Practice Press, an imprint of The Haworth Press, Inc., 2004, pp. 203-217. Single or multiple copies of this article are available for a fee from The Haworth Document Delivery Service [1-800-HAWORTH, 9:00 a.m. - 5:00 p.m. (EST). E-mail address: docdelivery@haworthpress.com].

versity partnership and a community-based participatory research project conducted in the aftermath of Hurricane Floyd. The description of methods used and the implications for practice will highlight the importance of including those most affected by a natural disaster. Members of several groups worked collaboratively to define the social and public health concerns of a rural North Carolina community and to create changes in disaster-recovery policy and practice. *[Article copies available for a fee from The Haworth Document Delivery Service: 1-800-HAWORTH. E-mail address: <docdelivery@haworthpress.com> Website: <http://www.HaworthPress.com> © 2004 by The Haworth Press, Inc. All rights reserved.]*

KEYWORDS. Community-based participatory research, public health, environmental justice, natural disasters, policy change

INTRODUCTION

An environmentally unjust policy or practice is one that disproportionately affects individual citizens, groups, or communities in places of life, work, and play (Bryant, 1995), and excludes certain populations from environmental policymaking on the basis of race/ethnicity or income (Institute of Medicine Committee on Environmental Justice, 1999; Bullard, 1994; Kuehn, 1996; USEPA, 1998). Indeed, decision-making around the environmental and social consequences of natural disasters such as hurricanes, fires, and floods also tends to exclude those populations that are more impacted by and less likely to quickly recover from the disaster (Enarson & Fordham, 1999; Blaikie, Cannon, Davis, & Wisner, 1994).

Recently, some environmental health research has united communities and researchers to address this inequity, and to include those who are most affected by environmental concerns. University-community partnerships challenge a few of the basic assumptions of traditional science, such as the assumption that research must maintain objectivity and remain detached from participants (O'Fallon & Dearry, 2002; Keeler et al., 2002; Lynn, 2000; Minkler, 2000). Community-based participatory research (CBPR) is a collaborative approach to research that equitably and meaningfully involves all partners in the research process. CBPR seeks to identify a topic that is important to the affected community, combine knowledge with action, and achieve social change to improve health outcomes (Israel, Schulz, Parker, & Becker, 1998). This presentation will describe the process of using CBPR to address unequal treatment and suffering in the aftermath of Hurricane Floyd in 1999. The partnership involved the University of North Carolina, Black Workers for Justice, and the Workers and Community Relief and Aid Project. These groups worked collaboratively to define the social and public health concerns of the community, to identify solutions to these concerns, and to change disaster-recovery policy and practice.

RECOVERY POLICY AND PRACTICES

In the aftermath of a natural disaster, such as a hurricane or a flood, long-term recovery starts when a community begins to reestablish infrastructure, reinstitute social services, and rehabilitate business and homes (NHRAIC, n.d.). These natural events are frequently followed by a recovery process that inadequately assists or excludes certain populations. Groups typically excluded from community decision-making are often more negatively affected by the consequences of natural disasters. Disasters do not discriminate, yet a community's vulnerability is determined in part by the ability to access resources and cope with losses. The conditions of people's lives before the disaster occurs–their employment status, education, social support system, housing situation, access to health care, financial credit, and legal services–determine their level of vulnerability or security in the recovery process (Blaikie et al., 1994; Bolin & Stanford, 1998).

In a review of research studies, Fothergill and colleagues (1999) documented differences in disaster experiences between racial and ethnic groups. Minority populations were found to experience longer recoveries from natural disasters, have limited access to insurance, and use aid and relief organizations differently than majority populations. Inequitable treatment of populations can occur when public safety messages are not translated effectively, when people are denied access to emergency service areas, and when cultural practices are ignored with regard to separation of sexes in emergency shelters (NHRAIC, n.d.).

Bolin and Stanford (1998) examined two communities–Fillmore and Piru–that were disproportionately impacted in the Northridge, California earthquake. Both have significant Latino working-class populations and a history of class and ethnic divisions, with the marginalization of Latinos into low-wage agricultural employment. Lower-income households have limited housing options and often occupy substandard housing. The earthquake intensified the shortage of affordable housing as several hundred mostly small older homes were damaged or destroyed.

In addition, cultural marginalization (English is the official language of all Fillmore City meetings) and political vulnerability (passage of state referendum to deny health, education, and social services to illegal immigrants) increased these groups' exclusion from disaster recovery efforts (Bolin & Stanford, 1998).

The ideal equitable recovery process encourages all interested stakeholders to participate in town meetings, planning sessions, and other public events that help inform a community's disaster mitigation plan. Coalitions and partnerships among university researchers, community-based organizations, and non-governmental organizations can help mobilize residents to voice their concerns, document experiences, develop collective strengths, and participate in the recovery process (Bolin & Stanford, 1998). However, an analysis of a CBPR project conducted in Harlem and Washington Heights notes that community residents can be hesitant to participate because they feel overwhelmed by political and societal challenges, it is difficult to involve neighbors, and they feel like they are fighting against the odds (Green, Fullilove, Evans, & Shepard, 2002). The following describes the development and outcomes of a community-university partnership established to document the concerns of a community recovering from a natural disaster.

HURRICANE FLOYD

Hurricane Floyd hit rural eastern North Carolina on September 16th, 1999, causing extensive flooding in that region. More than 7,000 homes were destroyed, 17,000 were left uninhabitable, and 47,000 residents were forced out of their homes to seek protection in temporary housing sites (Segrest, 1999). These sites, consisting largely of trailers and mobile homes located in several counties, were established and maintained by the Federal Emergency Management Agency (FEMA) and state and local government agencies. The initial response from citizens and charity organizations was tremendous; students and volunteers arrived from around the United States to provide assistance and encouragement. However, the long-term recovery efforts carried out by local, state, and federal governance have been inadequate. In July 2001, nearly two years after the flooding caused by Hurricane Floyd, most of the 1,000 citizens who were still without permanent housing were African American. Many of the displaced persons had been turned down for financial assistance, received misinformation about opportunities for recovery aid, had been unable to secure affordable and decent housing due to a lack of affordable rental units, and were excluded from recovery decisions (Lindenfeld, 2001; Farquhar & Wing, 2002).

This eastern region of North Carolina suffers from racial discrimination, poverty, unemployment, and inadequate housing. One out of 4 residents of this area of North Carolina lives below poverty level and 44% are not served by a public sewer system (Segrest, 1999). The region's towns are also highly segregated; the communities most affected by the flooding were predominantly African American. The historic town of Princeville, for example, is the oldest incorporated all-Black town in the country and was founded by former slaves after the Civil War. It was also one of the most heavily impacted communities (Farquhar & Wing, 2002). Several of the towns do not have an independent source of income from industry, as many local industries have folded and moved, resulting in a limited tax base. These towns must now replace destroyed infrastructures, address a lack of housing, transportation, food, and jobs, and repair the damage to the social and community fabric.

In January 2000, a coalition of local organizations was formed to respond to the flood survivors' unmet needs and frustrations related to longer-term recovery efforts. The Workers and Community Relief and Aid Project (RAP) was comprised of survivors of the flood and partners from member organizations, including Black Workers for Justice (BWFJ), North Carolina Fair Share, North Carolina Low Income Housing, Concerned Citizens of Tillery, University of North Carolina, and the North Carolina Student Rural Health Coalition. RAP began conducting meetings at the temporary housing sites and encouraged survivors to contribute to the development and implementation of RAP's mission and action plan. The longtime history of community organizing in Eastern NC helped RAP member organizations bring together these disparate groups to address a common goal of disaster recovery in the context of larger struggles for social justice.

RAP collaborated with university researchers on two projects. These projects followed the fundamental CBPR principle of "starting where the people are" (Nyswander, 1967), ensuring greater participation, project success, and sustainability of the partnership. One project, with the help of students from a graduate-level environmental justice class, uncovered state records indicating that hundreds of African American flood survivors had been relocated to an industrial coal ash landfill (For a description, see Segrest, 1999; Farquhar & Wing, 2002). This manuscript focuses on the second project, which documented the experiences of flood survivors and highlighted cases of discrimination by local and state agency representatives.

Documenting Discrimination and Need

More than one year after Hurricane Floyd, many of the individuals who survived the flooding caused by the hurricane were still without permanent housing. In September 2000, RAP invited the author, a post-doctoral fellow at the University of North Carolina's School of Public Health, to attend bi-monthly RAP meetings. During the meetings, survivors shared individual stories of unmet needs and of discriminatory treatment by local and state-level government agencies. At these initial meetings, RAP members and the university partner discussed the importance of collecting and reporting data that could systematically document these concerns and frustrations. The team resolved to create a survey with closed and open-ended questions that could be used to interview a target of 25%, or 250 of the still displaced flood survivors. RAP committed several meetings to specifically focus on the primary objectives of the Flood Survivor Survey. The survey was designed to systematically document the survivors' experiences of relocation, living conditions, and potential threats to health and loss of community as a result of the flooding; begin to mobilize the survivors for action; and give the survivors a voice. The University provided the author with additional support and resources, and a graduate research assistant facilitated aspects of the data analysis and post-survey meetings.

Early on in the research and documentation process a few flood survivors were hesitant to participate in RAP. Some worried that their financial or medical benefits might be reduced or discontinued by agencies involved in the flood recovery efforts. Others were concerned about being labeled a "mole" or an "informer" by fellow survivors who were suspicious of their involvement with RAP. It was stressed that no individual would be identified in RAP's organizational records. And since RAP was composed largely of local grassroots organizations and established based on survivors' expressed needs, RAP was not viewed as an imposing or exclusive organization. These factors helped alleviate barriers as the coalitions' efforts progressed.

Designing the Survey

Beginning January 2001, RAP members visited temporary housing sites to explain the purpose of the survey and to ask survivors for input. Based on this input, survey items were generated including questions regarding survivors' flooding experience, housing situation, health status, children's well being, finances and employment, environmental threats, interactions with agencies, and hopes for the future. For example, questions asked, "Has the flood affected your children's health?" and "Do you think community citizens should participate in decision making during an emergency situation?" RAP's university partner developed the survey based on general category themes and the survivors' language. RAP reviewed the revised survey and suggested minor modifications that were incorporated into the final instrument.

A draft of the survey and a description of the survey protocol were submitted to the University's Institutional Review Board (IRB). Limitations in the study's design included the requirement that the respondent reside in a temporary housing site, and did not include, for example, those survivors who had access to resources and were able to relocate to permanent housing. Similarly, the convenience sampling method was not able to capture or represent all of the possible perspectives of those living in temporary housing sites. However, given the urgent relocation deadline imposed by the state emergency management division, interviewing a randomized sample of survivors was not a viable option. In community-based participatory research such as this, it is sometimes necessary to find the middle ground between the "gold" standard of research methods and the demand for immediate information to respond to urgent needs. Nonetheless, the IRB process presented an ideal opportunity for helping community members and survivors understand the research process and the importance of confidentiality, informed consent, and voluntary participation. The survey design process was mutual. When flood survivors struggled with research concepts such as statistics, scientific validity, and confidentiality, the university partner shared knowledge and skills through discussion, interviewer training, and by providing examples of past CBPR research projects. Similarly, community members shared information about social norms, vernacular, and past research experiences to revise the survey instruments and protocol.

There were several occurrences when the university partner and the members of RAP disagreed about data collection protocol. Some RAP members did not want to require the interviewers to read the Informed Consent forms to respondents; others were hesitant to ask interviewers to read questions exactly as written, as they felt this might result in a formal and stilted interaction between interviewer and respondent. In response to these very valid concerns, the university partner talked about the importance of scientific validity and emphasized that data may be challenged because of its qualitative nature and community data collection. The group decided to use Informed Consent forms to make certain participants knew their rights and privileges, and to read the questions verbatim to interview respondents to ensure consistency in protocol. In instances such as these, researchers must work with community members to design procedures that respect community concerns while simultaneously utilizing sound data collection methodology. A healthy partnership involving such groups as academics, community, health agencies, and government officials should encourage discussion of conflicting viewpoints. Candid and non-threatening discussions about potential conflicts are more likely to contribute to an empowered and capable community than traditional research approaches (Israel et al., 1998).

Collecting Data

Five community members, four of whom were residents of the temporary housing sites, were recruited and trained to administer the surveys. Two members of RAP and the university partner facilitated the 4-hour training at one of the temporary housing sites. Each survey interviewer collected data from a site at which they lived or knew residents. Interviewers were not paid. Survey data collection lasted approximately three weeks; 270 surveys were completed from ten temporary housing sites located in four different counties. Over 90% of the survey respondents identified as African American. Only one individual was interviewed per household or trailer, and data were collected in face-to-face interviews at the respondent's housing site. Convenience sampling is a valid method to use to obtain information quickly (Singleton, Straits, & Straits, 1993), and respondents were selected by this method. There was consensus to gather and summarize the data promptly to understand and begin to address the temporary housing residents' concerns. Moreover, the director of the state emergency management division had set a relocation deadline, at which time all temporary housing sites would be shut down and residents forced out of the trailers. The deadline for this closure was six months away; data were necessary to demonstrate to those who were making decisions about funding and relocation whether there was still a lack of services and housing. The survey respondents represented many different temporary housing sites and counties; thus, the project partners felt confident that a variety of perspectives and experiences were captured. Interviews took 30 and 50 minutes to complete.

Survey items prompted the respondent to answer "yes/no" and then the interviewer asked the resident to elaborate using his or her own words. For example, in an effort to identify health problems associated with lost medications, destroyed insurance forms, and loss of access to affordable health care in the aftermath of the flooding, the interviewer asked, "Do you have immediate health needs that are not being met?" and then asked the respondent to describe these in greater detail. Because both qualitative and quantitative data were collected, the results can be presented with both words and numbers (Denzin & Lincoln, 1994). Early in the survey meetings, RAP partners recognized that different audiences respond to different forms of information delivery. For example, the media and emergency service representatives might be more affected by the survivors' words, while those who are writing policy might require numbers and percentages. Additionally, the use of combined qualitative and quantitative methods can also increase the validity of the study's conclusions and the range of information collected (Cook & Reichardt, 1979; Steckler, McLeroy, Goodman, Bird, & McCormick, 1992).

The partnership enlisted the help of the university partner to analyze the data. Quantitative data were entered into SPSS and descriptive statistics, such as frequencies and sums of responses, were tabulated. These basic computations provided the numbers necessary to better understand the general distribution of needs among residents of the ten temporary housing sites. The qualitative data were entered into Atlas/ti qualitative data software and analyzed using the focused coding method (Zimmerman, Israel, Freudenberg, Becker, & Janz, 1995; Glaser & Strauss, 1967). Seventeen code categories representing the respondents' experiences related to flooding and relocation were created. The qualitative data for each code category were then grouped and analyzed for similarities and differences between respondents' comments. This method of data analysis was flexible enough to allow new categories and ideas to emerge while maintaining a certain degree of structure based on the predetermined code categories as guided by the interview schedule. The following section briefly presents some of the survey findings.

RESULTS

Immediately after Hurricane Floyd, many of the survivors were forced to seek shelter in motels, with relatives, and in local schools. Respondents reported spending anywhere from one day to several weeks in a shelter and described the shelters as "overcrowded," "hectic," and lacking privacy. Some respondents felt that the first cases of discriminatory relief and aid occurred at the shelters. As one survivor reported, "My family stayed (in the shelter) for three days. Blacks stayed at school on floors and blankets, then they brought in the cots. Whites stayed in Hope House Plantation, an historical site." This quote highlights the perception of unequal treatment of survivors based on where each group was relocated and the conditions of the shelters.

Eighteen months after the flooding, all of the survey respondents were still residing in the temporary housing sites. Survey results indicated that 44% (n = 119) (see Table 1) of the respondents were unable to find affordable housing in their communities, and almost all of those individuals reported being turned down for housing loans or rentals because of poor credit histories or low income. Many respondents described the costs of housing and rentals as a continuing barrier to finding permanent housing, noting, for example, "since the flood, all the realtors and landlords have been allowed to raise their rent" and "I don't make enough to afford these high price apartments." Additionally, respondents expressed that there were multiple structural and administrative barriers to finding housing, such as complicated paperwork and restrictive eligibility criteria.

To add to the survivors' financial stress, most of those interviewed who were of working age reported losing work time because of the flood. Although many of the respondents were retired, disabled, or not working at the time of the flood, 109 (40%) respondents were forced to take weeks or months off of work to search for temporary housing, complete paperwork and seek assistance, and care for family members. Many of the local businesses and farms were destroyed in the flood. These respondents reported that they did not receive compensation for their lost time, resulting in a substantial drop in income. More than one-third (n = 96) of the respondents reported declining health associated with stress and living conditions. Following the flood, symptoms included a decrease in appetite, depression, crying spells, loss of sleep, nightmares, worry, panic attacks, arthritis, chest pains, headaches, and stomach aches. Many respondents reported that they continued to suffer from serious respiratory, sinus, and breathing problems related to exposure to mold and mildew associated with flood damage 18 months after the flooding.

The collapse of pivotal community structures, such as school and church, is devastating. As Eng (1993) has noted, for example, the church is a unit of identity, affirmation, and solution in African American communities and, thus, the loss of a church structure may be experienced on multiple levels. Similarly, the devastation of meeting places can result in a loss of personal identity and a decrease in sense of community cohesion (Chavis & Wandersman, 1990). Eighty-six (32%) of

TABLE 1. Quantitative and Qualitative Survey Results from the Flood Survivor Survey

Survey Item	Yes (%)	No (%)	Qualitative Responses
Have you been able to find affordable housing in your location?	149 (55%)	119 (44%)	"Since the flood, all the realtors and landlords have been allowed to raise their rent."
Did you lose work time because of the flood?	109 (40%)	161 (60%)	"I'm a farm worker. He lost the farm, so I lost my job. They never compensated me for being out of work."
Is your physical health worse today compared to before the flood?	96 (35%)	169 (63%)	"I think my health is worse because of not knowing what's available or where to get help."
Did the flooding damage your church or school?	86 (32%)	182 (67%)	"Both the church and school were destroyed, and it's torn apart our neighbors."
Do you think community citizens should be a part of the decision making process?	206 (76%)	59 (22%)	"The citizens cannot decide nothing or speak up for ourselves. Everything is governed by the local officials and that's not right."

Source: Author. Survey results are reported as number of respondents and percentage of total number of respondents. Results may not total 100% because of missing or unreported data.

the respondents reported that the flooding damaged their community's church and/or school. One flood survivor discussed the loss of both the community church and of a local elementary school, and noted that even though after two years the church was being rebuilt and the school was finally operating, "It's torn apart our neighbors."

Finally, the survey respondents felt that their participation in the allocation of funds and resources would have strengthened the post-flood recovery process. When asked if community citizens should be a part of the recovery agencies' decision-making processes, 206 (76%) respondents answered "yes" and most offered ideas about why citizen participation is so crucial to the longer-term recovery efforts. Many respondents mentioned that they were excluded from decisions made by the state emergency management agency because they were perceived as lacking intelligence or common "know how" about the system and institutions. One respondent noted that an agency representative, "Talked down to me as though I didn't have any intelligence to understand."

Disseminating and Applying the Findings

A summary of results was included in a 10-page report (Farquhar, 2001) designed to communicate the experiences and perspectives of the respondents to government agencies, local organizations, and other flood survivors. RAP members attended rallies and visited North Carolina legislators to advocate for the fair treatment of all flood survivors. RAP members also met with the North Carolina budget director and the senior policy advisors of Departments of Commerce and Low Income Housing to argue for the rebuilding of affordable, low-income housing. Results from the survey were used at these meetings to inform state level decision-makers of the flood survivors' concerns and the inadequacies of the state's response. The experience that survivors gained from participating in data collection and research improved their ability to communicate their concerns and requests.

Survey results were also presented to an audience of flood survivors, grassroots organizations, and agency representatives using slides and interview excerpts at the 2001 Hurricane Floyd Flood Survivor Summit. The summit was organized by RAP and convened at a local conference center. The purpose of the summit was to unite the voices of the hundreds of flood survivors throughout North Carolina and to plan a common agenda for unity and empowerment. To encourage coverage by the local news and print media sources, RAP partners worked together to create and widely circulate a press release. Several local newspapers and television and radio stations covered the summit. As a result of this coverage, the director of the state emergency management division was pressured to respond publicly and to grant flood survivors six additional months beyond the original deadline to remain at the temporary sites while locating permanent housing. Additionally, a member of RAP was invited to participate in monthly state-level emergency management meetings in Raleigh, NC. At those meetings, she has proven to be a very effective voice for the flood survivors' interests and in shaping policy.

Energized and empowered by the Hurricane Floyd Flood Survivor Summit and the survey report, a Survivors' Organizing Council was established. The Council met bi-weekly and continued to use the survey results to mobilize communities of survivors and to substantiate requests for affordable housing construction, grants and loans, and inclusion in decisions around the allocation of recovery funds. As a result of their participation in this project, the flood survivors, the survey interviewers, and the members of RAP experienced the ways in which data can shape decision-making and policy. Many of the participants also commented that they felt capable of carrying out their own small research projects. Currently, one of the members of RAP is participating as a community organizer on a federally funded research project examining the effects of large-scale hog farms on the mental and physical health of residents in North Carolina. The university partner, and primary author, increased her capacity to recognize when to make concessions around the research design and methodology to accommodate community desires. Experience in navigating the concerns of multiple stakeholders will be useful in future research involving community-university partnerships.

CONCLUSION

To pursue more equitable long-term disaster recovery, it is important to include marginalized populations in recovery planning and implementation. Participation in disaster recovery engages all people who have a stake in the recovery efforts, and can help to assure that the recovery approach is inclusive. Public health practitioners and researchers can play a critical role in meaningfully including survivors of disasters in recovery efforts. The results of this study and the disaster recovery literature strongly suggest that recovery programs should not only consider immediate recovery needs, but should also address the consequences on social, cultural, and emotional well-being. For example, the results indicate that the respondents continued to experience a decline in sense of community 18 months after the flooding and displacement. This suggests that future research could do a better job of assessing the long-term impact of disasters. A clearer understanding of these broader consequences could be used to tailor and improve recovery programs and services.

Throughout the RAP process, the partnership attempted to balance the more immediate concerns (e.g., pushing back state agency deadlines) with the more fundamental issues of discrimination and inequity. One of the primary challenges of CBPR is striking that balance between addressing the community's most urgent needs and sustaining the broader research goals and objectives (Israel et al., 1998; Altman, 1995). RAP managed the potentially competing objectives by recognizing that each organization involved had a unique set of goals. For example, the university researcher was responsible for gathering valid and reliable data that could withstand scientific scrutiny. Flood survivors were responsible for accurately relaying others' concerns. A central mission of Black Workers for Justice was to seek proper compensation and rehiring practices for those survivors who were out of work.

The aim of this research was to include those individuals who were most affected by Hurricane Floyd–the flood survivors themselves–to collect the data and seek policy changes. By highlighting inequities and providing solutions in the disaster recovery process, community-university partnerships can serve to set the stage for how the next disaster will be addressed. The research partnership provides examples of the potential power of collaborative endeavors in terms of influencing decision-making and public health practice. Public health and other social science researchers have the social responsibility to promote democracy and social justice through the formation of community-university partnerships.

REFERENCES

Altman, D.G. (1995). Sustaining interventions in community systems: On the relationship between researchers and communities. *Health Psychology*, *14*, 526-536.

Blaikie, P., Cannon, T., Davis, I., & Wisner, B. (1994). *At risk: Natural hazards, people's vulnerability, and disasters.* NY: Routledge.

Bolin, R., & Stanford, L. (1998). The Northridge earthquake: Community-based approaches to unmet recovery needs. *Disasters*, *22*(1), 21-38.

Bryant, B. (1995). *Environmental justice, issues, policies, and solutions.* Washington, DC: Island Press.

Bullard, R.D. (1994). *Dumping in Dixie: Race, class, and environmental quality.* Boulder, CO: Westview Press.

Chavis, D.M., & Wandersman, A. (1990). Sense of community in the urban environment: A catalyst for participation and community development. *American Journal of Community Psychology*, *18*(1), 55-81.

Cook, T.D., & Reichardt, C.S. (Eds.). (1979). *Qualitative and quantitative methods in evaluation research.* Beverly Hills, CA: Sage.

Denzin, N.K., & Lincoln, Y.S. (Eds.). (1994). *Handbook of qualitative research.* Thousand Oaks, CA: Sage.

Enarson, E., & Fordham, M. (1999). *Lines that divide, ties that bind: Race, class, and gender in women's flood recovery in the US and UK.* Paper presented to the European Sociological Association meetings, Amsterdam.

Eng, E. (1993). The Save our Sisters Project. A social network strategy for reaching rural black women. *Cancer*, *72*(Suppl. 3), 1071-1077.

Farquhar, S. (2001). RAP flood survivor survey report. Paper presented at the 2001 North Carolina Environmental Justice Conference, Whitakers, NC.

Farquhar, S.A., & Wing, S. (2002). Methodological and ethical considerations of community-driven environmental justice research: Examination of two case studies from rural North Carolina. In M. Minkler, & N. Wallerstein (Eds.), *Community-based participatory research for health* (pp. 221-241). NY: Jossey-Bass.

Fothergill, A., Maestas, E., & Darlington DeRouen, J. (1999). Race, ethnicity and disasters in the United States: A review of the literature. *Disasters, 23*(2), 156-173.

Glaser, B.G., & Strauss, A.L. (1967). *The discovery of grounded theory: Strategies for qualitative research.* NY: Aldine De Gruyter.

Green, L., Fullilove, M., Evans, D., & Shepard, P. (2002). Hey, Mom, thanks!: Use of focus groups in the development of place-specific materials for a community environmental action campaign. *Environmental Health Perspectives, 110*(Suppl. 2), 265-270.

Holistic disaster recovery: Ideas for building local sustainability after a natural disaster. (n.d.). University of Colorado, Natural Hazards Research and Applications Information Center. Retrieved July 20, 2002, from *http://www.colorado.edu/hazards/holistic_recovery*

Institute of Medicine Committee on Environmental Justice. (1999). *Toward environmental justice: Research, education, and health policy needs.* Washington, DC: National Academy Press.

Israel, B.A., Schulz, A.J., Parker, E.A., & Becker, A.B. (1998). Review of community-based research: Assessing partnership approaches to improve public health. *Annual Review of Public Health, 19*, 173-204.

Keeler, G., Dvonch, T., Yip, F., Parker E., & Israel, B. et al. (2002). Assessment of personal and community-level exposures to particulate matter among children with asthma in Detroit, Michigan as part of Community Action Against Asthma (CAAA). *Environmental Health Perspectives, 110*(Suppl. 2), 173-181.

Kuehn, R. (1996). The environmental justice implications of quantitative risk assessment. *University of Illinois Law Review, 103*(1), 103-172.

Lindenfeld, S. (2001, February 13). Floyd recovery in their own hands: Survivors "stand up." *Raleigh News and Observer*, p. B1.

Lynn, F.M. (2000). Community-scientist collaboration in environmental research. *American Behavioral Scientist, 44*(4), 649-663.

Minkler, M. (2000). Using participatory action to build healthy communities. *Public Health Reports, 115*, 191-198.

Nyswander, D. (1967). The open society: Its implications for health educators. *Health Education Monographs, 1*, 3-13.

O'Fallon, L., & Dearry, A. (2002). Community-based participatory research as a tool to advance environmental health sciences. *Environmental Health Perspectives, 110*(Suppl. 2), 155-159.

Segrest, M. (1999). *Looking for higher ground: Disaster and response in North Carolina after Hurricane Floyd.* Durham, NC: Urban-Rural Mission USA.

Singleton, R.A., Straits, B.C., & Straits, M.M. (1993). *Approaches to social research.* NY: Oxford University Press.

Steckler, A., McLeroy, K.R., Goodman, R.M., Bird, S.T., & McCormick, L. (1992). Toward integrating qualitative and quantitative methods: An introduction. *Health Education Quarterly, 19*(1), 1-8.

United States Environmental Protection Agency. (1998). Final guidance for incorporating environmental justice concerns in EPA's NEPA compliance analyses. Washington, DC: US Government Printing Office.

Zimmerman, M.A., Israel, B.A., Freudenberg, N., Becker, M.H., & Janz, N.K. (1995). Methodology. In N. Freudenberg, & M. Zimmerman (Eds.), *AIDS prevention in the community* (pp. 199-203). Washington, DC: APHA Press.

Addressing Barriers
to University-Community Collaboration:
Organizing by Experts
or Organizing the Experts?

Donna J. Cherry, MSW
Jon Shefner, PhD

SUMMARY. University-community partnerships, and COPC programs in particular, offer important opportunities for traditionally segregated groups to work together in collaborative relationships. The challenge of bringing people who possess distinct differences in background and social power together is a long-standing issue. Class, status, and organizational differences may impede collaboration. This article discusses the history of COPC as social policy and reviews an evaluation report of successful community-university partnerships. Drawing from the community organizing literature in sociology and social work, this article suggests community organizing methods that address structural obstacles to collaborative work. Especially in COPC programs characterized by multiple interactions, it is the community based organization (CBO) which has greatest facility to

Donna J. Cherry is a PhD student at the College of Social Work, University of Tennessee, Knoxville, TN, 37996. Jon Shefner is Associate Professor, Department of Sociology, University of Tennessee at Knoxville.

Address correspondence to: Donna J. Cherry, MSW (E-mail: dcherry@utk.edu).

[Haworth co-indexing entry note]: "Addressing Barriers to University-Community Collaboration: Organizing by Experts or Organizing the Experts?" Cherry, Donna J., and Jon Shefner. Co-published simultaneously in *Journal of Community Practice* (The Haworth Social Work Practice Press, an imprint of The Haworth Press, Inc.) Vol. 12, No. 3/4, 2004, pp. 219-233; and: *University-Community Partnerships: Universities in Civic Engagement* (ed: Tracy M. Soska, and Alice K. Johnson Butterfield) The Haworth Social Work Practice Press, an imprint of The Haworth Press, Inc., 2004, pp. 219-233. Single or multiple copies of this article are available for a fee from The Haworth Document Delivery Service [1-800-HAWORTH, 9:00 a.m. - 5:00 p.m. (EST). E-mail address: docdelivery@haworthpress.com].

equalize the playing field between disparate groups. The role of community organizers in CBOs is to acknowledge and disrupt the structural inequalities inherent in these relationships. The community organizer must resist the role of expert or buffer between the community and university and instead strive toward authentic collaboration. *[Article copies available for a fee from The Haworth Document Delivery Service: 1-800-HAWORTH. E-mail address: <docdelivery@haworthpress.com> Website: <http://www.HaworthPress.com> © 2004 by The Haworth Press, Inc. All rights reserved.]*

KEYWORDS. University-community partnerships, community organizing, collaboration, Community Outreach Partnership Center, community based organizations

INTRODUCTION

University-community collaborations offer important opportunities for traditionally segregated groups to work together in collaborative relationships. Examining the differences of collaborators' class, status, and educational backgrounds engenders the following questions. First, how do people possessing distinct differences in background and social power work together in an arena defined by egalitarian goals? Second, what is the role of the community organizer in university-community partnerships? Community organizing literature has long addressed collaborations among organizations and individuals possessing different backgrounds and resources. Structural inequalities are rooted in different levels of status, education, and class. Often, such structures are monolithic and overpowering. Current discussions of the global economy are illustrative. In the face of identifiable global trends, how can nations, let alone even less powerful actors in states and local communities, change such trends? Yet, structural inequalities are neither inevitable nor immutable; humans consistently shape the structures around them.

Similar to global inequities, relationships forged by Community Outreach Partnership Centers (COPC) partners inherit vast differences between community members and university workers. University administrators often ignore differences in attitudes regarding public safety issues, lifestyle differences, impacts on local economies, parking and traffic problems, and housing needs. Nichols (1990, p. 3) finds common a "lack of interaction and joint effort toward sharing resources, exploring opportunities, and enhancing the quality of life for all." Compounding these issues are the different cultural, class, status, and ethnic backgrounds that may be represented across faculty and administrators, students, and community members as they come together in a series of locations requiring ongoing interactions, including lab schools, teaching hospitals, and community-based agencies (Tippins, Bell, & Lerner, 1998). Often these locations are characterized by the university serving the community, rather than acting as an equal partner. Even though COPC programs emphasize forging egalitarian partnerships to achieve common ends, good intentions do not fully address the many structurally defined differences between partners. Some communities view universities with great skepticism during their entry into community collaborative work. Reardon (1997), for example, cites East St. Louis community leaders who " . . . believed university scholars had used the serious problems facing their community to secure research funding for projects that produced few, if any, community benefits. Local leaders viewed these academics as intellectual 'carpetbaggers' who used the city's problems to justify summer salaries, graduate student stipends, and other research support for the university while offering the city nothing in return" (p. 234).

One of the most difficult elements of the university-community relationship is the existence of multiple constituencies (Nyden, Figert, Shibley, & Burrows, 1997; Knapp, 1998; Lerner & Simon, 1998; Nichols, 1990). Local communities, university administrators, faculty, graduate and undergraduate students work in varying ways with universities, federal and local governments, and emergent and long-standing community groups. Such complicated environments not only pose difficult questions of how to build partnerships, but who gets what out of the relationships. At the same time, these complicated organizational environments pose opportunities. This article looks at the history of COPC as social policy, and summarizes the results of The Urban Institute's (2002) evaluation of community-university partnerships. Community organizing research from social work and sociology offers some strategies to assist community based organizations (CBOs) to work with COPC programs. We argue that CBOs are best positioned to bring together disparate groups. Creative strategies for bridging structural differences include multicultural organizing, feminist organizing, civic engagement, and community planning. The use of these strategies by CBO-based organizers moves away from project facilitation on the part of the university to community organizing to address the structural obstacles inherent in collaborative university-community partnerships.

ORIGIN AND PURPOSE OF COPC PROGRAMS

In 1994, the U.S. Department of Housing and Urban Development (HUD) established the Office of University Partnerships (OUP) to serve as a catalyst to bring colleges and universities together with their communities to address urban problems. Although partnerships between universities and urban communities have existed since the 1950s, no comprehensive national direction for this type of affiliation previously existed. In keeping with broader trends toward community collaboration in the public and public/private sectors, the Housing and Community Development Act (P.L. No. 102-550) was enacted in 1992. Through this Act, HUD established the OUP. The COPC program, established in 1994, is one of several initiatives administered by OUP (Marker Feld, 2002; Vidal, Nye, Walker, Manjaerrez, & Romanik, 2002).The purpose of the COPC program is to foster partnerships between colleges and universities and their urban communities, and encourage universities to integrate civic engagement in their missions by focusing on pressing community development issues. The COPC program is open to accredited public or private nonprofit institutions of higher education that grant 2- or 4-year degrees. These institutions may partner with communities ranging from a single neighborhood to an entire metropolitan area. Given annually since 1994, three-year awards of up to $400,000 must be matched by non-federal funds. Since its inception, HUD has invested over $45 million in more than 200 grants (Marker Feld, 2002; OUP, n.d.).

Each partner stands to gain substantially from collaboration. In addition to strengthening their research and teaching capacity, as place-based institutions colleges and universities have a strong interest in improving the quality of life in their surroundings. These improvements simultaneously assure current and potential students and staff of the neighborhoods' safety, and strengthen institutional reputations by producing better educated professionals possessing practical experience in solving community problems. As recipients of significant public funding, universities and colleges are increasingly expected to make a contribution to the social welfare of their communities (Marker Feld, 2002). Communities benefit from the valuable assets that universities and colleges have to offer in their efforts to revitalize neighborhoods. Academic institutions bring substantial intellectual, technical, and technological resources to community problem solving. They play significant economic roles in their locales, as well-hiring staff in many occupations, purchasing a wide array of goods and services, and attracting students who may have considerable purchasing power (Vidal et al., 2002). In order to support local community building efforts, the COPC program allows for great flexibility and encourages creativity and multi-faceted approaches to community problems (OUP, n.d).

COPC funds enhance previously-established outreach programs, and create programs that get their initial impetus through COPC funding. One exemplary model of a new collaboration is the Woodlawn COPC. This collaboration partnered the University of Rhode Island's (URI) Urban Field Center with Woodlawn, a diverse neighborhood with many needs (e.g., programs for literacy, life skills, and drug and school-drop-out prevention) but also with promising assets (e.g., local faith-based institutions and a prominent community activist). Community residents determined the projects and policy direction while the university provided the necessary technical assistance. The Woodlawn COPC addressed multiple issues including community planning, neighborhood revitalization, housing, and education and social services. The effects of the COPC program are evident: the residents have come together as a community, the URI opened an Institute of Housing and Community Development, and Woodlawn and the URI developed a long-term relationship. The mandate for citizen participation is critical. Although HUD historically encouraged community involvement, the COPC program requires it. For example, community residents must agree with the planned programs and join the advisory committee, which controls the programs and their funds (Marker Feld, 2002).

AN EVALUATION OF COPC PROGRAMS

In order to learn about the challenges and successes of COPC-supported university-community partnerships, The Urban Institute studied a representative sample of the 1994-1997 COPC grantees. Data were collected using three methods: a review of basic information from the grantee application materials; site visits and semi-structured interviews with key actors from the academic institution and the community; and follow-up site visits or telephone interviews. Three broad research questions were addressed: (1) Activities–Had the COPC funding increased the community outreach activities? (2) Partnerships–What kinds of partnerships were forged between academic institutions and communities? and (3) Institutionalization–How, and to what extent, had colleges and universities changed their values in order to sustain community outreach and partnership activities? Questions asked about activities addressed capacity building, community outcomes, community change, and outcomes regarding information and knowledge. Partnership questions included the university's history in the community, leadership, the process for creating the COPC, partnership structure, staffing, resources, and performance. Questions about institutionalization included "profitability" for the community and the university, fairness, future funding, and the future of the partnership. Twenty-five grantees were chosen that matched the sample on readily observable characteristics and who were at least moderately successful. Because many of the institutions had already been involved in outreach activities before the COPC program, data on both COPC and non-COPC activities was gathered and compared (Vidal et al., 2002).

Community development technical assistance (20%), life skills training (13%), and provision of professional services (10%) together accounted for over 40% of activities. Other activity categories representing either services or expertise provided included: facilities (infrastructure), education (K-12), workforce development, economic development, community planning, community development training, community service, and information technology. The analysis also revealed that highly motivated faculty most often initiated the activities and that most activities were considered a success by the universities and the community (Vidal et al., 2002). Compared to the non-COPC activities, the COPC program successfully encouraged colleges and universities to pursue new approaches to teaching and research activities. With the support of an outside grant, the institutions were more willing to take risks and experiment.

Rather than measuring success, the evaluation looked at challenges presented by the different configurations of partnerships. Partnerships were categorized into four dimensions, reflecting the amount of resident participation required (high or low) and the amount of academic technical expertise required (high or low). Activities that required high community involvement and high technical expertise included community planning and clinical services, and were considered to have the greatest "capacity risk." Capacity risk was defined as the probability that participants who make good-faith commitments are unable to carry out those commitments due to insufficient financial, human, or political resources.

The COPC grants presented universities with an opportunity to risk pursuing partnerships where academic institutions previously had little or no experience. COPC activities were more likely to be implemented with a community partner. About 50% were collaborations with CBOs. Although the COPC program played a significant role in helping to shape collaborations, partnerships were more likely to be formed for individual activities. COPC grants were seen as too small to provide sufficient incentive to develop longstanding partnerships. A Likert scale was used to measure institutionalization–that is, the sustainability of university-community partnership. COPC funding promoted institutionalization, but most of the grantees were already engaged in community outreach before obtaining COPC funding, and therefore, showed higher degrees of institutionalization, especially along dimensions of leadership, faculty involvement, and funding. Many institutions found external funding to continue COPC-initiated activities. The lowest ranking indicators–mission, policy, and hiring, promotion, and tenure–were factors that are more difficult to require as a condition of federal funding. These aspects are also slower to change because they involve a broad consensus of the institution as opposed to individual or departmental commitments (Vidal et al., 2002).

ORGANIZING BY EXPERTS OR ORGANIZING THE EXPERTS?

As the Urban Institute study shows, academic institutions often lack the resources to commit to a long-term framework for university-community collaboration. Thus, COPC funding may result in a university staying "open" to the community, positioning itself to be available without designing a comprehensive neighborhood strategy. Risk of failure can be minimized by limiting work with community members (Vidal et al., 2002). We posit another scenario. Faculty could gain better access to the community through community intermediaries. CBO-based community organizers can facilitate COPC activities because they provide access to community residents by utilizing their unique roots in the community to actively facilitate negotiation between university and community partners. To do so, organizers need to understand and address the structural inequalities that result in differential power among partners.

The Expert as Organizer

Community organizers have long acknowledged the differences between themselves and the communities with which they work (Delgado, 1986; Fish, 1973). COPCs are likely to be especially vulnerable to entrenched social hierarchies, given potential differences between university-affiliated workers and members of disadvantaged communities. We suggest that community organizing literature offers important strategies to supercede individual differences, while insufficiently recognizing the structural roots of hierarchies that are manifested in individual interactions. Although communication problems among organizers and communities may appear to reveal the most personal of interactions, these obstacles are best understood as representing structures of society rather than individual personal variations. Often these problems have their genesis in socially-defined hierarchies such as those of race/ethnicity, gender, class, and status.

Some community organizing literature recognizes the roots of inequalities, and addresses their implications. Delgado (1986), for example, notes that organizers' greater resources may engender beneficiary dependence and limit participation in decision making and agenda setting to those perceived as experts. "The organizer who creates a formal structure with definitive participatory roles may then render the formal structure irrelevant . . . by defining the terrain of discussion or steering the group toward a particular issue" (p. 578). Hyde (2001) echoes Delgado's warning and criticizes the model of expert organizer, writing that " . . . this creates a power dynamic between organizer and group" which "places too much emphasis on the organizer as expert" and "suggests that the group becomes too dependent on the organizers' expertise" (p. 79). Social hierarchies provide the roots of interpersonal communication problems; class and status differences often manifest themselves through the perception of the differential possession of expertise (French & Raven, 1959). Indeed, the expert status is a largely accepted characteristic of the organizer, even in social work texts that tenaciously hold to egalitarian values. Rothman (2001), for example, tells us that it is organizers' expertise that enables them to diagnose community needs, advise the community, and evaluate the effectiveness of a proposed action. This position is consistently repeated, as the following excerpt exemplifies:

> He or she must stand by the side of the people and see the world from their perspective. But he must be able to go outside that perspective to analyze and decide accurately what he should do in order to build organization. He . . . should place the organization in the hands of the membership, but he should also know when and how to intervene to protect the essential characteristics which he is responsible for ensuring in the organization. (Haggstrom, 2001, p. 368)

The possibility that the expert role may create barriers between organizer and the organized is addressed with fairly dismissive advice. Rubin and Rubin (2001, p. 134), for example, counsel "awareness." They tell organizers that they "must not take away ownership of the result from the newly empowered, activist community." They warn organizers to "avoid playing status games, acting as if they were bosses, showing favoritism, or ignoring important cultural values" (p. 131). Such warnings and advice address individual attitudes and may resolve the problems of the expert role for some organizers. Yet the expert role is not simply an individual expression of attitudes, but also a structural relationship. Expertise is rooted in different status and class location. Thus, it is not enough to re-shape attitudes of individuals working in impoverished communities. In spite of organizers' most dedicated efforts, the organizational framework within which they work may impede their efforts to achieve equality and cooperation. The very unification of individuals from distinct status and class backgrounds, and from organizations with divergent interests, generates a situation that can either challenge or recreate the hierarchy of wider society.

If organizers trained to avoid such problems still face dilemmas around expertise, potentially greater differences between members of universities and disadvantaged communities exacerbate the dilemma. Town and gown differences include perceptions of the university's expertise. One danger is the assumption that institutional knowledge surpasses the community's understanding of its needs. This perception may lead universities to dominate problem-solving efforts, to prioritize university interests over those of the community, and to "treat the community as deficient" (Tippins, Bell, & Lerner, 1998, p. 181). The expert role also defines university-affiliated workers as those who know the decisions to make, the direction to pursue, and the strategies to attain the defined goals. University faculty and staff are defined by expertise based on educational experiences; expertise provides the foundation of legitimacy in research, teaching, and service activities. Expertise is further reinforced by its organizational affiliation. Thus, university workers remain entrenched in relationships in which they are the dominant actors—they teach students rather than learning with them, and conduct research on subjects more often than collaborating with them. Acquiescence (Gaventa, 1980), the flip side of power, requires both empowered and disempowered actors to accept the cultural environment that reinforces that static relationship as the legitimate order of society. With greater legitimacy and power, universities are positioned to dominate their community partners.

CBO-Based Organizing

The recognition of these structural inequalities can help university-community partnerships deal with unjust power differentials. From the standpoint of the community, the actor more capable of addressing social injustices manifested in university-community relationships is the community organizer. Community organizing research offers some strategies for CBOs to work with COPC programs. Rather than simply act as project facilitators, community organizers are ethically obligated to strive toward authentic social justice. This ideal provides a formidable challenge given the resources and structural changes required. An organizer, for example, cannot force university policy changes that might demonstrate academic receptivity of community (e.g., university mission, and hiring and tenure policies). Nonetheless, strategies that bridge these structural differences exist in current community organizing models and in other fields. CBO-based organizers can work from their position in the community as adaptive generalists with the ability to integrate strategies from multiple practice models (see, for example, Parsons, Hernandez, & Jorgensen, 1988). The literature in social work and sociology offers practical methods for CBO-based organizing that can be applied to community work in COPC programs.

Multicultural Organizing. Multicultural organizing strategies are particularly relevant for the urban context of many COPC-funded programs. Multicultural organizing requires that the community organizer understands and value the cultures and social location of multiple community groups in order to address social justice and oppression (Gutiérrez, Alvarez, Nemon, & Lewis, 1996). The organizer must understand her individual social location and culture to fully realize the position of others. Ethnic competence by itself is insufficient; structural inequalities remain the fundamental obstacles to dismantling cultural barriers.

Urban communities are composed of multiple racial and ethnic groups, including immigrant populations and cultural groups that consist of numerous subgroups, each of which has its own unique culture and language (Rubin & Rubin, 2001). Frequently these groups are disempowered by racial, social class, and language barriers. Although organizers are warned not to oversimplify the characteristics of any group, a framework of some generalizations and strategies is useful. Successful multicultural organizing utilizes existing structures such as family, social organizations, and community networks. Within these structures, collectivity is valued over individuality, and respect and trust is vital for collaboration (Gutiérrez et al., 1996). Linking the university to the community means that university representatives must be willing to meet in, and actively engage, pre-existing community institutions (Thompson, Minkler, Bell, Rose, & Butler, 2003). Class-related obstacles such as transportation and childcare must also be considered. Barriers also exist in the design of meetings and collaborations. Stout (1996) found that college-educated people are comfortable with a classroom model where people speak at will in theoretical and impersonal terms, but this approach is unfamiliar to many low-income people. People of different cultures may be reluctant to speak with strangers as well as need more time to process their thoughts. Participation in final decisions may also work better by voting than by consensus as this may indicate an equal voice to all participants. The importance of communication and language requires organizers to be attentive to the pace of the meeting and translation needs (Rubin & Rubin, 2001; Stout 1996). Additionally, Hibbard and Lurie (2000) found that the expert jargon used by community planners and city officials intimidated the residents and eroded trust, leading to failure.

Feminist Organizing. Feminist organizing similarly addresses inequalities that perpetuate disempowerment of oppressed populations (Gutiérrez & Lewis, 2001). The overarching goal is to eliminate hierarchies that affect any oppressed group (Chaskin, 1997). For community practice, the organizer must be grounded in feminist principles that include valuing the process, consciousness raising, wholeness and unity, democratic structuring, and an orientation toward structural change (Weil, 2001). Feminist organizing principles facilitate achieving COPC program goals such as community involvement and joint decision-making. Because women, especially women of color, may dominate a community, collaboration attempts are likely to fail if the organizer and academic institution have underestimated their influence. Leadership roles must be shared. Adherence to feminist principles requires rethinking the traditional structure of meetings. Community-based meetings in familiar venues are useful because participants are not required to leave their communities, either physically or psychologically. Ordinary language and storytelling are useful feminist methodologies for problem definition and analysis (Fischer, 2000), reflecting the need to validate the human experience as a step toward empowerment. Proportional representation in meetings and intentional rotation of leaders and task assignment ensure that disadvantaged voices are heard and helps eliminate hierarchies. Finally, small group meetings are generally preferred over large forums (Gutiérrez & Lewis, 2001; Mansbridge, 1984).

Civic Engagement. The civic engagement literature offer further solutions for bridging the structural disparity between academic institutions and communities. Civic engagement implies making meaningful connections between citizens, issues, institutions, and the political systems (McCoy & Sully, 2002). Power differentials between planner (expert) and citizens (amateurs) are similar to barriers between universities and communities, as is the search for common ground and common language amidst diversity. A two-phase strategy called "deliberative dialogue" promises genuine structural change (McCoy & Scully, 2002, p. 117). First, participants are encouraged to honestly share ideas and try to listen and understand each other. Multiple forms of speech and communication tactics such as study circles, clearly articulated and employed ground rules, storytelling, encouraging reflection on personal experiences, and brainstorming help ensure that all participants have an opportunity for engagement. Deliberation, the second component, promotes the use of critical thinking and productive argument as a tool to reach decisions about public policy. The combination of these approaches allows participants to simultaneously build relationships and solve public problems despite structural differences.

Community Planning. Community planners also emphasize the need for common language. Important meanings and motives underlying human speech and behavior are likely to be obscured in situations marked by stark power imbalances. Community planning settings will likely reflect the shifting influence of several positions vying for influence within and among interest groups. These dynamics underscore the need for the planner to interact and gain rapport with a variety of groups in a given setting. Additionally, it is important to conduct varied citizen encounters to gain access to potentially hidden agendas. The degree of full and honest disclosure by participants in a diverse community is directly related to the level of meaningful results that may be expected (Baum, 1999, 2000; Briggs, 1998; Umemoto, 2001). Researchers consistently find that successful collaborations are based on the ability of each partner to make their needs and goals explicit, while maintaining the flexibility required to negotiate needed changes in the project's goals or strategies (Austin et al., 1999; Chaskin, 2003; Maurrasse, 2002).

CONCLUSION

COPC programs offer important opportunities for traditionally segregated groups to work together, yet also pose dangers that this common work will reinforce, not disrupt, societal inequalities. On one hand, they are mandated and funded by the same government that at times reinforces social oppression. On the other hand, they provide opportunities to bring people with multiple skills and knowledge together in ways that few other organizing venues offer. Although this dilemma may never be fully resolved, organizing work must include "an engagement in the struggle for social change . . . to challenge social inequalities and oppressive power" (Fisher & Shragge, 2000, p. 2). Community organizing can provide COPC programs with ways to confront social inequities, forge sustainable relationships, and resist the tendency to recreate hierarchy.

REFERENCES

Austin, M.J., Martin, M., Carnochan, S., Goldberg, S., Berrick, J.D., Weiss, B., et al. (1999). Building a comprehensive agency-university partnership: A case study of the Bay Area social services consortium. *Journal of Community Practice, 6*(3), 89-106.

Baum, H.S. (1999). Community organizations recruiting community participation: Predicaments in planning. *Journal of Planning Education and Research, 18*(3), 187-199.

Baum, H.S. (2000). Fantasies and realities in university-community partnerships. *Journal of Planning Education and Research, 20*(2), 234-246.

Briggs, X. (1998). Doing democracy up-close: Culture, power, and community in community building. *Journal of Planning Education and Research, 18*(1), 1-13.

Chaskin, R.J. (1997). Perspectives on neighborhood and community: A review of the literature. *Social Service Review, 71*(4), 521-547

Chaskin, R.J. (2003). Fostering neighborhood democracy: Legitimacy and accountability within loosely couple systems. *Nonprofit and Voluntary Sector Quarterly, 32*(2), 161-189.

Delgado, G. (1986). *Organizing the movement: The roots and growth of ACORN.* Philadelphia: Temple University Press.

Fischer, F. (2000). *Citizens, experts, and the environment.* Durham, NC: Duke University Press.

Fish, J. (1973). *Black power/white control: The struggle of the Woodlawn organization in Chicago.* Princeton: Princeton University Press.

Fisher, R., & Shragge, E. (2000). Challenging community organizing: Facing the 21st century. *Journal of Community Practice, 8*(3), 1-19.

French, J.R.P., & Raven, B. (1959). The bases of social power. In D. Cartwright (Ed.), *Studies in Social Power.* Ann Arbor: Institute for Social Research.

Gaventa, J. (1980). *Power and powerlessness: Quiescence and rebellion in an Appalachian Valley.* Urbana: University of Illinois Press.

Gutiérrez, L.M., Alvarez, A.R., Nemon, H., & Lewis, E.A. (1996). Multicultural community organizing: A strategy for change. *Social Work, 41*(5), 501-516.

Gutiérrez, L.M., & Lewis, E.A. (2001). A feminist perspective on organizing with women of color. In F.G. Rivera & J.L. Erlich (Eds.), *Community organizing in a diverse society* (pp. 95-111). Boston: Allyn & Bacon.

Haggstrom, W. (2001). The tactics of organization building. In J. Rothman, J.L. Erlich, & J.E. Tropman (Eds.), *Strategies of community intervention*, (6th ed.), (pp. 364-379). Itasca, IL: F.E. Peacock Publishers, Inc.

Hibbard, M., & Lurie, S. (2000). Saving land but losing ground: Challenges to community planning in the era of participation. *Journal of Planning Education and Research, 20*(2), 187-195.

Housing and Community Development Act of 1992, Pub.L. No.102-550, § 993, 106 Stat. 3891 (1992).

Hyde, C. (2001). Experiences of women activists: Implications for community organizing theory and practice. In J.E. Tropman, J.L. Erlich, & J. Rothman (Eds.), *Tactics and techniques of community intervention* (4th ed.), (pp. 75-84). Itasca, IL: F.E. Peacock Publishers, Inc.

Knapp, M.S. (Ed.). (1998). *Paths to Partnership: University and Community as Learners in Interprofessional Education.* Boulder: Rowman and Littlefield.

Lerner, R.M., & Simon, L. A. (1998). *University-community collaborations for the twenty-first century.* New York: Garland Publishing, Inc.

Mansbridge, J. (1984). Feminism and the forms of freedom. In F. Fischer & C. Sirianni (Eds.), *Critical studies in organization and bureaucracy* (pp. 472-481). Philadelphia: Temple University Press.

Marker Feld, M. (2002). Partnerships and collaboration rebuild communities: A case study in Pawtucket, Rhode Island. *Federal Reserve Bank of Boston Community Development,* 18-21. Retrieved March 8, 2004 from *http://www.bos.frb.org/commdev/c&b/2002/summer/RI.pdf*

Maurrasse, D.J. (2002). Higher education-community partnerships: Assessing progress in the field. *Nonprofit and Voluntary Sector Quarterly, 31*(1), 131-139.

McCoy, M. L., & Scully, P. L. (2002). Deliberative dialogue to expand civic engagement: What kind of talk does democracy need? *National Civic Review, 91*(2), 117-135.

Nichols, D. (1990). *University-community relations: Living together effectively.* Springfield, IL: Charles Thomas Publishers.

Nyden, P., Figert, A., Shibley, M., & Burrows, D. (Eds.). (1997). *Building community: Social science in action.* Thousand Oaks, CA: Pine Forge Press.

Office of University Partnerships. (n.d.). *Community Outreach Partnership Centers program.* Retrieved March 8, 2004, from *http://www.oup.org/about/copc.html*

Parsons, R.J., Hernandez, S.H., & Jorgensen, J.D. (1988). Integrated practice: A framework for problem solving. *Social Work, 33*(5), 417-421.

Reardon, K. M. (1997). Participatory action research and real community-based planning in East St. Louis, Illinois. In P. Nyden, A. Figert, M. Shibley, & D. Burrows (Eds.), *Building Community: Social Science in Action* (pp. 233-239). Thousand Oaks, CA: Pine Forge Press.

Rothman, J. (2001). Approaches to community intervention. In J. Rothman, J.L. Erlich, & J.E. Tropman (Eds.), *Strategies of community intervention*, (6th ed.), (pp. 27-64). Itasca, IL: F.E. Peacock Publishers, Inc.

Rubin, H.J., & Rubin, I.S. (2001). *Community organizing and development* (3rd ed.). Boston: Allyn and Bacon.

Stout, L. (1996). *Bridging the class divide and other lessons for grassroots organizing.* Boston: Beacon Press.

Thompson, M., Minkler, M., Bell, J., Rose, K., & Butler, L. (2003). Facilitators of well-functioning consortia: National Healthy Start program lessons. *Health and Social Work*, *28*(3), 185-195.

Tippins, P., Bell, M., & Lerner, S. (1998). Building relationships between university and community. In M.S. Knapp (Ed.), *Paths to Partnership: University and Community as Learners in Interprofessional Education* (pp. 165-192). Boulder: Rowman and Littlefield.

Umemoto, K. (2001). Walking in another's shoes: Epistemological challenges in participatory planning. *Journal of Planning Education and Research*, *21*(1), 17-31.

Vidal, A., Nye, N., Walker, C., Manjaerrez, C., & Romanik, C. (2002). *Lessons from the community outreach partnership center program.* Retrieved March 5, 2003, from *http://www.huduser.org/publications/commdevl/lessons_complete.html*

Weil, M. (2001). Women, community, and organizing. In J.E. Tropman, J.L. Erlich, & J. Rothman (Eds.), *Tactics and techniques of community intervention* (4th ed.), (pp. 204-219). Itasca, IL: F.E. Peacock Publishers, Inc.

REFLECTIVE ESSAY

Engaged Research in Higher Education and Civic Responsibility Reconsidered: A Reflective Essay

David P. Moxley, PhD

How can we think about the research enterprise in civic engagement? The purpose of many institutions of higher education is to engage in research and, in particular, research for the common good, or to use a somewhat out of fashion word, for the commonweal. So this is not a challenging question until we deconstruct it. Who initiates the research? Who decides on its purpose and focus? Who controls the research–how it is undertaken? And, how it is used? Answers to these questions are easy, some may say. The answers are apparent. Research expertise and research authority lie within the university or within other institutions of higher education, and all the tenets of positivism suggest that the researchers, the people who possess the mandate, control the inquiry.

David P. Moxley is Professor, School of Social Work, Wayne State University, 4756 Cass Avenue, Detroit, MI 48202.

[Haworth co-indexing entry note]: "Engaged Research in Higher Education and Civic Responsibility Reconsidered: A Reflective Essay." Moxley, David P. Co-published simultaneously in *Journal of Community Practice* (The Haworth Social Work Practice Press, an imprint of The Haworth Press, Inc.) Vol. 12, No. 3/4, 2004, pp. 235-242; and: *University-Community Partnerships: Universities in Civic Engagement* (ed: Tracy M. Soska, and Alice K. Johnson Butterfield) The Haworth Social Work Practice Press, an imprint of The Haworth Press, Inc., 2004, pp. 235-242. Single or multiple copies of this article are available for a fee from The Haworth Document Delivery Service [1-800-HAWORTH, 9:00 a.m. - 5:00 p.m. (EST). E-mail address: docdelivery@haworthpress.com].

http://www.haworthpress.com/web/COM
© 2004 by The Haworth Press, Inc. All rights reserved.
Digital Object Identifier: 10.1300/J125v12n03_14

At best others are users or audiences of the researchers' findings and, from this perspective, a good and proper researcher invites utilization, fosters it, and helps translate the data into recommendations for subsequent action. Such a response to these critical questions is quite consistent with past generations of researchers lodged in the universities and colleges and thinking of themselves primarily as discoverers or revealers of knowledge undertaken through their own initiative and under their control and administration.

But civic engagement not only challenges this paradigm, it also changes it–perhaps radically, demanding a new orientation from the investigator. Fusing research with practical aims of helping, service, or intervention in which whole communities become involved in a research project changes the nature of the model of inquiry. Researchers who undertake investigations through the lens of civic engagement may see their social responsibility as paramount and, as a consequence, they may gravitate towards those models of research that turn on action, incorporate service and research, and that are driven as much by the participants as they are by the investigators whose expertise actually may be limited by the controls and rigor colleagues in the academy may prize. Participants may twist the research. They may imbue it with the aims of advocacy and create an oxymoron in the eyes of positivist researchers. Advocacy research? Is it even possible when one prioritizes detachment, control, and the reduction if not elimination of bias?

Civic engagement requires universities and other institutions of higher education to cross boundaries and to fill nontraditional roles. Boundaries change, old role definitions dissolve, and new perspectives emerge while university researchers and the people or communities they engage (or who engage them) struggle with ambiguities they may have never anticipated. More affluent communities may not expect much of the university down the road or situated in the city. Certainly the members of these communities may look to the college or university as a source of entertainment, as a source of identity, perhaps expressed through identification with an athletic team, or even as a source of cultural or intellectual enrichment. Members of affluent communities may come to campus to make use of these resources. Affluent communities have bargaining chips–their members can afford the price of admission, likely possess the social capital to navigate campuses, and likely have alternatives to campus-sponsored events.

Poor or embattled communities, particularly those adjacent to a campus or within close proximity, may look to the university or college as a source of healing or recovery for the social ills they face. Like one conference flyer recently announced, many of these poor or embattled communities exist in the "shadows of great campuses," and often suffer from the economic and political decisions these institutions make that, in turn, can have great implications for the quality of life and well-being of those residents whose lives may be dependent on institutional actions.

Poor communities, poor people, and poor families may look to universities as great opportunity structures, as deliverers of services they cannot get readily or easily from other sources, particularly health and social services. Indeed, many of the nation's great university medical centers and campuses expanded through entitlements for people coping with poverty. While universities and colleges cast great shadows, often too they can create substantial positive externalities for communities struggling with poverty or limited resources.

Some campuses may back unawares into civic engagement through their own efforts to create campus community life, enrich student development, and ensure campus safety. Once I undertook similar research projects in two different locales within the same state. Both were small cities and both were located in rural areas of the state. Both had very similar employers and economies. One city, however, was home to a medium-size state university and I was to find that this one difference created substantial differences in the quality of life the recipients of the social service agencies I was working with experienced in their daily lives.

In comparison to the focus groups from the city without a college or university, the members of focus groups from university-city (a pseudonym) had very different perspectives of their quality of life. University-city informants noted the availability of transportation, community policing, a vibrant and interesting student center that offered amenities like movies and entertainment, preventive health services, and recreational and cultural opportunities. The university provided all of these resources to its students and the fluid and ambiguous boundaries between "town and gown" gave low-income citizens easy access to amenities and opportunities with little cost and little hassle.

Now this particular university was not undertaking research–but it did inadvertently produce benefits for those with the least, many of whom struggled with health concerns, disabilities, and mental health issues. Engaged research, inquiry driven by social and civic responsibility in higher education, can produce these benefits intentionally and through the production of benefits as an intentional and primary aim such research creates more knowledge about the dynamics of social issues, and about ways to improve social circumstances, particularly for citizens who have the least among us. My example can be reframed in terms of civic engagement and in terms of intentionally framed outcomes–the particular university could have undertaken action research on how to improve the quality of life of those individuals and communities who reside in the shadows of campus.

Why would a college or university undertake such an endeavor? Civic responsibility indicates that the purpose and role of higher education is changing dramatically in our society. No longer are institutions of higher education secular monasteries sealed from their communities. These institutions possess considerable resources–knowledge, expertise, and capacity to name a few of the obvious–and, also, they are critical actors nationally, regionally, and at state and local levels. Their legal, statutory, and political mandates increasingly require engagement in partnership with various communities and in collaboration with other local and societal institutions. The joining of service and research is one expression of this civic responsibility and it translates increasingly into new models of inquiry, ones that incorporate the properties of engagement, partnership, collaboration, and participation, particularly involving people who were once treated as "subjects" in more traditional research paradigms.

Of course, many of us are familiar with the excesses of these more traditional research paradigms: the coercion of low income or poor people and their communities into research projects, the unilateral nature of the research, which invested too much power and authority into the role of researcher, and the absence of community need as the driving force of the research. Engaged research based on tenets of civic responsibility changes this calculus dramatically. Driving engaged research undertaken with civic responsibility are the needs of communities, particularly those with tremendous needs, but also ones with tremendous strengths, typically ones embedded in the lived experience of locales that possess indigenous leadership, coherent traditions, and rich cultures.

Engaged researchers join with these communities with an understanding that they must not come with a rigid agenda or a rigid method. Joining literally means blending of the researchers' questions, capabilities, and resources with those of a community. The researcher is mindful that validity is a product out of this joining in which the interests of multiple parties are served through a particular project. Engaged researchers come to a community in a spirit of service and mindful of their strengths and limitations. And, they come mindful of their own and their institution's civic responsibility. Communities may claim the resources of these researchers with more assertiveness than ever before since for many of them academics can offer powerful tools to address local concerns, many of which can take serious tolls on the vitality of neighborhoods, schools, and local economies.

Some researchers may not be ready for such assertiveness. Their academic training may not have incorporated an ethical perspective framing both civic responsibility and engaged research and framing their linkage. Their academic training may not have equipped them with the process skills and human relation competencies to interact with assertive community stakeholders who do not want knowledge for the sake of knowledge but who want collaboration for the sake of *improving the real lives of citizens*–infants, mothers, families, children, and elders, of *improving real institutions*–such as schools, businesses, and social services, of *improving immediate situations*–such as employment, health, and infrastructure. These stakeholders likely see the researcher and the institution of higher education as a source of hope.

The engaged researcher imbued with a sense of civic responsibility will be mindful of the necessity of partnership and collaboration. It is a "two sided street," to paraphrase if not distort Myles Horton's notion of his "two eyed theory of teaching." Myles prescribed keeping an eye on where the student was and where the student was going. The "two sided street" makes the engaged researcher mindful of the linkage between creating knowledge for the public good (for the commonweal) and the immediate good the community requires–typically a community in distress. (Perhaps there is a third street–the researcher also is trying to figure out how to keep on the tenure track through engaged inquiry and civic responsibility, two approaches that may produce some concern within the university.) Coming to a community as a partner and collaborator changes the nature of the research–its design, process, and execution.

The book, *Building Community: Social Science in Action* (Pine Forge Press, 1997), authored by Nyden, Figert, Shibley, and Burrows, captures the spirit and substance of engaged research informed if not driven by a sense for civic responsibility. Perhaps the two introductory chapters capture the spirit the best. The authors devote the introduction to reflecting on a rationale guiding collaboration and on "how to" models.

The two chapters examine university and community collaborations (Chapter 1) as well as effective models of collaboration (Chapter 2). The authors show how the traditional divisive tensions between community groups and university investigators can be reframed and joined to foster new synergies. The authors make some obvious yet important observations: expanding the scope of partnership, changing the content and style of communication, and recognizing that "research is done with the community and not to it." Completing chapter one will remind readers of the pragmatics of collaboration and the necessity of mutual purpose and joining together without working at cross purposes.

Chapter two expands the lessons of the first chapter. It offers specific models guiding collaboration including collaborative research models and action networks. While there is nothing really new in this chapter, readers will find a refreshing perspective on pragmatism and lessons learned from the field. The authors remind us that the essence of collaboration resides in mind set and attitude that shape how we approach people and groups who are more a like us than different. We all want to be heard, to share our perspective, and fulfill our needs. The authors suggest practical things to strengthen a university and community collaboration including taking time, enjoying the challenge, achieving flexibility, figuring out a mutual perspective on relevant issues, forming close and strong relationships, a sustaining and generating a strong membership.

In the subsequent five parts of the book, the editors offer numerous case studies–27 of them to be exact. They cut across diversity, ecology, the joining of research with community-based learning, health and social issues, and community control and voice. The case studies are well done, and can illuminate many of the issues inherent in collaboration. They offer a great resource for lessons learned, best practices, and exemplary models of practical collaborations that achieved good outcomes or resolved what some contributors refer to as "land minds." There are examples of university-community collaborations for revitalizing low-income neighborhoods, addressing environmental racism, promoting scientific literacy, bringing the community into the university, addressing Lesbian health risk, and facilitating microenterprise development. The sheer diversity shows the utility of collaborations formed from university investigators and community activists.

Within this volume, there is no grand theory steering university-community collaboration, but the case studies reveal some potential contours of such a potential theory. One aspect of this theory is demand-communities look to the university for assistance, or faculty members stimulate demand through their own interests in engagement and civic responsibility. Indeed, one of the ideas I was reminded about repeatedly through the multiple cases is that engaged academics can make a vital difference and a profound local impact that have consequences for practical application, teaching and learning, and the development of action. What academics pay attention to matters and the investment of the time, attention, and resources can make a significant difference in the life of a particular community. In addition, the cases remind me of how important community initiative is to the successful design and execution of a project. Community members cannot be passive. They too must be as engaged as their university or college counterparts. This book is a reminder that engagement is mutual, interactive, and developmental. Without framing it in this manner, and without building these properties, it is unlikely that engaged research is sustainable. Communities must engage universities. And, universities must engage communities. But engaged collaborative research must blend into its own community of practice in which researchers and community members form and sustain strong relationships of mutuality and a keen sense of purpose.

Another excellent resource for thinking about university and community partnerships is *Collaborative Research* authored by Myrtis Sullivan and James G. Kelly, and published by the American Public Health Association in 2001. Much of the volume is based on the work of the Maternal and Child Community Health Science Consortium, which, since its inception, has employed and developed a strategy of collaborative research within a framework of university and community partnership. The three opening essays of the book complement what Nyden and his associates present in their case studies on building community.

The authors of these three essays emphasize pragmatic aspects of collaboration and the necessity of community and university participants to cross a gulf formed by differences in power, financial resources, motivations, and forms of knowledge. In the first essay, Gills offers an important perspective on the differences between what universities and communities expect of academic researchers. There are substantive differences in the areas of research, fund development, teaching and training, and service. Inspection of these differences, however, suggests the absence of great differences in either perspective or kind. Indeed, astute academics and community members can readily integrate these expectations if they remain mindful of the necessity to integrate and create synergies and if they remain committed to a unified purpose. It is critical, however, for both entities to frame engagement as a mutually beneficial activity in which the needs of universities and communities are central to the collaboration. Both entities can benefit from new research, can collaborate in joint funding, and can form new ways of teaching and serving.

Allocating ample time to the development of partnership is the central focus of the second chapter. The authors, Amuwo and Jenkins, argue that ample time is necessary for sustainability–that any partnership that does not rest on strong and enduring relationships is likely to be unstable and unsustainable. They offer an interesting perspective on the use of a multi-phase model including initial networking, involvement, cooperation, and then the formation of partnership in which there is an articulation of research needs, the creation of a joint agenda, and the development of a specific project. Their model affirms my own experience–engaged research is a product of building networks of relationships in which all parties find meaning and relevance. University and community participants need to appreciate and affirm the process-orientation of collaboration and engagement.

In the third essay, Riger identifies the core competencies of any productive collaboration. She identifies the importance of trust, shared power and control, ample time, and the blending of the expertise of researchers and advocates. The author identifies these as challenges and tensions within any collaboration. But their achievement also forms capacities and assets that strengthen collaboration and make university-community engagement sustainable.

Following these three introductory chapters, nine case studies amplify substantive projects in child and maternal health and illuminate the dynamics of collaboration and the challenges of university and community partnerships. These cases give readers a good sense for time, trust, power, control, and the blending of knowledge and expertise. They reveal the strain between knowledge for the sake of knowing and knowledge for the sake of action. Tying these together is the idea of action, and the case studies amplify that without purposeful action focusing on a substantive issue that calls for practical solutions university and community collaborations will simply fail.

Both of these volumes imply a lot about civic responsibility within higher education but they do not address it in any depth. Let me be so bold as to make a statement that could get me in some trouble. Engaged research comes out of an institutional commitment to civic responsibility. Engaged research is not an end in itself. For community practice and community practitioners, civic responsibility is likely well understood. While many universities and their faculty may gravitate towards community engagement their aims and motivations will be frustrated if they do not recognize research as a form of service. Research for service and service as research, therefore, go hand in hand, something colleges and universities may come to understand if they take both engagement and civic responsibility seriously.

REFERENCES

Nyden, P., Figert, A., Shibley, M., & Burrows, D. (Eds.). (1997). *Building community: Social science in action.* Thousand Oaks, CA: Pine Forge Press.

Sullivan, M., & Kelly, J.G. (Eds.). (2001). *Collaborative research: University and community partnership.* Washington, DC: American Public Health Association.

Confluence:
An Afterword

We look at this Afterword, not so much as a closing to this special issue, but as an invitation to further explore the literature and emerging river of work of university-community partnerships and civic engagement in higher education. This volume has provided examples of partnerships being carried out in many disciplines, including the sometimes lost voice of social work. It has addressed a myriad of issues that excite and frustrate both academic and community partners. It has provided examples of individual faculty, of teams joined together in common pursuits of research and policy change, and of the work of consultants. The many authors who have contributed to this publication have shared their own sense of the opportunities and challenges for enhancing teaching and research as their programs, schools, and institutions entered community service arenas. They have also added to the ongoing dialogue on civic engagement in higher education, as well as to the growing literature in this field. There are many rivers of thought that branch through this field, and we hope this collection of articles invites our readers to explore some of them.

Armanda Carriere's introduction on behalf of the U.S. Department of Housing and Urban Development and its Office of University Partnerships provides an excellent launching point for this exploration. Initiated as an urban academic catalyst akin to that of County Extension Agents which mobilized academic resources for their farm and rural community partners, the Office of University Partnership, or OUP, maintains a rich website (*www.oup.org*) with information on its unique grant opportunities for community outreach, student fellowships, and

[Haworth co-indexing entry note]: "Confluence: An Afterword." Soska, Tracy M., and Alice K. Johnson Butterfield. Co-published simultaneously in *Journal of Community Practice* (The Haworth Social Work Practice Press, an imprint of The Haworth Press, Inc.) Vol. 12, No. 3/4, 2004, pp. 243-248; and: *University-Community Partnerships: Universities in Civic Engagement* (ed: Tracy M. Soska, and Alice K. Johnson Butterfield) The Haworth Social Work Practice Press, an imprint of The Haworth Press, Inc., 2004, pp. 243-248. Single or multiple copies of this article are available for a fee from The Haworth Document Delivery Service [1-800-HAWORTH, 9:00 a.m. - 5:00 p.m. (EST). E-mail address: docdelivery@haworthpress.com].

http://www.haworthpress.com/web/COM
Digital Object Identifier: 10.1300/J125v12n03_15

applied research–particularly doctoral and post-doctoral. Moreover, this site contains an archive of articles and publications with links to some of the current initiatives on university civic engagement, such as the *CEOs for Cities* report with HUD on today's economic importance of universities in the development of cities. OUP's and HUD's own publications examine best practices in university-community partnerships, including a 2002 issue of *Cityscape* that was devoted exclusively to articles and studies from HUD-funded Community Outreach Partnerships Center (COPC) programs. The site also provides links to every college and university with a COPC grant since its inception in 1994, as well as links to the many and varied minority-serving institutions of higher education funded through OUP. The COPC initiative has also spun-off a new organization, the Association of Community and Higher Education Partners (ACHEP), which is working to advance information/resource exchange among partnerships and promote funding (*www.achep.com*).

On the medical and health side of civic engagement, the Community-Campus Partnerships for Health (CCPH) (*www.depts.washington. edu/ccph*) based at the University of Washington, is pursuing a parallel university-community agenda among the health professions. CCPH and COPC joined forces for a combined symposium when their 2003 national conferences overlapped in San Diego, and both websites have reports of these proceedings. Literature in public health journals, as well as pharmacy, nursing, and medicine has featured many articles on service-learning and community-based applied research that have stemmed from these campus-community health partnerships. Some higher education institutions, such as the University of Pittsburgh, with its US-UK symposium on university-community health partnerships, are developing international exchanges around higher education civic engagement that addresses community health and health disparities.

Another key civic engagement resource has grown out of the cooperative extension work of leading land-grant institutions. Not surprisingly, the major public institutions fostered by the Morrell Act that established the land-grant college tradition, are continuing this legacy of outreach and engagement. The "Wisconsin Idea" that seeded the engaged public institution has taken strong root in today's work at the University of Wisconsin, which along with Ohio State and Penn State, have established the annual "Outreach Scholarship" conference (*www.outreachscholarship.org*). *The Journal of Higher Education Outreach and Engagement* (*www.uga.edu/jheoe*), published out of the University of Georgia, provides an important forum for scholarship and dialogue from this public and land-grant tradition.

One of the strongest and earliest currents of civic engagement flows from the service-learning field and is often linked with university-community partnerships. Among the major resources is the National Service Learning Clearinghouse (*www.servicelearning.org*), which is connected with Learn and Service America and focused on K-12 educational institutions as part of the Corporation for National and Community Service's agenda. Campus Compact (*www.compact.org*), based at Brown University, is another key source that documents and disseminates best practices of civic and community engagement. Hundreds of college and university presidents are parties to the Campus Compact, and their Wingspread Conference Declarations, such as the "President's Declaration of Civic Responsibility of Higher Education" (1999) and "On Renewing the Civic Mission of the American Research Institution" (1999), have fueled the national dialogue on civic engagement and on the recognition of this work in the academy. A Google or Yahoo search of "service learning" taps into a wellspring of links to college and university programs across the country and the world. Also, publications like the *Michigan Journal of Community Service Learning* (*www.umich.edu/~mjcsl*) afford opportunities for contributions to the literature and what Ernest Boyer so eloquently termed the "scholarship of engagement."

A few higher education institutions have even managed to connect some of these rivers of engagement. A notable example is the University of Pennsylvania where one of the leading lights of this work, Ira Harkavy and his colleague have helped their institution partner in remaking the West Philadelphia neighborhood that once isolated their campus. Penn has joined its COPC with Learn and Serve America (*www.learnandserve.org*) and other civic engagement programs into a range of outreach, research, and scholarship, including their *University and Community Schools Journal* (*www.upenn.edu/ccp/bibliography.shtml*) that focuses on university and K-12 service-learning connections. At the University of Illinois at Chicago, the Great Cities Institute (*www.uic.edu/cuppa/gci*) supports interdisciplinary, urban-centered research in a variety of ways. Its Faculty Seed Fund provides start-up funding for interdisciplinary and urban-centered research projects that have potential to generate new partnerships. Through a competitive process, Faculty Scholars are selected from academic departments throughout the University to work on their research projects for a full academic year.

Several national higher education organizations have also charted these waters of outreach, partnership and engagement. The Carnegie Foundation for the Advancement of Teaching (*www.carnegiefoundation.org*), which in many ways defines and classifies our higher education arena, is noted for such publications as

Civic Responsibility and Higher Education (2000) edited by Thomas Ehrlich and, of course, as the home for many years of its late president, Ernest L. Boyer, whose *Scholarship Reconsidered: Priorities of the Professoriate* (1990) is considered the vanguard of the civic engagement movement in higher education and, perhaps, the most cited source in the literature of this field. The National Association of State Universities and Land-Grant Colleges (*www.nasulgc.org*) has also been very active in exploring this topic and guiding institutional members through its Kellogg Commission on the Future of State and Land-Grant Universities. Kellogg Commission publications, such as the "Returning to Our Roots" series and, especially, *Returning to Our Roots: The Engaged Institution* (1999), have been very influential on senior academic leadership. In addition, the American Association of Higher Education, particularly through its conferences on "Faculty Roles and Rewards" like its 2002 conference "Knowledge for What? The Engaged Scholar," have provided fertile ground for growing the academic dialogue on outreach and engagement as it relates to difficult promotion and tenure issues (*www.aahe.org/convenings.htm*). Finally, the Society for College and University Planners (*www.scup.org*), an organization of university administrators who address today's "town-gown" relations in developing universities and their physical forms, provides a different voice and an active list-serve in the national dialogue.

As Moxley's essay noted, the journey through academia, especially its research institutions, is a particularly perilous one. Barry Checkoway provided one of the key discussions on this issue in his 1997 foundational article "Reinventing the Research University for Public Service" in the *Journal of Planning Literature* (*www.acs.ohio-state.edu/jpl/index*). The focus on applied research in university-community partnerships has become an important topic in the literature. A 2003 report from the Pew Partnership for Civic Change, *University + Community Research Partnerships: A New Approach* edited by Jacqueline Dugery and James Knowles, reports on the state of applied research field in relation to such partnerships (*www.pew-partnership.org/pubs/pubs.html*).

Over the years a substantial core of literature has been built in this field, and this has lent greater scholarly credibility to community outreach and civic engagement work. Just as the *Journal of Community Practice* has made this a special issue topic, a number of national journals and periodicals have featured special volumes on university-community partnerships and civic engagement. Among the more notable, in addition to those noted earlier, are:

- *American Behavioral Scientist* (*www.sagepub.com/journal. aspx?pid= 171*)–two special issues, "Universities Respond to Troubled Times"

(1999) and "Service-Learning Pedagogy as Universities' Response to Troubled Times" (2000).

- *Journal of Planning Education and Research* (*www.acsp.org/JPER*) (Summer 1998)–special issue on "Symposium on University-Community Partnership Centers" published by the Association of Collegiate Schools of Planning.
- *Metropolitan Universities Journal: An International Forum* (*http://muj.uc.iupui.edu*), from Indiana University and Purdue University at Indianapolis offers numerous issues on themes related to service-learning, community partnerships, and civic engagement.

For those academics seeking a serious exploration along these waterways, several books in addition to those like Boyer's noted above, can provide deeper inquiry into the historic and current trends of higher education in relationship to community. A few of the more notable are:

- *The University and the City: From Medieval Origins to the Present* (1988), edited by Thomas Bender, New York: Oxford University Press.
- *Universities and Communities* (1998), edited by Jacquelyn McCroskey and Susan Einbinder, Westport, CT: Praeger Publications.
- *Serving Children and Families through Community-University Partnerships: Success Stories* (1999), edited by Thomas R. Chibucos and Richard M. Lerner, Norwell, MA: Kluwer Academic Publishers.
- *Beyond the Campus: How Colleges and Universities Form Partnerships with Their Communities* (2001), by David Maurrasse, New York: Routledge.
- *Collaborative Research: University and Community Partnership* (2001), edited by Myrtis Sullivan and James Kelly, Washington, DC: American Public Health Association.
- *A Future for Everyone: Innovative Social Responsibility and Community Partnerships* (2004), edited by David Maurrasse with Cynthia Jones, New York: Routledge.

If you're still eager to further immerse yourself in these waters, the National Service Learning Clearinghouse (*www.servicelearning.org*) has recently added a new "Doctoral Dissertation" link for those who are interested in the emerging research and thinking from younger "engaged" scholars.

We hope this closing discussion of the established resources, growing literature, and emerging thinking on "University-Community Partnerships: Universities in Civic Engagement" will be useful to your own institutional, school or collegial dialogue on these ideas flowing and, sometimes, surging through the higher education landscape. In adding our own editorial contributions to the rivers running through this field, we hope we have found some confluence for the ideas and voices of those doing this good academic and community work in service to society.

Tracy M. Soska
Alice K. Johnson Butterfield

Index

BOOK ORDER FORM!

Order a copy of this book with this form or online at:
http://www.haworthpress.com/store/product.asp?sku=5538

University-Community Partnerships
Universities in Civic Engagement

____ in softbound at $34.95 ISBN: 0-7890-2836-0.
____ in hardbound at $54.95 ISBN: 0-7890-2835-2.

COST OF BOOKS _____

POSTAGE & HANDLING _____
US: $4.00 for first book & $1.50
for each additional book
Outside US: $5.00 for first book
& $2.00 for each additional book.

SUBTOTAL _____
In Canada: add 7% GST. _____

STATE TAX _____
CA, IL, IN, MN, NJ, NY, OH, PA & SD residents
please add appropriate local sales tax.

FINAL TOTAL _____
If paying in Canadian funds, convert
using the current exchange rate.
UNESCO coupons welcome.

❏ BILL ME LATER:
Bill-me option is good on US/Canada/
Mexico orders only; not good to jobbers,
wholesalers, or subscription agencies.

❏ Signature _____

❏ Payment Enclosed: $ _____

❏ PLEASE CHARGE TO MY CREDIT CARD:
❏ Visa ❏ MasterCard ❏ AmEx ❏ Discover
❏ Diner's Club ❏ Eurocard ❏ JCB

Account # _____

Exp Date _____

Signature _____
(Prices in US dollars and subject to change without notice.)

PLEASE PRINT ALL INFORMATION OR ATTACH YOUR BUSINESS CARD

Name	
Address	
City	State/Province	Zip/Postal Code
Country	
Tel	Fax
E-Mail	

May we use your e-mail address for confirmations and other types of information? ❏ Yes ❏ No We appreciate receiving
your e-mail address. Haworth would like to e-mail special discount offers to you, as a preferred customer.
We will never share, rent, or exchange your e-mail address. We regard such actions as an invasion of your privacy.

Order from your **local bookstore** or directly from
The Haworth Press, Inc. 10 Alice Street, Binghamton, New York 13904-1580 • USA
Call our toll-free number (1-800-429-6784) / Outside US/Canada: (607) 722-5857
Fax: 1-800-895-0582 / Outside US/Canada: (607) 771-0012
E-mail your order to us: orders@haworthpress.com

For orders outside US and Canada, you may wish to order
through your local
sales representative, distributor, or bookseller.
For information, see http://haworthpress.com/distributors

(Discounts are available for individual orders in US and Canada only, not booksellers/distributors.)
Please photocopy this form for your personal use.
www.HaworthPress.com

BOF05